OUT OF HAND
MATERIALIZING THE POSTDIGITAL

OUT OF HAND

MATERIALIZING THE POSTDIGITAL

EDITED BY RONALD T. LABACO

museum of arts and design

black dog
publishing
london uk

CONTENTS

FOREWORD

In 1956, the Museum of Arts and Design (then the Museum of Contemporary Crafts) organized its premiere exhibition *Craftsmanship in a Changing World* exploring the then-present state of the crafts in a post-Industrial Revolutionary world. It was intended to "feature the unique work of the craftsman in both its established and experimental forms." The exhibition underscored the reality that, after an often contentious past, traditional crafts and industrial design had arrived at a mutually beneficial and symbiotic relationship: studio crafts practitioners served as operators of production businesses and designers for industry, in addition to maintaining the creative independence of the artist. Over the decades since its founding, the Museum has continued to examine and interpret material creativity in its diversity on an international platform.

Fast forward to the last decades of the twentieth and first decade of the twenty-first century, when radically new technologies, materials, and processes again maneuvered the worlds of craft, art, and design into creative collision. While it is true that technology has always been the muse to creativity, its impact in the past three decades is especially dramatic and far-reaching. The digital "revolution" of our time has inalterably changed the shape of the material world: forms that were once difficult or even impossible to make are now readily achievable; new materials challenge our preconceived notions of value; and, territories and hierarchies that once separated art, craft, and design are obscured, if not meaningless. As this exhibition proves, the changes in practice, products, and purpose provoked by digital technologies are inevitable, evolving, and exciting. The exhibition also underscores the fact that these changes are global, affecting fields ranging from medical design to fashion to architecture.

MAD curator Ronald T. Labaco has selected the works that comprise *Out of Hand: Materializing the Postdigital*, with brilliance and intelligence. He deserves kudos for organizing a groundbreaking and visually compelling exhibition that furthers the mission of the Museum of Arts and Design—to reveal the ways that materials and processes intersect with culture, creativity, and content. *Out of Hand: Materializing the Postdigital* is both a document of creative evolution in our time, and a unique resource of information on the complex and exciting world of art and design in the postdigital era.

David Revere McFadden
William and Mildred Lasdon Chief Curator

OBJECTHOODS FROM THE DESKTOP

CHRISTIANE PAUL

At least since antiquity the sculptural act in art has occupied a space on the threshold between the artificial and the living. Sculptors transform raw material into a form that, representational or not, takes on a life of its own. The blurring of the boundaries between the sculptural form and the living being has been a recurrent subject in Greek mythology and literature, from Pygmalion to Talos and Pandora. Digital technologies have introduced significant shifts in the creation of sculpture and consequently the understanding of the sculptural act and the concept of sculptures themselves. They have offered a refinement and an acceleration of experimentation with perspectival systems and the representation and manufacture of form. The theme of the "living sculptural form" has gained new meaning at a time when sculptural form can produced through generative software processes and artificial life algorithms.

To determine the date (or even year) of birth of an artistic technique is always a problematic if not futile endeavor, but it might be safe to say that the 1990s were the decade when "digital sculpture" officially began to exist, even if it had its roots in earlier experiments. In the early 90s, Tim Duffield, Bruce Beasley, Rob Fisher and David Smalley founded the Computers and Sculpture Foundation (CSF) and in 1993, Intersculpt, a biennial computer sculpture exhibition conceived by Christian Lavigne and Alexandre Vitkine, was organized by the French organization Ars Mathématica. While some sculptors make use of the technologies both in the initial design and the output of the physical objects, others create sculptures that exclusively exist in the virtual realm and can take the form of a CAD (computer-aided design) model or an animation.

The relationships between the physical and the virtual played an important role in the discussions surrounding digital sculpture in the 1990s. Most practitioners used the term digital sculpture for objects manufactured through CAD/CAM, CNC milling and/ or Rapid Prototyping processes and virtual sculpture for work that existed on the Internet, in Virtual Reality environments or as 3D animation. Practitioners in the field early on seemed to understand themselves primarily as sculptors minus classifying additions such as computer, virtual, or digital. A few of the artists represented in *Out of Hand*, such as Michael Rees, were deeply involved in the field in its beginning stages and made major contributions to shaping it.

While the basic concepts, themes, and methods of production in the field of digital sculpture have prevailed since the early 1990s, there certainly has been an evolution of the art form and its context. Due to the technological developments over the past two decades, the tools for the production of digital culture have become more refined, common, and accessible, as well as cheaper. Twenty years ago the status of digital sculpture in terms of "art world credibility" was fairly low. Today it is hard to find artwork whose production hasn't involved digital tools at some point in the process of its creation and the questioning of its status has become moot. One reason for the resistance to digital sculpture—or digital art in general—within the traditional art world was the possibility of the infinite reproduction of digital work, which raises the question of the copy and the original. Today digital reproducibility has become more of an accepted fact, and editioning has become the accepted model for selling many forms of digital artwork.

The new digital tools for modeling and output have broadened creative possibilities for sculptors and changed the construction and perception of three-dimensional experience. While machines and industrial manufacturing have been used in the process of creating sculptures for a long time, digital technologies add a layer of data abstraction that brings new qualities to mechanical production. Digital media translate the notion of three-dimensional space into the virtual realm and thus open up new dimensions for relations between form and space. Tangibility, which has been a major characteristic of the concept and creation process of sculpture, isn't necessarily a defining quality of the creative process or even presentation any more. The transphysical aspect of the virtual environment changes traditional modes of experience that were defined by gravity, scale, material, etc. Scaling operations, proportional shifts, eccentric vantage points, morphing processes, and 3D montage are some of the techniques employed in the realm of digital sculpture. Sculptures become instantly scalable and printable. Their objecthood, regardless of scale and material, can be initially defined on the computer, from the desktop of one's working table.

In an information-based and technologized "post-media" society, it is virtually impossible to separate technology from one's environment, which has become a frictionless system of information retrieval, dissemination, and exchange. Therefore, any attempt to understand an artistic medium through the lens of technology alone may be ultimately futile and counterproductive, imposing limits on the conceptual understanding of the work. Good art is always both deeply rooted in and at the same time transcends its medium, and most sculptors would not want to rely on the qualifier of the "digital" to understand their work.

In addition, the loss of the "mark" in digital creation—meaning the lack of personality in the mark one produces on a computer screen as opposed to materials such as clay, paper, or canvas— has been a much discussed subject in digital artistic practice. However, the comparison to painting and drawing itself is slightly problematic and it may be more productive to understand the supposed "loss" as a "shift". Art created by means of computer technologies is more comparable to other technologically mediated art forms such as film, video, and photography where the individuality and voice of an artist also does not manifest itself in a direct physical intervention. All elements of the composition process, the writing of software and many other aspects of digital art's creation are still highly individual forms of expression that carry the aesthetic signature of an artist. The exhibition title *Out of Hand* perfectly captures this shift by suggesting a process where materiality is not shaped by the hand of the artist in the traditional way, even though the parameters for the sculptural work are established and controlled by its creator.

While some digitally produced objects do not exhibit distinctive features of the medium and could have been created by traditional means, others immediately point to the process of their creation. Wim Delvoye's *Twisted Dump Truck (Counterclockwise Scale Model 1:5)*, 2011—made from laser-cut steel—for example, couldn't have been produced without digital technologies, a fact that is obvious to the viewer's eye. The sculpture achieves a perspectival distortion that does not resolve into a three-dimensional object as we know it and challenges our senses. Delvoye's dump truck, reminiscent of a late-Gothic cathedral, as well as Chris Bathgate's

ML622254434732323, 2012—a CNC-milled metal sculpture of offset cylindrical shapes that fuses the Medieval with the machinic and futuristic—and Ron Arad's *Oh Void 1*, 2006—a play on modernist form—all suggest a "reboot" that takes previous forms to new levels. All of the works cease to appear man-made, yet have a distinct artistic approach and signature and transcend their materiality.

Chris Bathgate
ML622254434732323
(detail, see pp. 148–151)

Based on mathematical functions, software-generated design allows for the development of new forms of geometries that would be hard if not impossible to conceive or produce with the same precision by means of traditional methods. Frank Stella's *K.162*, 2011, a burst of twists and extensions made of resin and steel, both continues the fusion of geometry with accumulations of curved lines that Stella already pursued in painting and, at the same time, takes these explorations to a new level of geometry that blurs the organic and mathematical. A radically different aesthetic emerges from *Hiroshi Sugimoto's Mathematical Model 009 Surface of revolution with constant negative curvature*, 2006, which represents a curvature of almost otherworldly and futuristic perfection.

One of the inherent characteristics of the digital medium is its generative quality, the possibility to produce evolving forms and structures by activating a computerized process. Artists are able to establish rules by writing or activating software that, with some degree of autonomy, produces an artwork. Possibilities for interaction between elements are outlined in programming, and structures evolve through actions and movements of the elements within the given parameters. Processuality thereby becomes one of the defining aspects of digital creation and not only allows for the creation of new geometries and structural patterns, but also connects generative software processes to natural systems. Principles of emergence function as underlying frameworks for both biology and software. Many artists create abstractions of systems that occur in the natural world, or actively model nature through computerized generative processes.

In *K.179*, 2011, another Frank Stella sculpture included in the exhibition, these organic qualities of the curved steel structures move to the foreground. The fusion of nature and geometry in Maya Lin's *Imaginary Iceberg*, 2009, both points to the connections between these systems and plays with the tension between them. The competing forces of the natural and computerized find a different form of expression in the seemingly organic intestinal structures of Anish Kapoor's Prototypes for *Greyman Cries, Shaman Dies, Billowing Smoke, Beauty Evoked*, 2008–2009, whose materiality is the result of a custom type of cement rapid

prototyping and counteracts the sculptures' evocation of organic decay. The amalgamation of nature, algorithmic instructions, and automated production processes becomes most obvious in projects that employ nature itself for rapid prototyping. An example would be Markus Kayser's *Solar-Sinter*, 2011, a solar-powered machine that uses the sun's rays as a laser and sand as resins for the rapid prototyping of objects.

2 Anish Kapoor

Greyman Cries, Shaman Dies, Billowing Smoke, Beauty Evoked, installation view, Royal Academy of Arts, 2009 (see pp. 48–51)

Photography Dave Morgan

3 Markus Kayser

Solar Sinter in Sahara Desert near Siwa, Egypt, 2011 (see pp. 40–43)

Photography Amos Field Reid

A number of works in *Out of Hand* reflect on the processuality of the digital production process itself, which has been made seemingly instantaneous or even portable through rapid prototyping or 3D printing. Roxy Paine's *S2-P2-MAR1*, 2011, a work that formally connects to Kapoor's sculpture, is produced by Paine's sculpture-making Scumak machine, which is often shown producing polyethelane (plastic) sculptures "live" in the exhibition space. Software designed by Paine determines the size and direction of the opening through which the plastic is poured, as well as the length of the "pour" itself.

Processuality also is one of the defining elements in Allan McCollum's *Laminated Plywood Shapes*, 2006, CNC-milled laminated birch plywood structures. To realize his *Shapes Project*, McCollum designed a system for developing unique two-dimensional shapes in Adobe Illustrator, each of them taking form through a series of actions that involve the drawing and then cutting and pasting of combinations of parts. An essential aspect of the project is its quality as a playground for creative experimentation. The shapes do not only function as fine art and design projects, but are also meant for fulfilling a range of social functions, as emblems, logos, toys, and educational tools. Algorithmic process and the potential for transformation also play a central role in Michael Rees and Robert Gero's *Intervening Phenomena*, 2012, a form based on a site-specific architectural floor plan, which became the core structure to be morphed and modified in multiple iterations by means of 3D modeling software. Combining play theory with systems theory, *Intervening Phenomena* is grounded in "operativity" as a significant component of the system that generates the work and transforms the structure. Michael Rees' sculptures can be considered a reconfiguration and expansion of scientific disciplines. He has frequently used science and its imagery as a way of weaving systems—analytical and intuitive. In other works, including *Converge*, 2013, he has borrowed imagery from medical anatomy and fused anatomical elements and organic forms into complex sculptural structures. Pattern, as a recurring and persistent characteristic of structure, becomes more pronounced in the works of Geoffrey Mann and Marc Fornes, as well as Chuck Close's tapestry.

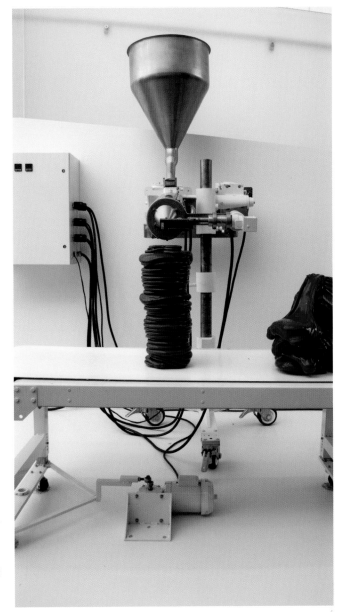

4. Roxy Paine, American (b. 1966)
Scumak No.2, 2001. Aluminum, computer, conveyor, electronics, extruder, stainless steel, polyethylene, and Teflon
7 feet 6 inches x 23 feet x 6 feet 1 inch (228.6 x 701.04 x 185.42 cm)
Image courtesy The Nelson-Atkins Museum of Art, Kansas City, Missouri.
Photography Alberto Orihuela

5

6

While digitally produced sculpture lends itself to explorations of systems, structures, geometries, and patterns, the notion of the figurative has not been abandoned by sculptors working with technologies. The body has always been a reference point for traditional sculpture, and still plays a crucial role in our perception of sculptural work even though the domain created by new technologies extends from nano-scaled to macro structures. A group of works in *Out of Hand* illustrates how the depiction of the human form has been affected by the potential of digital technologies. Where Barry X Ball explores and exaggerates the geometry of the human form, Richard Dupont distorts it into shapes that would have been hard to realize without the use of the digital medium. Stephen Jones augmented the original 1827 marble bust of Lady Belhaven—on view at the Victoria and Albert museum in London—by creating a 3D scan of the bust and manipulated the scanned data to augment it with an intricate hat that captures Lady Belhaven's heritage and her interest in music in abstracted forms extruding from her head. Nick Hornby takes advantage of the digital medium's combinatory potential by mixing the body and legs from Rodin's *Striding Man* with Brancusi's *Bird*

5. Allan McCollum

Shape (see pp. 256–259)

Photography Will Lytch, Courtesy Graphicstudio

6. Nick Hornby

I never wanted to weigh more heavily on a man than a bird (Coco Chanel) (see pp. 218–219)

in Space and the negative space from Hepworth's *Single Form* in a sculpture whose title—*I never wanted to weigh more heavily on a man than a bird*—both perfectly describes his quotation of famous sculptures and is itself a quote from Coco Chanel.

As an artistic practice, sculpture has always been striving to challenge and supersede its own traditions, and digital technologies have provided new tools for pushing the boundaries of the medium, both in terms of concept and materiality. As the projects discussed here illustrate, digital technologies have opened up new possibilities for the design and production process. Computability makes data 'sculptable' in numerous ways and the modular, process-oriented nature of digital media allows for a continuous, generative process of combinations. Virtual 3D forms can be instantaneously and remotely translated into a haptic experience—an idea and form, conceived anywhere, can literally be at your fingertips. Digital technologies have also brought about a reconfiguration of boundaries between various disciplines—among them art, design, science, and architecture—and artists creating digital sculptures draw their source material from or work with concepts related to science, medicine, archaeology and the history of technology. For many of these artists the immersion into the histories of the forms they use—and the various disciplines they are associated with—is the basis for their interest in this area of practice. It is important to them to saturate their work with some sense of the social significance of both forms and the means of their production. Altogether, these possibilities change the social references for sculpture, which can carry multiple social functions, from art object to tool and design solution. In some cases digitally created sculptures literally take on a life of their own, originating from a framework created by artists, but generating and printing forms in a process out of the artists' hands.

1. In Ovid's *Metamorphoses*, Pygmalion appears as a sculptor who falls in love with a statue he had carved. In Greek mythology, Talos was a giant man of bronze and Pandora was made from clay at the behest of Zeus.

EVERYBODY'S AN ARCHITECT THESE DAYS

GREG LYNN

In architecture, and to a great degree in both art and design, visual and formal complexity has come through the assembly of parts. In the work collected in *Out of Hand: Materializing the Postdigital* another form of complexity is proposed whose reliance is not on the assembly of discrete elements. So the exhibition is not so much about losing the handmade to machines processes but the discovery by designers and artists that things need not be complicated in their assembly and construction to be complicated in their form and expression. The work in *Out Of Hand* could roughly be characterized by an increase in inflections, openings, pockets, or what might best be called features combined with a marked reduction in components, often to simply one. This contemporary work is simultaneously complex in its articulation and monolithic in its construction.

Both the modeling of shapes digitally and their construction using computer-controlled machines allow for the texturing, shaping, puncturing, deformation and merging of multiple features into a single surface, or what more accurately would be described as a topology or polygon mesh. The manner in which objects are constructed with a 3D printer, for example, is the deposit of relatively thin, almost invisibly stepped layers of material allowing for several things: very small-scale features; forms that would be impossible to mold due to die-lock and the inability to remove the tooling from the object; and trapped hollow volumes or voids within objects. It is no surprise that we are now seeing objects conceived for production by 3D printers having a surplus expression of intricate branches, holes, voids, lattices, pockets, and perforations if for no other reason than it can now be done. The principle of the 3D printer is the conversion of complex objects into 2D slices that are simply filled as either solid or void. This mechanical operation of manufacturing is wedded to virtual modeling operations that combine forms through polygon modeling tools with merging and smoothing operations that allow for multiple objects to become "Booleaned" together into composites and then smoothed with Chaiken's algorithms into facsimiles of continuous surfaces. The results are very finely inflected and perforated shapes one would associate with the assembly of large numbers of parts yet these objects are more often than not one-piece constructions. The language germane to contemporary modeling software is no longer the simple, smooth, taught, fusiform,

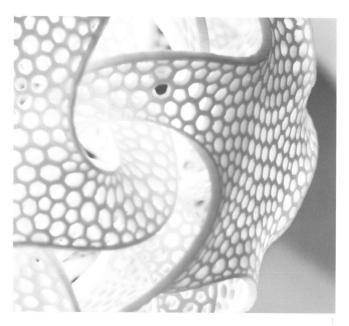

1. Bathsheba Grossman
   Quin.MGX lamp, (detail, see pp. 20–21)

2. Softkill Design
   Protohouse 1.0 (detail, see pp. 194–197)
   Photography Softkill Design

surface shapes that were associated with digital modeling in the 80s and 90s in design and architecture. What is being used for formal expression today is more often intricately perforated enfolding surfaces. When multiple forms are combined in digital modeling software they are now frequently intersected, merged, smoothed, and combined into a monolithic volume. Instead of assembling volumes and describing their intersections discretely and interpenetration, the joints and intersections are filleted, smoothed, and blended into continuous volumes. There is an increase in formal turbulence and modulation and a decrease in individuation of elements common to much of the work.

From a Nike shoe upper that is machine-knitted from yarn rather than cut fabric panels stitched together to Roxy Paine's *Scumak* sculptures extruded from a computer-controlled head, there is a radical economy to these objects where it is not clear that they have come from a more primitive sheet, tube, bar, block, or other raw material. Because of their zero-waste construction and their reduction of parts and pieces there are formal effects one associates with raw materials but a dissonance in the actual materiality. This brings a familiar sculptural quality to some of the work reminiscent of the "Baroque" folds of fabric rendered in marble in a Baroque sculpture; only now, Paine's sculptures are not carved from a block of raw material but frozen extrusions reliant on the chemistry of plastic materials. Through heat and chemistry many of the materials aspire to become solidified or arrested from a liquid to a solid state. This character of melted, slumped, and poured forms is achieved in many cases with the use of a secondary tool, vessel, or form into which these objects were cast.

These machine processes dispense with the expense and standardization of tooling and instead can deposit, carve, weave, sinter, or otherwise construct materials without secondary forms. Even though the title *Out of Hand* alludes to the loss of the hand there is a distinct return to the body for many of the objects both in art and design. When in the past, machine-based industrial processes have been associated with an abstraction of ergonomics into ideal postures and profiles. Now there is a return of the bespoke, often for its own sake; that is for its formal and expressive potential. Scanning technology allows for high resolution digital models of the human body that can be used to define specific contours and shapes of objects that have the identity and sometimes forms of specific users embedded into them for function, comfort, or personalization. In the same way that one expects digital experiences and interfaces to be customized to their preferences so too do design objects now address their users with bespoke form and contour. In some cases, algorithms that define an envelope of potential forms are specified by medical scanning such as EKG and CAT data as well as scanning technology for video game control and feature recognition. The personalization and participation in the act of creation or specification is extended to users who can design custom forms themselves within the constraints defined by the designers. In many ways, the objects that surround us reflect the digital media culture that we experience manifest in physical form.

3

3. Scott Summit for Bespoke Innovation
Bespoke Fairings (detail, see pp. 246–247)

What is most salient in *Out Of Hand* is a new kind of expression that would have previously been associated with visiting a building but that now one feels when viewing contemporary sculpture, when interacting with industrial design, or when watching a film. There is a very discrete skill necessary to experience and understand architecture that is not articulated and that has been unique to the discipline distinct from painting, sculpture and other arts. To appreciate architecture intellectually and creatively, one must learn to perceive the abstract organizing geometries that preceded the construction of the building. Once someone learns to perceive the spatio-geometric relationships underlying buildings a complex and vibrant experience of spaces begins in which one is in the building and experiencing both the literal building and what might best be called the virtual design that underpins it. This simultaneous presence of abstract alignments and organizations and physical forms and spaces is the eerie pleasure of those trained to be sensitive to architecture. There are many other ways to appreciate architecture besides its abstraction but this trait of abstract order and physical form is unique to, or used to be unique to architecture.

Recently, this experience can be had in other fields. The implicit labor of a Tom Friedman sculpture, the implicit composition of a Rauschenberg *Combine* and the implicit crushing force of a Chamberlain sculpture has been related to the handling of materials without recourse to geometry or geometric modeling. Sculptors like Charles Ray, Jeff Koons, and Olafur Elliason are scanning, CNC cutting, 3D printing, and in general becoming involved with the geometric description of objects as a necessity of their production; what has otherwise been the purvue of architects. When visiting their studios, seeing their sculptures being fabricated in factories, and visiting these objects in cities and museums one can't help but think: everybody's an architect these days. Not because of scale but due to the necessity of geometric description on the way to production. Before architects, buildings were made without drawings by guilds of craftsmen; the architects invented a job for themselves as the geometers that described the construction through drawings. Now, in order to make a sculpture, it seems one needs a similar character to define the geometry that controls the machines that assist in production. Artists in *Out Of Hand* like Roxy Paine and

4. Unfold & Tim Knapen
Vases created by *l'Artisan Electronique*
(see pp. 284–285)
Photo courtesy Unfold

5. J. Mayer H. Architects
Metropol Parasol, evening view
(see pp. 210–213)
Photography Fernando Alda

Anish Kapoor resist the virtual geometric underpinnings by focusing on the alchemy of materials arresting in forms that are not geometric *per se* but are determined by feed rates of material and patterns of extrusion. However, some of the artists and many of the designers work like architects with elaborate digital geometries that underly their forms so that when one experiences them there is a feeling of a virtual geometry being brought into physical form with a high degree of intricacy and abstraction. From Wim Delvoye's torqueing figures evoking architectural precedents forming other figures of transportation T-shirts with faceted polygon wolf heads emerging from them, the experience of a virtual geometry within literal forms brings the experience of a cathedral to the scale of objects for those attuned to the play between virtual description and physical forms.

Perhaps the hierarchies of architecture, a field where for thousands of years many elements are organized to form larger volumes and forms is now possible at the scale of a chair, where thousands of perforations and surfaces are combined into one monolithic object. Instead of building a chair out of perhaps a dozen tubes and panels that are welded and bolted together; today a chair is far more complex in its articulation but is instead built in one monolithic material in one volume; like a single donut with a thousand holes.

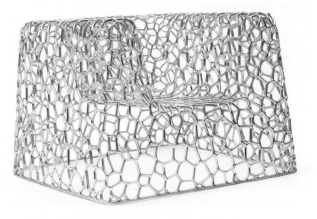

6

6. Marc Newson
Random Pak Chair (see pp. 104–109)
Photography © Fabrice Gousset
Courtesy Marc Newson Ltd.

MODELING NATURE

In today's computational world, biological and ecological phenomena often serve as models for creative expression. Generative art and design approaches provide ways to mimic biomorphic structures ranging from microscopic unicellular organisms to the macroscopic environment, and to simulate physical occurrences such as bone development, plant growth, and water flow. These procedures involve the use of automated planning systems—from computer-based algorithms to such schemata as mathematics, data mapping, symmetry, and tiling—that direct the machines to produce the work. In addition, some generative models introduce subtle "genetic" changes to the fabrication process, allowing for the possibility of endless mass-customization.

BATHSHEBA GROSSMAN

I am an artist exploring the region between art and mathematics. My work is about life in three dimensions: working with symmetry and balance, getting from the origin to infinity, and always finding beauty in geometry. That is to say, I like to think about shapes, and occasionally I think of a new one, and usually they come out very symmetrical. I am like any artist in that it is difficult to explain how and why this happens.

Apparently I have studied more math than most artists. I do not use it very directly—I wouldn't call myself a mathematician, and most of my designs are drawn rather than computed—but it is plain that my creative engine is interested in this.

I like technology. 3D printing in metal is my main medium now, and I also work with subsurface laser damage in glass. This is not because I love gadgets, it is much more trouble to do this than to use the mature tech that most sculptors enjoy. I do it because the shapes I have in mind aren't moldable, and I want to make a lot of them. Those two constraints, taken together, turn out to be remarkably constraining: most traditional sculpture technology simply does not operate on un-moldable objects.

I have a grass-roots business model. My plan is to make these designs available, rather than restrict the supply. It is more like publishing than like gallery-based art marketing: we don't feel that a book has lost anything because many people have read it. In fact it becomes more valuable as it gains readership and currency. With the advent of 3D printing, this is the first moment in art history when sculpture can be, in this sense, "published".

My designs are visions of order in the universe, my peaceful places. I feel calm and hopeful in making them, and I hope they will bring some of that satisfaction into your life.

I have become known in geek culture and in the 3D printing industry. I have not made much of an inroad into the traditional art world, but then showing in galleries is not a focus for me. I made a conscious decision many years ago to work directly for the viewer—you—rather than try to get the attention of cultural gatekeepers. The logical outcome of this decision was that only a small group of mathematicians and enthusiasts would ever take an interest. It's been a huge surprise, and a testament to the love of math and geometry that's out there, that it didn't turn out that way.

Bathsheba Grossman

Quin.MGX Lamp, 2005
Polyamide; laser sintering
Made by .MGX by Materialise
5½ x 5½ x 5½ inches (14 x 14 x 14 cm)
Courtesy .MGX by Materialise

MICHAEL HANSMEYER

The *Subdivided Column* explores the use of algorithms to develop a previously unimaginable architecture. The column is evolved purely procedurally, without drawing a single line. Historically the column orders were used to manifest architectural ideals about beauty and technology. The columns were composed according to a series of established geometric and mathematical rules. Today, we can re-appropriate this idea of a rule-based design and encode new rules as algorithms. In harnessing computational power, these algorithms can generate architectures that would have been impossible to conceive of using traditional means. This column is a contemporary interpretation of what these new architectures can be.

The algorithm for the *Subdivided Column* consists of rules that iteratively articulate and refine the structure out of a primitive input form. This forming involves recursively splitting and growing, much in analogy to morphologic genesis in nature.

The single process sculpts the form at manifold scales: from the overall proportions to the development of surfaces, down to the miniscule textures at a seemingly endless resolution.

The architect effectively designs a process to compose an object, rather than designing the object directly itself. This process can be performed over and over again with slightly varying parameters to create an entire family of objects. These objects can be combined and bred to create new generations of objects, and the final form can be successively refined in this manner.

The resulting column has a distinct language of form unlike anything created by traditional processes. It exhibits highly specific local conditions as well as an overall coherency and continuity. Its ornament is in continuous flow, yet consists of very distinct local formations. The geometric complexity of the column contrasts with the simplicity of the generative process and the initial input. It strikes a balance between order and chaos.

Michael Hansmeyer

Subdivided Column, 2010
2,700 sheets of 1mm coated grey board, wood;
computer numerical control (CNC), laser cutting
106 5/16 x 23 5/8 x 23 5/8 inches (270 x 60 x 60 cm)
Courtesy Michael Hansmeyer

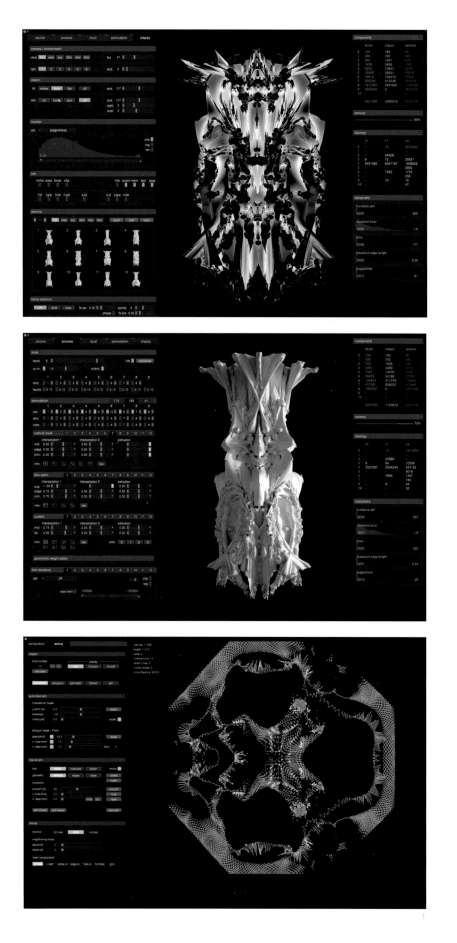

1. Screenshots of application used to design column, including mapping of column's topographical attributes to subdivision ratios (top), design of column's mid-section (center), and use of slicing tool to calculate cutting path for laser cutter (bottom)
2. Stack of leftover sheet material from which column was cut (i.e. its negative)
3. Fabrication in progress, showing several hundred stacked 1mm sheet slices; sheets are aligned using wooden rods, with cut-out voids to reduce overall weight

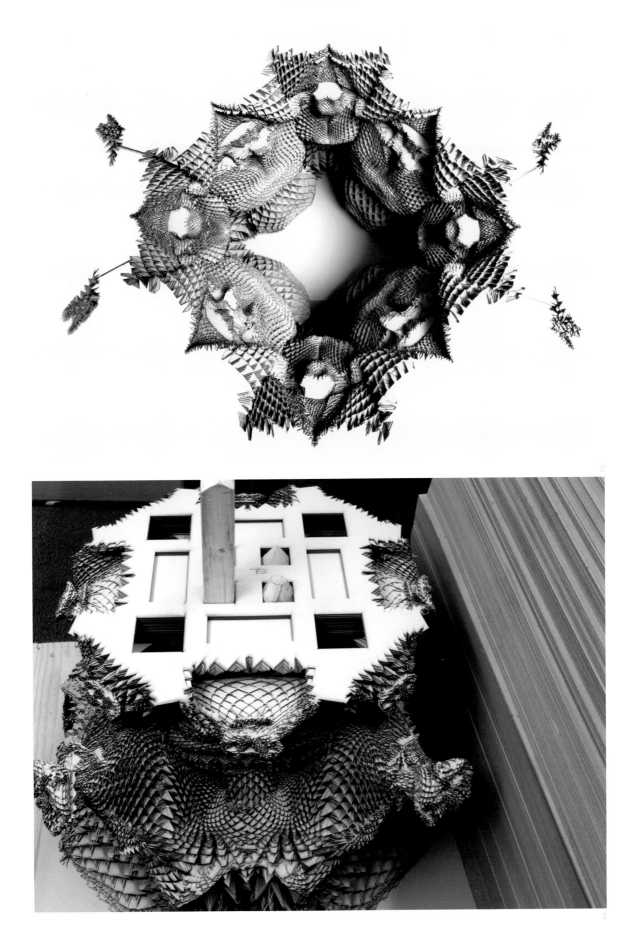

AMMAR ELOUEINI, AEDS

An exploration of dematerialization in architecture was a source of inspiration for the staircase in the Dickens Apartment in Paris. The massing of the stairs uses the logic of a solid and firm ground at the top and thinner, more ethereal massing at the bottom. The first step is less than one inch thick and flexes when a person steps on it. As one moves up the stairs each step becomes more firm and solid.

The same idea was carried out with the Corian screen that functions as a handrail and visual separation between the main living space and the stairs leading to the master bedroom. Based on a computer-generated script, the pattern is more solid and opaque at the top and gradually dematerializes towards the bottom of the stairs. The aesthetic quality of the screen references ornament and its typical presence in Haussmannian Parisian apartments.

The Corian screen design also refers to notions of beauty concerned with ideas of the incomplete and unfinished. Like in some Eastern philosophies such as wabi-sabi in Japan, the idea of imperfection and lack of finitude were a source of inspiration for the way the Corian screen was conceived and implemented. The relationship between the Corian screen and the steps was designed with the intention of creating an imperfection, and having this imperfection as a source of beauty.

Integrating oak and Corian together in this staircase allows it to bridge the two materials of the floors it is connecting. Oak was utilized for the underside of the stairs to reflect the existing wood floor in the living room on the lower level, and the upper face of each tread is finished with Corian to provide a transition to the Corian floor of the master suite above.

Ammar Eloueini

Dickens Apartment, Paris, 2011

Corian screen/handrail by Ammar Eloueini

with Marc Fornes

Robotic fabrication by Machineous, Los Angeles

Photography Christian Richters

JORIS LAARMAN

The Bone Furniture project started in 2004 with the research of Claus Mattheck and Lothar Hartzheim, published on Dutch science site Noorderlicht.

Seeing this, we were totally amazed by the efficiency, beauty and accuracy that this optimization software could generate. Ever since industrialization took over mainstream design we have wanted to make objects inspired by nature: from Art Nouveau and Jugendstil to streamline and the organic design of the 60s. But our digital age makes it possible to use nature not only as a stylistic reference, but also as an underlying principle to generate shapes through an evolutionary process. The project was initially developed with the help of Droog and Friedman Benda Gallery.

Trees have the ability to add material where strength is needed, and bones have the ability to take away material where it is not needed. With this knowledge the International Development Centre Adam Opel GmbH, a part of General Motors Engineering Europe created a dynamic digital tool to copy these ways of constructing used for optimizing car parts. In a way it quite precisely copies the way evolution constructs. We didn't use

it to create the world's next most perfect chair, but as a high tech sculpting tool to create elegant shapes with a sort of legitimacy. After a first try-out and calculation of a paper *Bone Chair*, the aluminium *Bone Chair* was the first made in a series of 7. The process can be applied to any scale up to architectural, in any material strength.

The Bone Furniture series consists of seven different pieces in all different materials and finishes. All pieces where made possible with the help of digital fabrication. The *Bone Chair* was developed using a custom developed 3D printed ceramic mold in which the complete chair could be cast as one single piece.

The following piece, a chaise longue, was developed at the workshop of Vincent de Rijk, who is known for his expertise with resin and his architectural models for Rem Koolhaas. It is cast in UV-resistant clear polyurethane, soft enough to shape itself to the body. Then we made a rocking and armchair. They were cast in a homemade recipe of marble powder and resin.

Both pieces are printed in a 79 (armchair) and 91 (rocker) part 3D mold assembled with countless little bolts.

Joris Laarman Lab

Bone Armchair, 2008

Cast marble resin

29 1/2 x 31 1/2 x 39 3/8 inches (75 x 80 x 100 cm)

Edition: 10 of 12

Courtesy Friedman Benda and the artist

Photography Jon Lam

1. Structure optimization of chair
   design generated by custom
   algorithm using soft kill option
   (SKO) method (top), rendering of
   chair mold (center), and rendering
   of chair mold assembly (bottom)

2. (opposite) Detail of 3D-printed
   polyamide mold, assembled
   with stainless steel nuts and bolts
   Photography Joris Laarman Lab

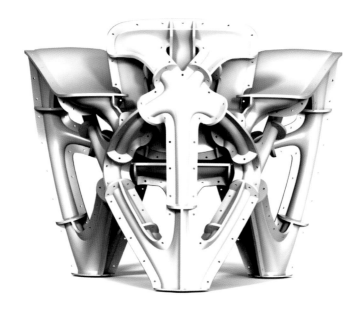

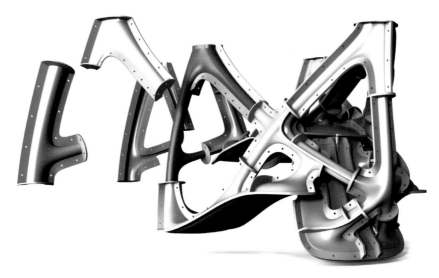

3

3. Casting chair using Carrara marble
   powder and resin mixture
   Photography Joris Laarman Lab
4. Month-long process of sanding
   and polishing chair
   Photography Joost van Brug

NAIM JOSEFI

Melonia are the first 3D-printed couture shoes in the world and come from the ecologic concept of no material waste. They are products for an industrial ecology. Due to the homogeneous material they are easier to recycle and create a closed loop.

A new vision for shoe production is to be able to go to a shop where you can scan your foot and print your own shoes. These could, after wear from long term use, be reprinted into a new pair. The shoes are a part of my Collection Melonia—a futuristic collection that visualizes an ideal society.

Naim Josefi

Melonia Shoe, 2010
Polyamide; laser sintering
9 1/16 x 3 9/16 x 8 11/16 inches (23 x 9 x 22 cm)
Courtesy Naim Josefi
Photography Johannes Helje and Clara Nova

1. Artist's sketch of shoe design
2. Screenshot in Rhino

HAWK UNIVERSITY OF APPLIED SCIENCES AND ARTS, GERMANY

We owe our thanks to the eruption of the Eyjafjallajökull volcano on Iceland on 20 March 2010 for the idea of the *Rapid Racer*. Because we couldn't fly back from Budapest, we spent 16 hours together on the train and had a lot of time to talk as a result. For the 2011 power screwdriver race—a race in which students compete using vehicles that are motorized by a power screwdriver and can accommodate at least one person—we wanted to be at the starting line with a particularly lightweight vehicle. We were imagining inner bionic structures such as those in a jawbone and the plan could only be reproduced in 3D printing. Then we found Stratasys in the USA, a partner who accompanied us in this experiment. In the largest possible build chamber at that time of 900 x 600 x 900 mm (35 1/2 x 23 1/2 x 35 1/2 inches), we created the world's first vehicle to be produced in one piece in 3D printing. Except for the pinions, wheels, chain, and some of the screws, it is created completely in the printer, including the steering wheel and the throttle. This comes very close to the idea that Andreas had in his childhood; after all, he always thought that products just dropped out of a machine, complete and ready to go. In our case, the machine took ten days since the vehicle is made up of 3,600 layers.

But what also fascinates us about the 3D printing was the fact that only one data set has to be sent for production (in our case, the file was only 44 MB in size) and the product can then be produced on location and changes can be easily made to the size and the features included. We believe that this presents us with two opportunities, but at the same time, they also involve a certain risk. On the one hand, 3D printing means that the consumer can have a much greater influence on the individual customization of the design itself, and on the other, it is also possible to generate spare parts yourself or to use the company's open-source product data. Both of these factors will have an enormous impact on our idea of design and products in the future.

Barbara Kotte and Andreas Schulz

Rapid Racer, 2011
Acrylonitrile butadiene styrene (ABS)
15 3/8 x 51 3/16 x 33 1/16 inches (39 x 130 x 84 cm)
27.56 lbs (12.5 kg)
Manufactured by Faculty of Design, Hochschule für angewandte Wissenschaft und Kunst (HAWK), and Stratasys Ltd, USA
Courtesy HAWK
Photography Johannes Roloff

MARKUS KAYSER

In a world increasingly concerned with questions of energy production and raw material shortages, this project explores the potential of desert manufacturing, where energy and material occur in abundance.

In the *Solar Sinter* experiment sunlight and sand are used as raw energy and material to produce glass objects using a 3D printing process that combines nature with high-tech production technology. The *Solar Sinter* aims to raise questions about the future of manufacturing and triggers dreams of the full utilization of the production potential of the world's most efficient energy resource—the sun. Whilst not providing definitive answers, this experiment aims to provide a point of departure for fresh thinking.

In the deserts of the world two elements dominate—sun and sand. The former offers a vast energy source of huge potential, the latter an almost unlimited supply of silica.

Silica sand when heated to melting point and allowed to cool solidifies as glass. Here the idea arises of a "translator" using the desert as a host to produce objects from the energy above and the material below. By using the sun's rays instead of a laser and sand instead of resins, it becomes the basis of an entirely new solar-powered machine and production process for making glass objects. The proposition of "desert manufacturing," of using what is there already in abundance in terms of energy and material, seems like a logical step rather than an eco-friendly version of something else. The 3D printing process makes sense as it suggests "you can make almost anything" which in turn can start a thinking process about possibilities, posing the question of what this might be.

The combination of technology and nature is at the core of this exploration and gives meaning to the proposal beyond questions of sustainability. Today advanced technology is an everyday companion and there is a need to integrate nature into technological processes. To explore natural environments as the host of all things and to make them part of technological achievements seems necessary in terms of understanding more about the direct applications of the natural given.

In the case of the *Solar Sinter* as little conversion as possible is done to the provided energy—sunlight. The "primary" energy to produce the heat to melt the sand is purely concentrated sunlight and the "secondary" energy is converted by photovoltaic cells producing the electricity needed for electronics and motors to drive the machine. The concept is not to harness sunlight, convert it to electricity, store it, and then turn it into heat again. Instead *Solar Sinter*'s concept is to directly use the sunlight where it occurs the plentiful in the given environment and the cycle of day and night. This allows for the fabrication of products using advanced technology that lives symbiotically with nature.

When excluding either nature or technology in the production of products there is an imbalance of what men want or respectively what nature can provide. The combination and finally even union of technology and nature could bring about processes that produce high quality products and even architecture at very little or no lasting damage to the planet.

Markus Kayser Studio

Solar Sinter in the Sahara desert
near Siwa, Egypt 2011
Photography Amos Field Reid

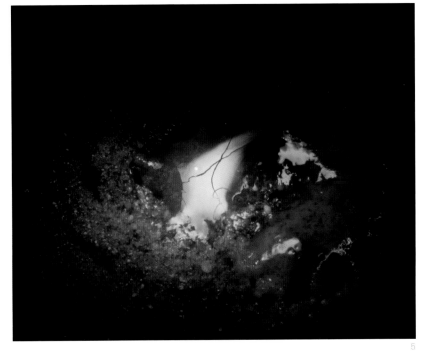

1. Flattening a new layer of sand.
2. First object printed by *Solar Sinter* from a 3D file is a glass bowl
3. Top view of bowl showing concentric layers
4. Electronics and laptop with wet-stone cooling improvisation
5. Close-up of sand being melted by heat of focused sunlight

ORDINARY LTD

Ordinary is a London-based design studio founded in 2011 by long-time collaborators Magnus Larsson and Alex Kaiser. Our partnership was born in Oxford, UK, where the hottest topic on the architecture school curriculum was Digital Culture. A decade later, that's an impossible tautology. We live in a digital society, in a digital era, in which culture is per definition digital, and where anything analogue is an interesting deviation from the norm. We are not just producing and consuming more digital culture, we are becoming digital beings that inhabit that digital culture.

This explosive development has affected architecture in ways that are simply irreversible. We were once taught that architects make drawings of buildings rather than the buildings themselves. This is no longer true. Architects make digital buildings, using digital tools and digital materials, and then communicate those buildings digitally to a digital society.

We are therefore decidedly unconcerned with architecture that needs to redundantly communicate its digitalness. In our material investigations, we are already mixing digitally controlled processes with analogue ones, such as the natural growth of materials across 3D-printed substrates. Knowing that the model is the building, we recently invested in a CNC router, with which we aim to close the gap between modeling and making even further.

The *Dune* project was presented at TED Global in July 2009, having already reached an architectural audience through an enthusiastic review on BLDGBLOG, where Geoff Manaugh called it "a kind of bio-architectural test-landscape."

The scheme seeks to investigate an adaptive way of living with desertification through the engineered solidification of existing wall to be created through microbial lithification of sand dunes in the Sahara Desert. The resulting sandstone building, literally spanning the African continent from east to west, would offer a green wall against the future spread of the desert.

Dune is an architectural speculation aimed at creating a network of solidified sand dunes in the desert—a proposition that suggests a manipulation of the ground through methods that perhaps brings to mind images of what Manaugh called "rogue basement chemists of the future." The selective solidification of a sand dune into a building volume using bacteria is indeed a novel building technology and a groundbreaking material strategy. Furthermore, the scheme advocates a radical shift in structural thinking, away from existing construction methods and material palettes, towards the localized cementation of granular materials using the bacterium, *Bacillus pasteurii*.

The idea is to use this biocementation strategy to create a very narrow and very long pan-African city with the capacity to mitigate against the shifting sands of Sahara. Through digitally controlling the sedimentation processes, the city/building is essentially perceived as a gigantic biological computer frozen in time. The image presented here shows an urban nodal point within the sandstone network—a city within the city—a habitable anti-desertification structure made from the desert itself, a sand-stopping device made out of sand, dunes turned into a city.

Ordinary Ltd

Magnus Larsson and Alex Kaiser
Dune: Arenaceous Anti-Desertification
Architecture, 2008
Courtesy of Ordinary Ltd

ANISH KAPOOR

The hand of the artist is much estimated as the means by which the expression of art finds a voice. To make art without hand is a goal that sets art beyond expression.

Artists have found ways to subvert the means of production.

Some three years ago, Adam Lowe and I wondered if it were possible to make a machine that could generate form. The printing machine formed a model for the basis of our thinking. After much trial and error, we found a surprisingly simple way of making a workable engine.

Once we had started making objects, a new reality began to emerge.

These were objects like no others; they seemed to obscure the border between artifice and event.

These are objects that are more akin to natural things than to those made by design.

This is the state of matter that has mind. It keeps a loose relation to both intention and control. Closest in its formal considerations to the work of the Raku potters of Japan.

The Hyper-Materiality of these event-things gives them a physical presence that is bodily (shit, intestines, flesh) and the feeling of objects that might have been made by animals.

Technological methods give technological solutions. This is not the case here.

Geometry gives structure and architecture. Entropy and decay put geometry to trial.

There is no hierarchy of form, but form has a propensity to meaning.

And meaning is the translation of art.

Anish Kapoor, Adam Lowe and Simon Shaffer, *Uncomformity and Entropy: Greyman Cries, Shaman Dies, Billowing Smoke, Beauty Evoked*, (Madrid: Turner, 2009), p. 39

Greyman Cries, Shaman Dies,
Billowing Smoke, Beauty Evoked,
2008–2009
Concrete
Installation view, Royal Academy of Arts,
London, 2009
Photography Dave Morgan; © Anish Kapoor

1. Artist's sketchbook, 2009
2. Artist's studio, 2009–2011
   Photography Anish Kapoor Studio
3. Artist's studio, 2009–2011
   Photography Anish Kapoor Studio
4. *Greyman Cries, Shaman Dies,*
   Billowing Smoke, Beauty Evoked,
   2008–2009
   Installation view, Royal Academy of Arts,
   London, 2009
   Photography Dave Morgan; © Anish Kapoor

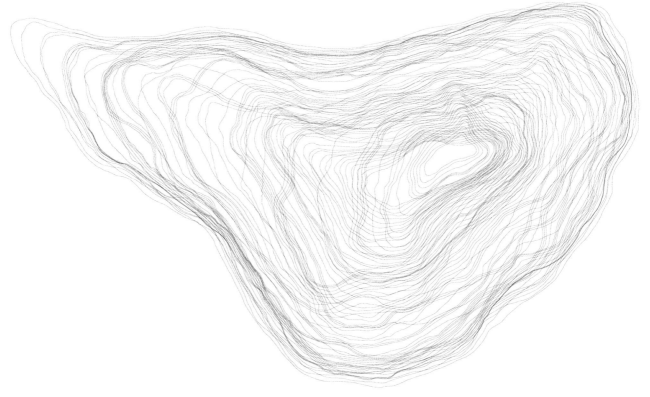

MAYA LIN

Originally exhibited in the exhibition *Bodies of Water* at the Storm King Art Center. For this exhibition, the works—both small and large scale installations—revealed new and at times unexpected views of the natural world, from the topology of the ocean floor, to the imagined form of a large body of water, to the shape of an iceberg both above and below sea level.

Utilizing twenty-first century technologies to look at the natural world, I create works inspired by studies and explorations of natural terrain and topographies—from sonar views of the ocean floor to aerial and satellite views—revealing aspects of the natural world that are at times invisible to us.

The form of glaciers fascinated me because so much of the body of a glacier is submerged, and only a minuscule fraction is visible above the waterline. I began by studying actual icebergs and then proceeded to create imagined ones. This work was part of that study.

Maya Lin

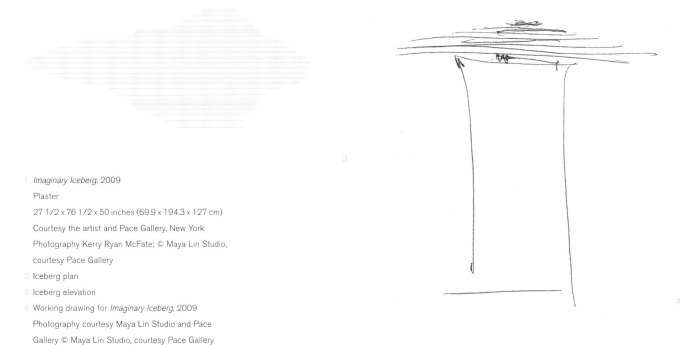

1. *Imaginary Iceberg*, 2009
   Plaster
   27 1/2 x 76 1/2 x 50 inches (69.9 x 194.3 x 127 cm)
   Courtesy the artist and Pace Gallery, New York
   Photography Kerry Ryan McFate; © Maya Lin Studio,
   courtesy Pace Gallery
2. Iceberg plan
3. Iceberg elevation
4. Working drawing for *Imaginary Iceberg*, 2009
   Photography courtesy Maya Lin Studio and Pace
   Gallery © Maya Lin Studio, courtesy Pace Gallery

ZAHA
HADID

The *Liquid Glacial* design embeds surface complexity and refraction within a powerful fluid dynamic. The elementary geometry of the flat table top appears transformed from static to fluid by the subtle waves and ripples evident below the surface, while the table's legs seem to pour from the horizontal in an intense vortex of water frozen in time. The transparent acrylic material amplifies this perception; adding depth and complexity through a flawless display of infinite kaleidoscopic refractions. The result generates a wonderful surface dynamic that inherits a myriad of colors from its context and continually adapts with the observer's changing viewpoint. The form is of its creator; a design that does not compromise functionality or ergonomic requirements and a coherent evolution of her architectural narrative exploring movement through space.

Courtesy David Gill Galleries Ltd.

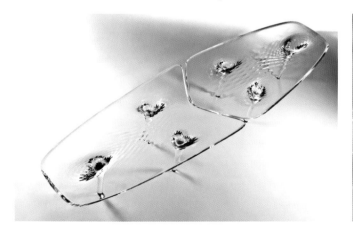

Zaha Hadid & Patrik Schumacher
Liquid Glacial Coffee Table, 2012
Polished plexiglass
15 1/2 x 106 5/16 x 35 7/16 inches (40 x 270 x 90 cm)
Courtesy David Gill Galleries Ltd.
Photography Jacapo Spilimbergo

IMPOSSIBLE PRODUCTIONS INK

POUR is part of a series of explorations around the idea of "saturation." So far, others in this series include Condensate, Hydrate, Dilute, and Caustic, all representing an interest in working with water in all its forms, although here primarily through multiple understandings of water as a "model" for design. "Model" here is seen in all its complexity, from idea through to what can be meant by "materialization," and in particular processes of 3D printing. Hopefully, then, these objects are not just functional, formal, aesthetic, etc., but work on a number of different levels simultaneously; not just Idea, the Sensory, an Idealization, the basis of Simulations or Understandings, Prototyping, Miniaturizations. It is not just qualities or properties of the thing which sits on a table, nor is it just a simulation frozen and made actual. Whilst this tea set obviously performs as such, it is the forced "saturation" of each of these levels which bring about the object in the first place, a kind of appreciation of the object even before its coming to be, as an actual 3D printed physical thing.

In this way this series of experiments are not just the creation of real objects, complex, simple, rarified, beautiful, or otherwise, but something which enables us to think about the object in many different ways at the same time, whilst simultaneously enabling us to question if these new forms of materialization truly bring something new to the table. As an office we do in fact belief that these technologies are truly new, and not just due to the current wide spread use of these technologies. The same object, created one-to-one by other means would still be a very different object, arguably lacking, and necessarily so, what 3D printing introduces us to, a whole new world not just of making physical complex things, but to truly further our appreciation of such.

Veronika Schmid

POUR, 2011
Aluminum; direct metal laser sintering (DMLS)
Vessel: 11 3/4 x 10 x 5 1/2 inches (29.8 x 25.4 x 14 cm)
Cup: 2 5/8 x 3 3/4 x 3 3/4 inches (6.7 x 9.5 x 9.5 cm)
Courtesy Impossible Productions Ink LLC

NERVOUS SYSTEM

The *Hyphae* lamps are a series of generative table lamps inspired by how veins form in leaves. Each lamp is digitally grown in a computer simulation and fabricated with 3D printing. Every lamp is unique. Efficient LED fixtures illuminate the lamps, casting dramatic, ethereal shadows on the surrounding environment.

Our work at Nervous System combines scientific research, computer graphics, mathematics, and digital fabrication to explore a new paradigm of product design and manufacture. Instead of designing specific objects, we craft computational systems that result in a myriad of distinct creations. These forms are realized using computer-controlled manufacturing techniques such as 3D printing, laser cutting, and CNC routing.

We are fascinated by natural processes that produce complex forms from simple rule sets and local interactions. Our projects center around adapting the logic of these processes into computational tools; we do this by translating scientific theories and models of pattern formation into algorithms for design. We abstract a natural phenomenon into a set of rules that specifies discrete instructions for a computer to carry out. The design systems we encode are "generative," meaning they have no fixed outcome. Rather than thinking of them as mere tools, we consider them our medium. These systems are digital materials with inherent properties and behaviors.

Our *Hyphae* system began with an algorithm for mimicking how veins form in leaves by a process called auxin flux canalization. The auxin flux canalization theory links the development of leaf veins to the flow of the growth hormone auxin. We have adapted and further developed this algorithm, taking it in new directions that allow us to control the simulation in order to produce varied and novel results. Using this simulation, we generate forms reminiscent of diverse natural phenomena including trees, leaf veins, sea fans, roots, and fungal rhizomes.

Our simulation begins with isolated root veins in an environment of digital hormone sources. Veins gradually emerge from the roots and colonize space as hormone flows towards nearby veins. They branch as these flows meet from different directions and subsequently merge as the network surrounds individual hormone sources. Growth continues until every source has been overtaken. The result is a space-filling network that is both hierarchical and rhizomatic.

Because our design process is entirely digital, computer-controlled manufacturing is the natural way to realize our products. Using 3D printing, we can create complex, organic forms that would be impossible to fabricate by traditional manufacturing methods. Because 3D printing does not require any investment in tooling, it costs the same amount per piece to produce a single item or thousands of identical objects. Where mass production favors uniformity, 3D printing favors diversity, freeing us to create one-of-a-kind designs like the *Hyphae* Lamps.

Nervous System

Pollen, Reaction, and Seed Lamps, 2010

Nylon; laser sintering

Diameter, largest: 10 1/2 inches (26.7 cm)

Courtesy Nervous System

Photography Jessica Rosenkrantz

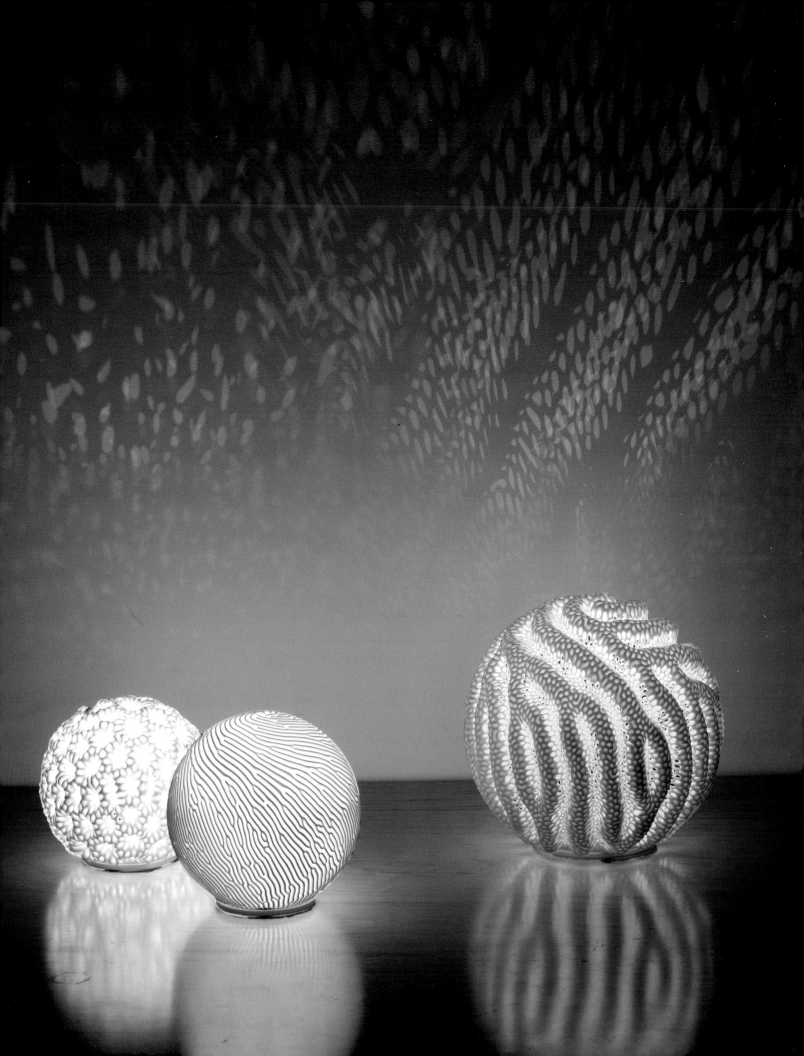

1. *Seed Lamp* surface construction
2. *Seed Lamp* sketch
3. *Seed Lamp* growth
4. *Seed Lamp* rendering

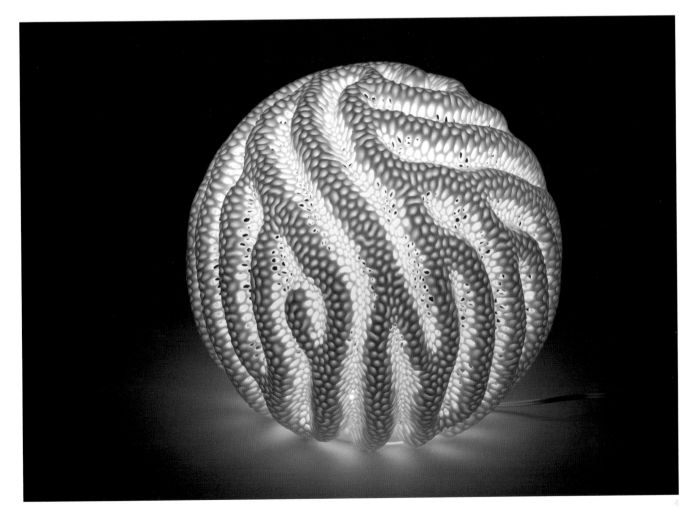

REBECCA STRZELEC

Inspired by early botanical illustrations, *Army Green Orchids* consists of 18 brooches that redefine the corsage. The series brings awareness to the practices surrounding commercially cultivated flowers and the daunting number of casualties caused by military activity in Iraq. Flowers have been worn as decoration since ancient Greece. Over time they have grown to signify achievement, class, mourning, celebration, and wealth. The preciousness of the corsage as self-expression has been watered-down with the onset of overnight delivery. Our society has created the mass-produced flower.

In parallel, as a nation, we have grown accustomed to the decade long casualty count in Iraq. Approximately 4,400 American soldiers and well over 100,000 Iraqi people have been killed since the start of the war in March 2003. Color brings attention to these overwhelming numbers. "Army" green speaks to military activity in general but also to the familiar toy soldier, sold in bags by the millions. In many ways, like our commercialized flowers, we have created the mass-produced soldier/civilian.

Army Green Orchids serve as a lasting corsage to memorialize these individuals. The Army Green Orchids brooches are created through computer aided design and 3D printing. The "Cross-section" pieces contain a unique interior scaffolding grid pattern. This complex form characteristic is created by intentionally pausing the 3D print build at a predetermined layer revealing the computer generated structures automatically built within "hollow" parts.

Rebecca Strzelec

(right) Sketch for *Army Green Orchids*

(opposite) *Army Green Orchids* Brooches, 2005–2006

Acrylonitrile butadiene styrene (ABS), corsage pin;

fused deposition modeling (FDM)

Largest: 4 13/16 x 4 1/8 x 11/16 inches (12.2 x 10.4 x 1.7 cm)

Courtesy Rebecca Strzelec

Photography Doug Yaple

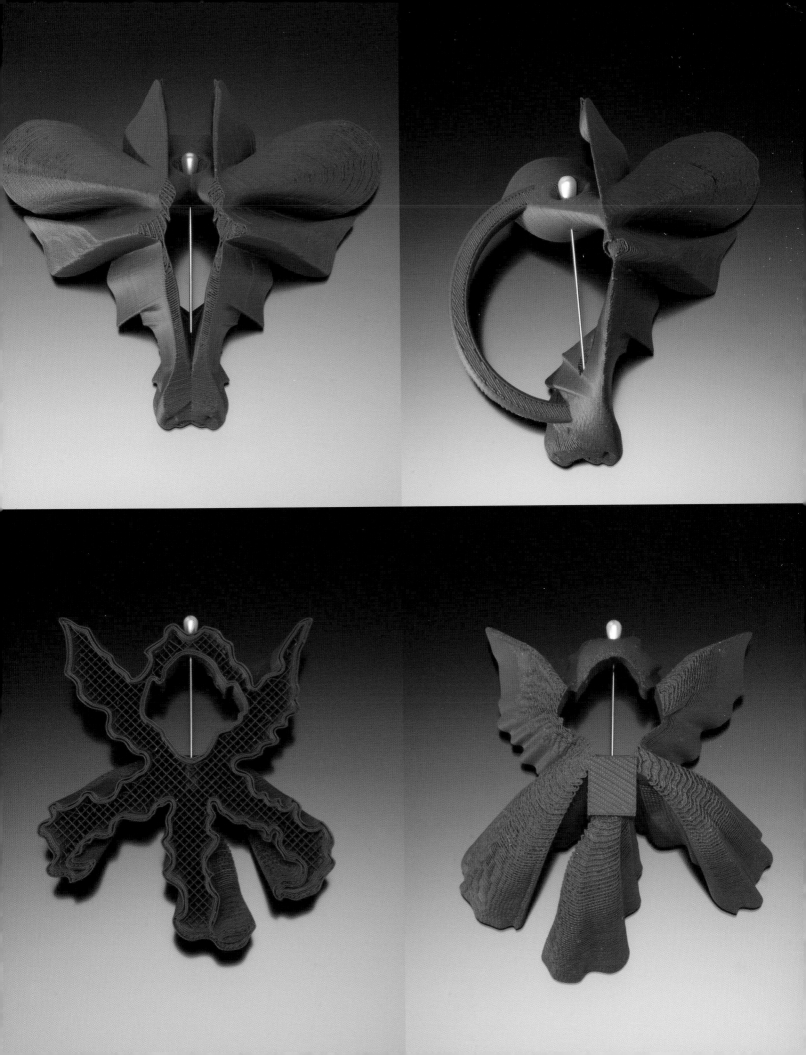

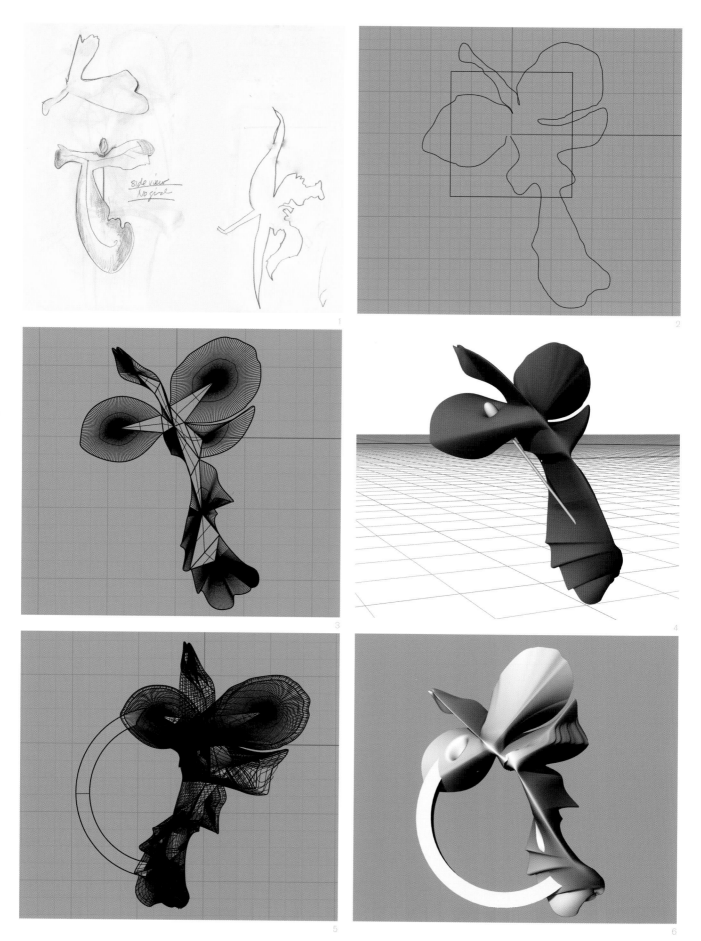

CS2

CS3

CS #4

CS7

1. Early sketches of orchid shapes
   based on botanical drawings
2. Drawing boundary curves in Rhino
3. Creating tent-like surfaces from
   boundary curves
4. Testing location of pin in quick
   shaded view

5. Adding circular element to
   balance composition
6. Shaded view of final surfaces
7. Comparing wireframe rending printouts
   on bulletin board

RICHARD ELAVER

Starting with computation and natural mutation as sources for design development, forms emerge through computational systems. Using text as building blocks, this work explores the translation between the virtual and physical, utilizing visualization and prototyping tools from industry to make one-of-a-kind objects. Each form is unique, built through an unfolding expression of potential, revealing semi-determinant authorship through similarities and deviations

By utilizing mathematical structures that replicate variance in nature, every object produced is an original, sharing characteristics and evolutionary history with its sibling (same genetic code, different expression). Exploring the space between control and chaos, this work allows the affordances of unpredictability to be a significant part of the process of form generation.

What is the physical manifestation of our understanding of fractals, chaos, and emergent systems? How can products be grown like trees? Through programmatic growth systems, this project is developing an expression of our understanding of nature through computation and desktop manufacturing.

The work begins with inspiration in the natural world, is processed through software, materialized through hardware, and finished by hand. Each piece is generated by code, the outcome of a custom software program. Through small changes in program elements, variations in form and pattern emerge. In the cycle of physical to virtual and back again, the process starts from observations of the natural world (physical); it then moves into a digital simulation (virtual) which begets three-dimensional forms in a CAD environment; that model is then output as a 3D print in wax (physical). The 3D printing process accretes tiny droplets of wax through a print-head, stacking layer upon layer to create a physical object from digital information. From there, the wax model returns to traditional craft methods and is used in a lost-wax process to cast the form in sterling silver.

Richard Elaver

Emergent Tableware, 2005
Cast sterling silver
Each approx. 6 x 1 x4 1/2 inches (15.2 x 2.5 x 1.3 cm)
Maxine and Stuart Frankel Foundation for Art
Photography Molly Reilly

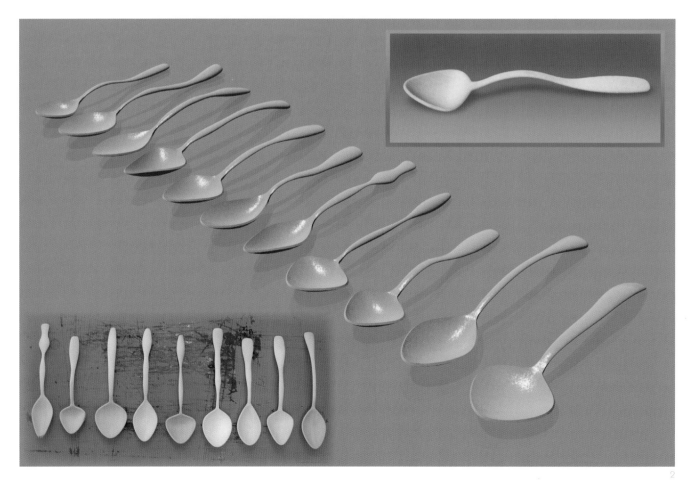

1. Computer rendering of five-piece
   settings showing variations in form and
   surface ornamentation
2. Early CAD from renderings using
   program scripting (RhinoScript) to
   create varied spoon forms, with initial
   3D test prints from Z-Corp printer
3. Fabrication process in stages, including
   CAD model (top), 3D print in wax
   (center), silver-cast utensil from 3D
   print using lost-wax process (bottom)

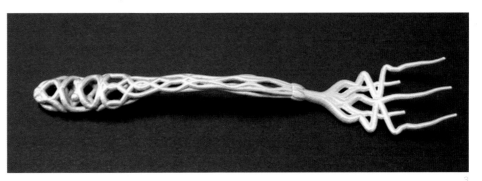

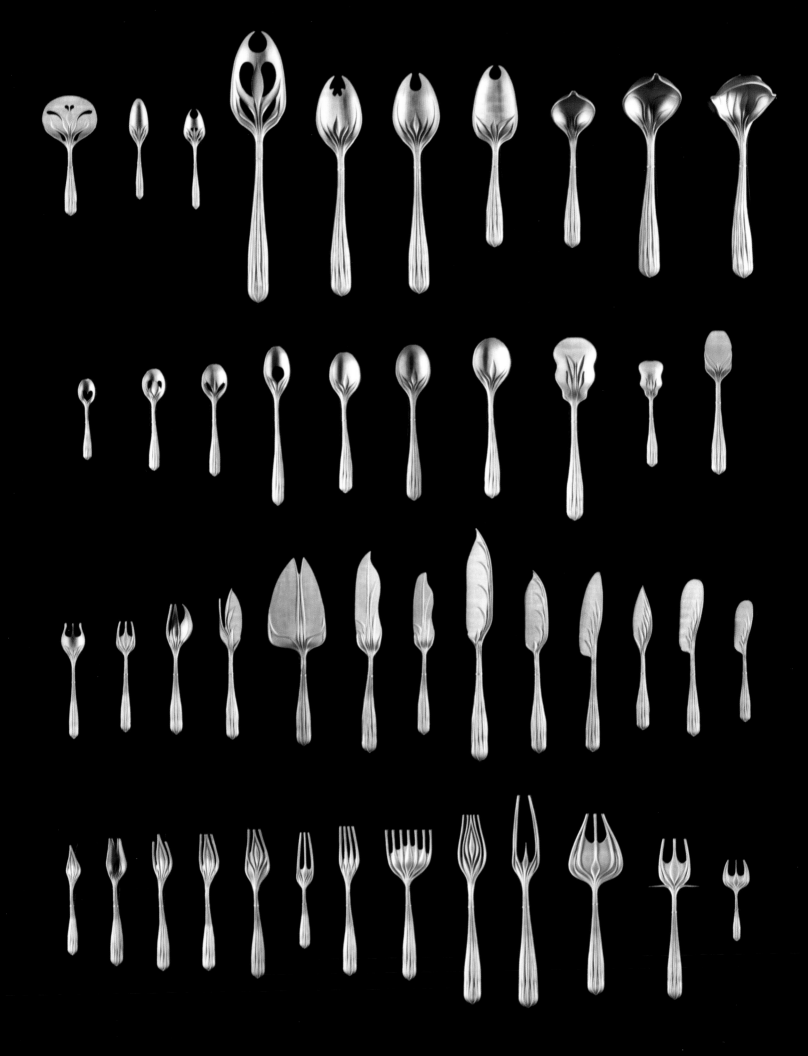

GREG LYNN

The design of flatware is most often a study in typology and variation. The basic utensil, such as a spoon, is used as the basis for a series of functional and cultural variations that range from the basic typologies of fork and knife into more exotic utensils for specialized practices. The design of the flatware set proceeded from a primitive, yet-to-be-specified, beginning. This primitive form was made up of a bundle of tines as a handle with webbing. The design of the individual elements in the set of flatware proceeded through the use of specialized software invented for the animated film industry where the primitive form was designed for specific functions and then mutated, blended, and evolved into the various functions of forks, spoons, knives,

and all elements in-between. The combined use of an original primitive design element that contained all the potential but none of the familiarity of the specialized functions with the dynamic modeling software led to the result of elements that are at once familiar and uniquely strange, specialized individually yet related as a family collectively.

The set was originally designed in sintered ceramic material that proved to be too brittle for daily use. The final set is manufactured as an edition where each piece is built using a computer controlled 3D printer that builds the pieces in micro-layers of sintered tool steel and bronze. There are no tools and no polishing used in the manufacture or production of the flatware.

Greg Lynn FORM

Flatware Prototypes, 2004–2007
Steel/brass alloy; direct metal laser
sintering (DMLS)
Variable dimensions
Los Angeles County Museum of Art,
Decorative Arts and Design Council Fund
Photography Greg Lynn FORM

NEW GEOMETRIES

Advanced mathematical theories play a fundamental role in the creation of three-dimensional forms that extend beyond the limits of traditional Euclidean geometry. Whether drawn from complex repeating arrangements found in nature or abstract concepts that determine spatial order, these algorithms map out mathematical space into diagrams with distinctive angles, facets, and whorls. This data is then translated into physical objects by machines using 3D printing for smaller works or CNC machining for larger structures. Scientific terminology such as fractal, space truss, hexagonal tiling, crystallography, and Voronoi diagram—once solely the language of mathematicians and engineers—are used in the titles and descriptions of these works, revealing the interrelationship between science, art, architecture, and design.

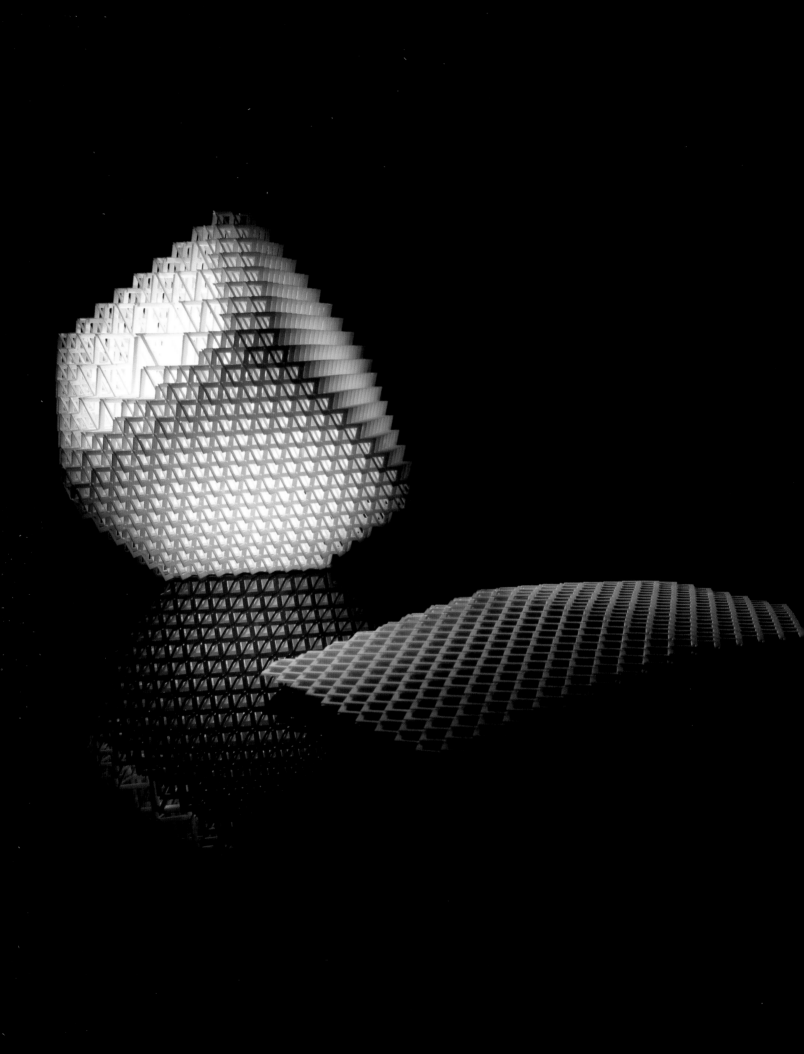

DROR
BENSHETRIT

The *Volume.MGX* Lamp uses the QuaDror geometry, which our team has been developing since 2008. With this product, we took the most complex way of interlocking the QuaDror joints and partnered with Materialise to realize this structure in one flat, 3D, SLS print. We pushed the boundaries with technology, creating 1,200 connecting joints that unfold into a self-supporting structure. Our team always strives to combine physics and poetry in every project, and for me this lamp is a perfect example. It is a great technical achievement in terms of engineering and the warm glow it gives when it functions as a light source is quite beautiful.

Studio Dror

Volume.MGX Lamp, 2009

Polyamide; laser sintering

Made by .MGX by Materialise

11 3/4 x 12 x 12 inches (29.9 x 30.5 x 30.5 cm)

Courtesy .MGX Materialise

SHANE
KOHATSU

The quest for acceleration and speed has long been the North Star for athletes across sport, and in order to excel in the game of football the mastery of these skills is seen in the 40-yard dash.

Nike Football debuts the *Nike Vapor Laser Talon* with a revolutionary 3D-printed plate that will help football athletes perform at their best. In a version built to master the 40, the Nike *Vapor Laser Talon* weighs a mere 5.6 oz. (standard men's size 9) and is specifically designed to provide optimal traction on football turf and to help athletes maintain their "drive stance" longer.

With more than 40 years of athlete insights and innovation across sport, NIKE designers worked with elite trainers within Nike SPARQ, as well as long time partner and gold medal sprinter Michael Johnson, to understand how he and his team at Michael Johnson Performance train football athletes for the 40. According to MJP Performance Director, Lance Walker, an athlete's "Zero Step" is a pivotal point that can make or break an athlete's 40 time. In the moments before that first step hits the turf, his propulsion and acceleration speed are determined. At that point it's all about geometry.

The plate of the cleat is crafted using Selective Laser Sintering technology (SLS). It is the sport's first 3D-printed plate. SLS is a manufacturing technique that uses high-powered lasers to fuse small particles of materials into a three-dimensional shape. Through proprietary material selection, NIKE was able to prototype a fully functional plate and traction system within a fraction of the traditional timeframe and at a fraction of the weight. The SLS process allows for the engineering and creation of shapes not possible in traditional manufacturing processes. It also provides the ability to make design updates within hours instead of months to truly accelerate the innovation process to never seen speeds.

Courtesy Nike

Vapor Laser Talon, 2013
Synthetic thermoplastic
polyurethane textile upper, with
Flywire and mesh, cubic dipped and
painted nylon plate; laser sintering
Made by Nike
Courtesy Nike

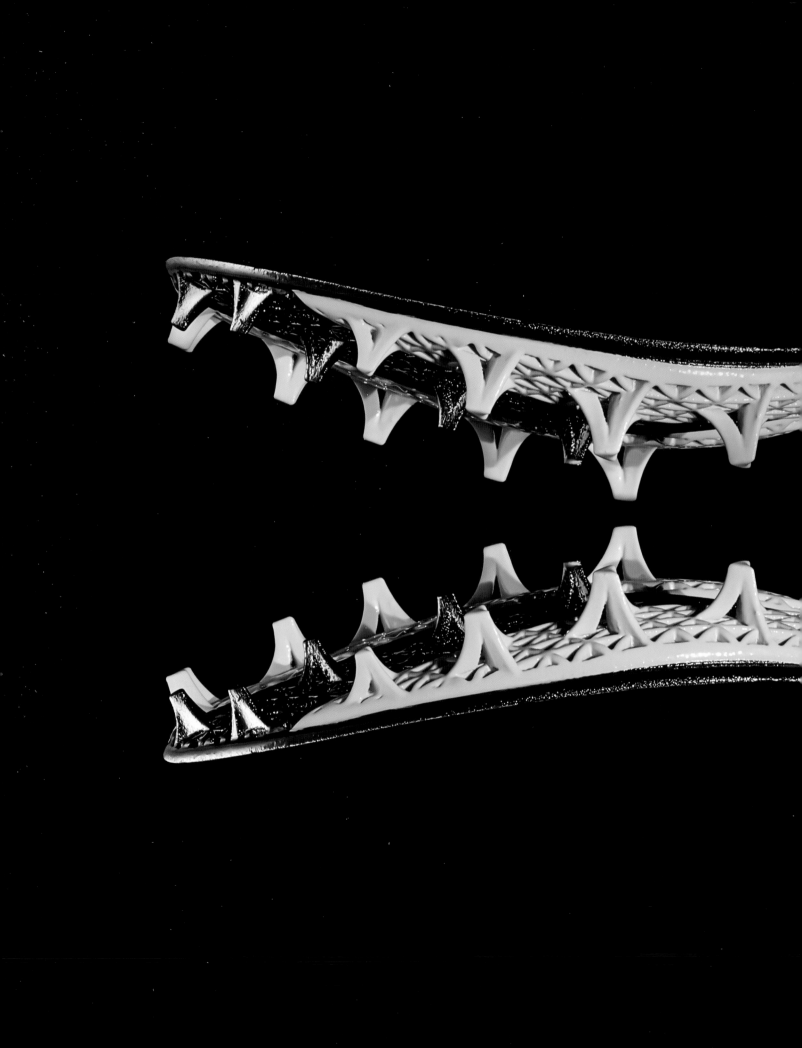

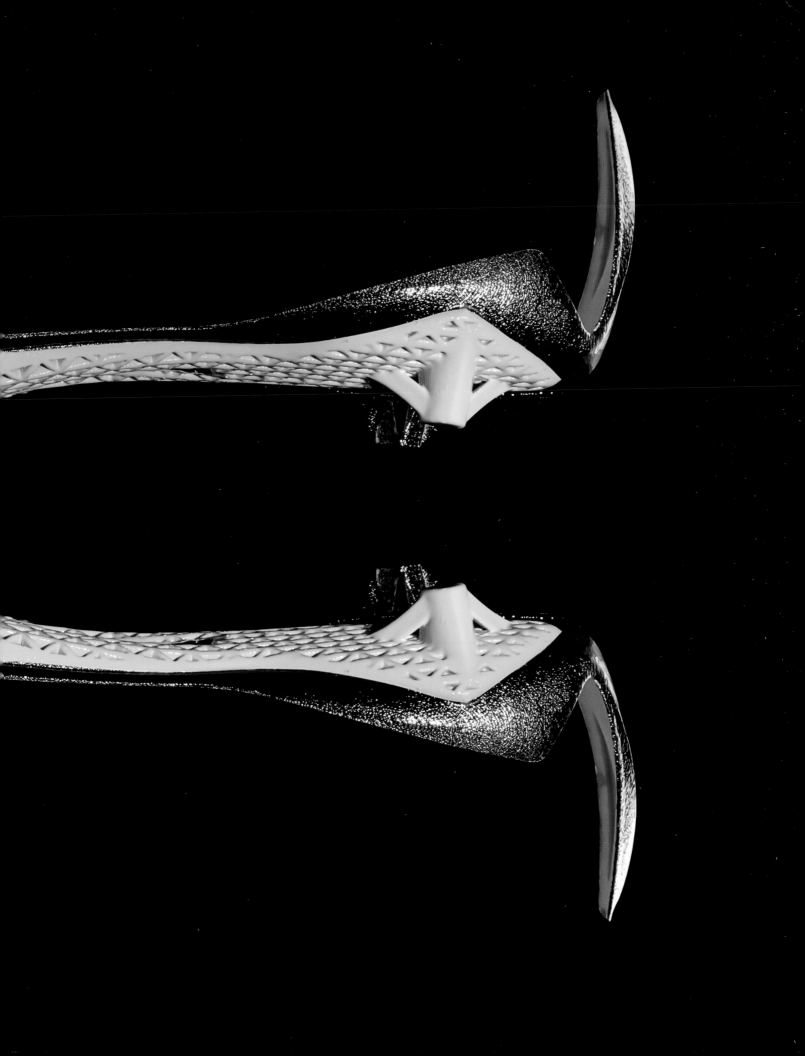

WERTEL OBERFELL
& MATTHIAS BÄRR

Fractal.MGX Table is a result of studies into fractal growth patterns that can be found in nature and which can be described with mathematical algorithms.

Per definition a fractal is a fragmented geometric shape that can be split into parts, each of which is (at least approximately) a reduced-size copy of the whole, a property called self-similarity.

Tree-like stems grow into smaller branches until they get very dense towards the top to form a quasi-surface.

The structure starts quite unorganized at the bottom and gets progressively organized until it ends in a regular grid, thus a progression from an approximate fractal to a fractal with exact self-similarity. To achieve this result different CAD software, both for nurbs modeling and polygon modeling, was used.

The fascination for us as designers lies in the object's grown and organic nature but also in its structured and mathematical quality. Both in terms of size and complexity *Fractal.MGX* Table pushes the manufacturing process to its limits.

Jan Wertel and Gernot Oberfell

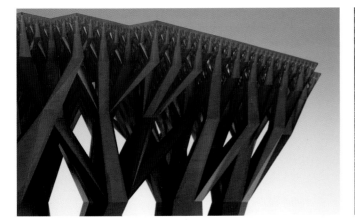

Fractal.MGX Table, 2008–2009

Epoxy resin; stereolithography

Made by .MGX by Materialise

16 1/2 x 38 1/2 x 22 3/4 inches (42 x 98 x 58 cm)

Courtesy MGX by Materialise

Photography © Stéphane Briolant Paris

MARC NEWSON

When French luxury jewellery and watch company Boucheron asked Newson to collaborate on a product, he decided to design a necklace. "Having just done the Gagosian show, I didn't want to be seen as jumping on the object bandwagon. Everyone would expect me to design some kind of sculptural object, hybrid half jewellery, half sculpture. For that reason, I decided to do a piece of traditional jewellery, to tackle it head-on." Newson had studied jewellery making in art school, where he'd learned to solder and set jewels. He was knowledgeable about metals and was familiar with stones as well.

In searching for inspiration, Newson chose fractals. "One thing that I'd always been fascinated by, like a lot of people, was fractal geometry, because it really underlined my fascination with scale. I like the way certain objects can transcend scale." Playing with the concept of scale itself, he came up with the idea to begin with the Julia set, a subset of the Mandelbrot set, "which in itself is a beautiful thing to look at—awe-inspiring, infinitely stunning". He selected a part of the Julia set and began translating it into a necklace. The problem was figuring out a way of accurately portraying the fractal character of the Julia set. "It's one thing to try and mimic fractals in two dimensions, but you risk losing the character, which is infinite and utterly irregular. There is an underlying order but it's all slightly unexpected, and that's what gives it its character. It's very difficult to translate that into an actual object. I spent the bulk of the time communicating the fractal language with the materials, but at the same time I thought there were wonderful parallels in the sense of using natural gemstones."

Newson set out by creating drawings, then with the help of his design assistant Nicolas Register did a survey of the literally infinite space of the Julia set. Once the region was found that had the character Newson was looking for, a fully developed digital model was created. Boucheron took this high-tech information and translated it into intricate hand drawings—a step usually eliminated by computers.

"They explained that that's the way they've always been doing it and it hasn't changed. Before they purchase the stones, the merchants work from hand-painted drawings, counting every stone. The way it ends up looking is entirely dependent on what's available in terms of the stones." Using age-old techniques, the Boucheron jewellers at Place Vendôme in Paris set over 2,000 precious stones to finish the piece.

Marc Newson Ltd

Doudou Necklace, 2009

Sapphires, diamonds, white gold

Made by Boucheron

9 7/16 x 7 1/16 x 1 15/16 inches (24 x 18 x 5 cm)

Mr. Tomasz Gudzowaty Private Collection

Photography Courtesy Boucheron

ACHIM MENGES & JAN KNIPPERS

In the summer of 2011 the Institute for Computational Design (ICD) and the Institute of Building Structures and Structural Design (ITKE), together with students at the University of Stuttgart realized a temporary, bionic research pavilion made of wood at the intersection of teaching and research. The project explores the architectural transfer of biological principles of the sea urchin's plate skeleton morphology by means of novel computer-based design and simulation methods, along with robotic manufacturing methods for its building implementation. A particular innovation is the possibility of effectively extending the recognized bionic principles and related performance to a range of different geometries through computational processes, which is demonstrated by the fact that the complex morphology of the pavilion could be built exclusively with extremely thin sheets of plywood (6.5 mm).

The project aims at integrating the performative capacity of biological structures into architectural design and at testing the resulting spatial and structural material-systems in full scale. The focus was set on the development of a modular system which allows a high degree of adaptability and performance due to the geometric differentiation of its plate components and robotically fabricated finger joints. During the analysis of different biological structures, the plate skeleton morphology of the sand dollar, a

sub-species of the sea urchin (*Echinoidea*), became of particular interest and subsequently provided the basic principles of the bionic structure that was realized. The skeletal shell of the sand dollar is a modular system of polygonal plates, which are linked together at the edges by finger-like calcite protrusions. High load bearing capacity is achieved by the particular geometric arrangement of the plates and their joining system. Therefore, the sand dollar serves as a most fitting model for shells made of prefabricated elements. Similarly, the traditional finger-joints typically used in carpentry as connection elements, can be seen as the technical equivalent of the sand dollar's calcite protrusions.

Following the analysis of the sand dollar, the morphology of its plate structure was integrated in the design of a pavilion. Three plate edges always meet together at just one point, a principle which enables the transmission of normal and shear forces but no bending moments between the joints, thus resulting in a bending bearing but yet deformable structure. Unlike traditional lightweight construction, which can only be applied to load optimized shapes, this new design principle can be applied to a wide range of custom geometry. The high lightweight potential of this approach is evident as the pavilion that could be built out of 6.5 mm thin sheets of plywood only, despite its considerable size. Therefore it even needed anchoring to the ground to resist wind suction loads.

Achim Menges

ICD/ITKE Research Pavilion, 2011
University of Stuttgart
6.5 mm birch plywood; computer
numerical control (CNC) laser cutting
Courtesy Achim Menges

1, 2. Robotic fabrication of cell walls with
grated edges for finger-joint assembly

3. Sanding edges for smooth surfaces

4. Application of glue to edges of
lower cell surfaces

5. Cells

6. Students lifting cell into structure
at construction site

7. Completed cells before assembly
of pavilion
Photography ICD/ITKE
StuttgartUniversity

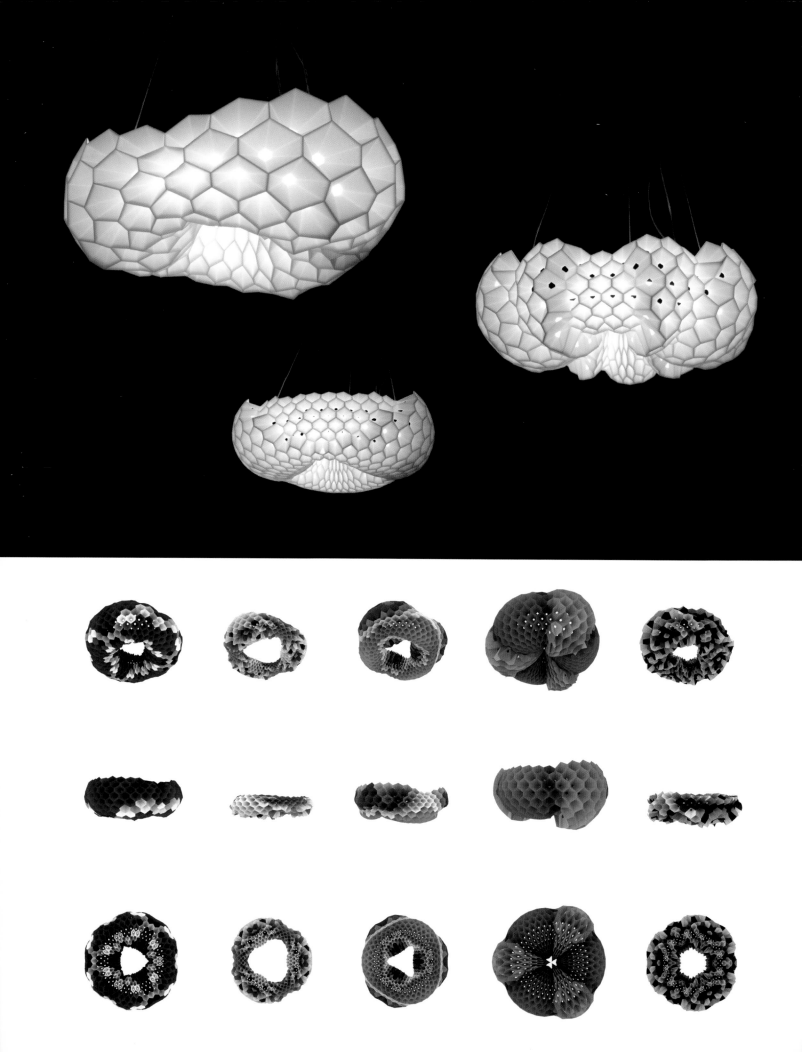

FRANÇOIS BRUMENT
& SONIA LAUGIER

Digital fabrication opens new ways of creation for the reassessment of standardization. For designers it involves a shift from conceiving one and only one object for everyone's use to developing systems in which the end user can participate and make his or her own unique object. How can we create new standards that are variable and easy to adopt? *KiLight* and *Vase#44* investigate design processes where the user can employ the most natural of tools: voice and gesture.

Shape a light with your body! *KiLight* lets the user determine the form and color of a virtual pendant lamp shade by manipulating a 3D model with the assistance of a Microsoft Kinect device that reads hand movements and captures the color of clothing. Move slowly, play with your hands or adjust the sleeves of your shirt. Once you're done freeze for three seconds and the program generates your *KiLight*'s 3D file ready to be 3D-printed.

François Brument

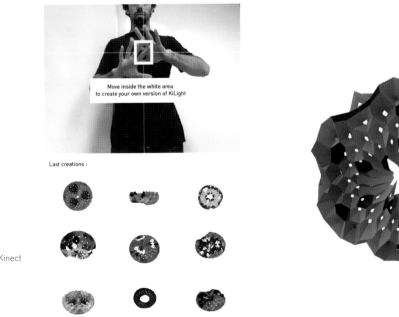

KiLight, 2011
Polyamide; laser sintering
Interactive installation: Microsoft Kinect
sensor, computer, projector
Courtesy François Brument &
Sonia Laugier

FRANK STELLA

The process begins with what's available, a piece of a model or piece of anything that I've worked on one way or another. Then I decide I want to work with it more, so that piece is then scanned by a computer.... There's a physical reality... to the pieces, and then there is a part in which the pieces are organized and arranged in a three-dimensional format with the aid of a computer.... That provides the geometry, the mathematical information needed to build it.

Then the piece is built, usually in a model form.... The pieces [are built] with fairly arbitrary holes in them so we can thread [steel] armatures through to support them and hold them together. That part [threading the steel armatures] takes place while we are working on them. The other part is the color—painting it—and there are various ways of painting it. I usually just work it out on a piece of paper. We paint it largely with industrial paint and of course fluorescent paint.

In 1990, we were working on an architectural project in Holland. The Medini brothers had asked me to do a project [for the Groninger Museum]. We made models, and the models were based on a few simple ideas, but one of the things that kept recurring was this notion of the wave form. The wave had come from the background in [my earlier] *Moby Dick* series.... In working out the model-making for the Museum, and for what amounted to a lot of walls and surfaces with compound curves, we had to scan models... to make them more manipulative and to make decisions about either the flexibility or strength of the materials.... Scanning models became a way of thinking and building pieces, and ultimately came to these pieces here.

There are considerable design challenges. The basic challenge is to find the orientation, the point where the piece is in equilibrium. You have to find the center of gravity of whatever object you're dealing with, so you can handle it properly. They're static, and the point is, it's a game of illusion. It may be a static piece but [it] has to create the illusion of movement. The movement is the vitality. In the art of the past, it had to look real. The figures had to breathe, and they were more highly prized the more natural they seemed; the way in which they moved was satisfying. Movement is somehow the given in both mimetic and abstract art.

In the end, the painting really counts.... I can leave it as form, but... they're not really unpainted; they're painted white so that's already a painted color. Once they have to interact with the stainless steel tubing, you have light and shadow and color and material.... You have a totality, which is very close to the totality you have in successful paintings that you achieve illusionistically. And these are illusionistic... there is an element here of negating their objectness, their object-like [quality]. There is kind of an anti-literalism to these pieces, to the conventional view of literalism anyway.

Adapted from an interview by Elsa Smithgall with Frank Stella appearing in *Stella Sounds: The Scarlatti Kirkpatrick Series at the Phillips Collection*, edited by Elsa Smithgall (Washington, DC: The Philipps Collection in collaboration with Yale University Press, 2001).

K.162, 2011
Epoxy resin, lacquer
22 x 22 x 24 inches (55.9 x 55.9 x 55.9 cm)
Courtesy FreedmanArt, New York
Photo:© 2013 Frank Stella / Artists Rights
Society (ARS), New York

ARANDA
LASCH

20 Bridges for Central Park proposes a series of interventions inspired by the brick, stone and cast iron bridges that dot Central Park. The original bridges by the Park's designers, Frederick Law Olmsted and Calvert Vaux, were built to make connections between landscapes and ease the intertwining of the Park's footpaths, carriageways and bridle paths, allowing for the traffic of people and nature to flow over, under and through each other. *20 Bridges for Central Park* extends this legacy by asking, "Are there other connections to be made?" The project connects existing landscape features in the Park by bridging them through a family of radically new structures that vary in size and configuration but retain the same fundamental identity and logic. While some are conventional footbridges, others are more unexpected bridges, such as stepping stones over a creek or a ladder up a hill. Like the original bridges of Central Park these structures are meant to be innovative and beautiful. Because they add to the existing repertoire in an unconventional manner, they underline an essential role of Central Park itself; that it is about connecting people, places, and nature together.

Aranda\Lasch

Concept for *20 Bridges for
Central Park*, 2011
Commissioned by Jumeirah
Essex House
Photography Aranda\Lasch

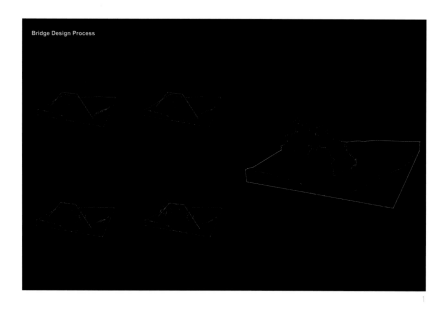

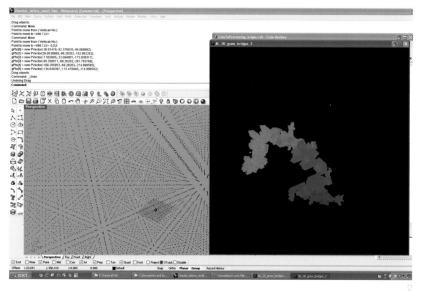

1 Bridge design process for
20 Bridges for Central Park
Photography Aranda\Lasch

2 Bridge design processing application
Photography Aranda\Lasch

3 Model for *Bridge* #2, 2011
Commissioned by Jumeirah Essex House
Expanded polystyrene (EPS) foam,
LINE-X finish; computer numerical
control (CNC) wire cutting
7 x 7 x 7 inches (17.8 x 17.8 x 17.8 cm)
Courtesy Aranda\Lasch
Photography Aranda\Lasch

4. *Baby Chair (Black)*, 2010 from *Modern Primitives*
installation, Venice Architecture Biennale, 2010
30 x 36 x 36 inches (75 x 90 x 90 cm)
CNC wire-cut EPS foam, Linex finish
Courtesy Aranda\Lasch
Photography Aranda\Lasch

5. Detail of Model for *Bridge #6*, 2011
Commissioned by Jumeirah Essex House
Expanded polystyrene (EPS) foam,
LINE-X finish; computer numerical
control (CNC) wire cutting
7 x 7 x 7 inches (17.8 x 17.8 x 17.8 cm)
Courtesy Aranda\Lasch
Photography Aranda\Lasch

4

5

MARLOES TEN BHÖMER

Rapidprototypedshoe is made using an additive manufacturing technology in which successive layers of a photopolymer material are UV cured. The shoe is built in one go, but is comprised of two materials, which are organized into different microscopic structures, thereby enabling different material properties. As a result, the shoe has both flexible and rigid sections. The shoe has been designed to be disassembled for the purpose of replacing parts, despite having never been assembled in the first place.

When moving from rapid prototyping to rapid manufacturing, inherent construction possibilities and aesthetics of the production method needs to be explored. Certain design and production details such as the punch holes and screws in this design are not a derivative of this production method, but still make constructive sense.

Marloes ten Bhömer

Rapidprototypedshoe, 2010
Photopolymer
7 1/16 x 11 13/16 x 9 13/16 inches
(18 x 30 x 25 cm) each
Courtesy Marloes ten Bhömer

ANDREIA CHAVES

The *InvisibleShoe* was born from a study of optics applied to shoe design. Andreia Chaves explores the concept of invisibility through the "chameleon effect": the shoe has a reflective finished surface, creating a deceptively obscured optical effect with every step taken. On the *NakedVersion*, the designer exposes the geometric structure's skeleton, exploring its contrast with the internal leather shoe.

The shoes were developed through a combination of leather-making techniques, to insure the best quality and comfort, while fusing this with the advanced 3D printing technology.

Andreia Chaves

Invisible NakedVersion from *InvisibleShoe*
Collection, 2011
3D-printed nylon exterior structure,
handmade leather internal
Heel: 5 inches (13 cm)
Courtesy Andreia Chaves
Photography Andrew Bradley

MARC NEWSON

For many years, Newson had been fascinated with the idea of "growing" materials, like metal, onto a substrate. The fabrication process for the *Random Pak* involves growing metal on a surrogate form, making an inorganic material behave organically. Growing metal around a sacrificial form allows a continuous, seamless surface to form. What is being created, in fact, is a metallic culture. The original object becomes redundant; it is merely a surrogate object or host to the metal growing on it. The process involved numerous steps: to start with, a series of algorithms was employed that made countless decisions about how to grow the desired objects. The digital part of this process alone took weeks, using a series of dedicated computers. Up to six machines ran concurrently to produce the various components for the works, and the largest component took over 1,500 machine hours to build. In addition to this was the detailed handwork required in finishing processes.

Courtesy Gagosian Gallery

Random Pak Chair, 2006
Grown nickel
34 5/8 x 34 5/8 x 24 5/8 inches (88 x 88 x 60 cm)
Edition: 1 AP
Courtesy Gagosian Gallery
Photography © Fabrice Gousset
Courtesy Marc Newson Ltd.

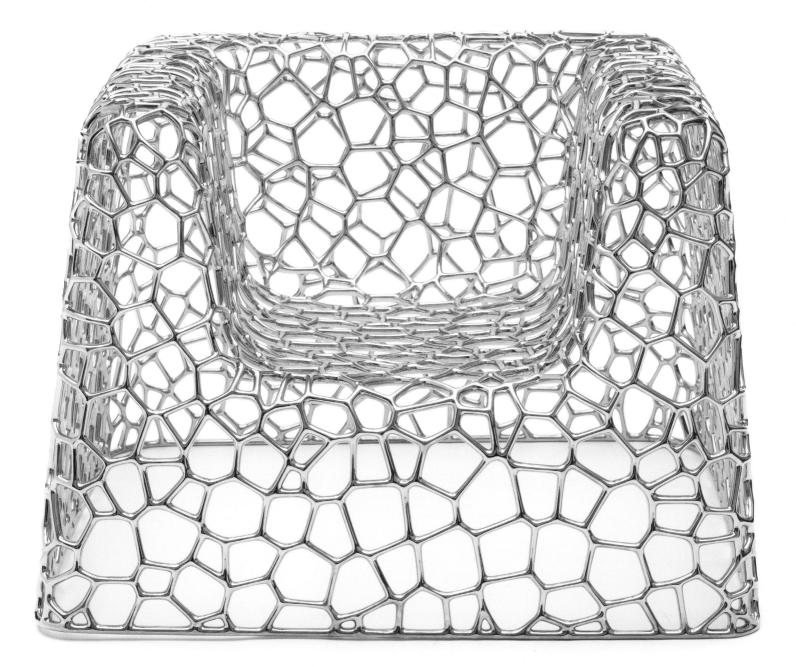

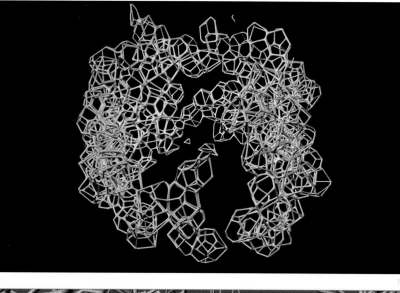

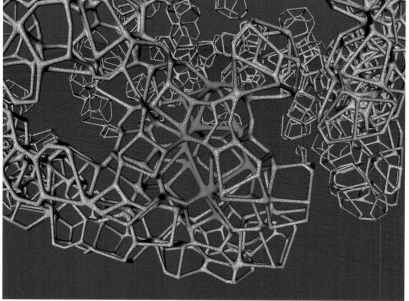

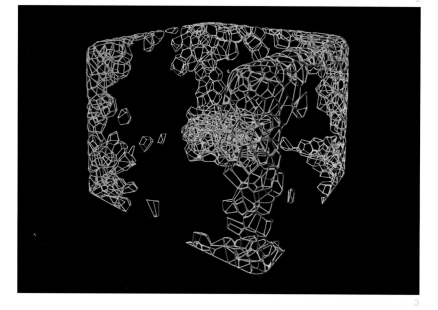

1, 2, 3. Refining algorithms used to generate
surface of *Random Pak* pieces
Photography © Marc Newson Ltd.
4. Full three-dimensional space-filled
study for *Random Pak Chair*
Photography © Marc Newson Ltd.

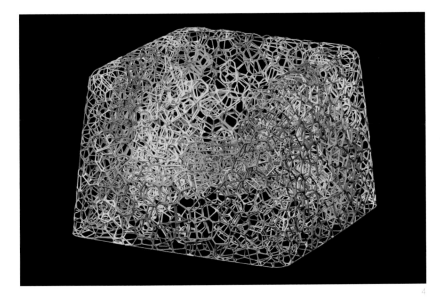

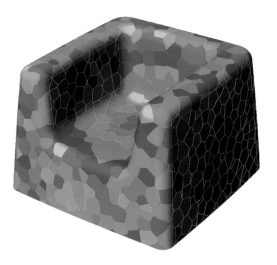

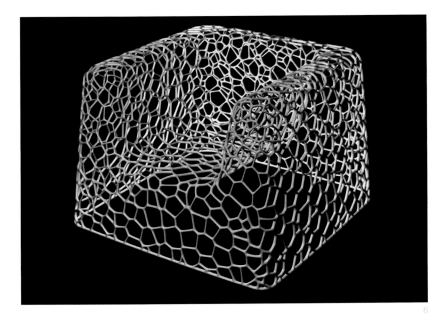

5. Intersection of *Random Pak Chair* form
   and space-filling Voronoi structure
   Photography © Marc Newson Ltd.
6. Development phase of internal
   structure for *Random Pak* series
   Photography © Marc Newson Ltd.

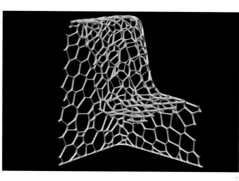

7. Development phase of internal structure
   Photography © Marc Newson Ltd.
8. Assembling internal structure
   Photography © Marc Newson Ltd.
9. Surface refinement prior
   to metal deposition
   Photography © Marc Newson Ltd.
10. Metal deposition in action
    Photography © Marc Newson Ltd.
11. Finished *Random Pak Chair*
    Photography © Fabrice Gousset;
    courtesy Marc Newson Ltd.

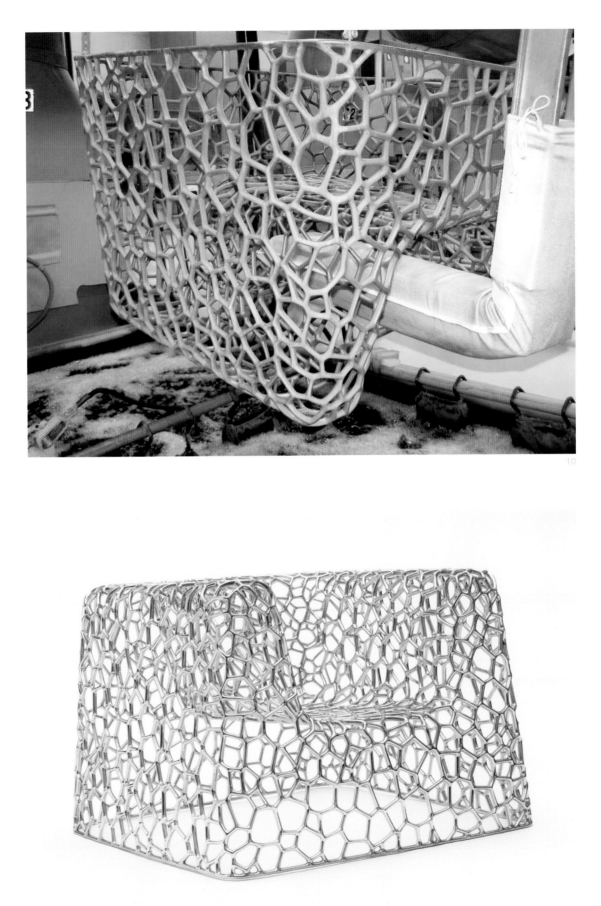

10

11

JANNE KYTTÄNEN

The *Macedonia* Space Divider was designed by Janne Kyttänen to maximize flexibility and freedom when dividing interior and exterior spaces. The modular system creates a highly decorative 3D effect.

Courtesy 3D Systems

Macedonia Space Divider, 2009
Polypropylene, Polyamide; laser sintering
Made by Freedom of Creation
Each: 19 3/4 x 19 3/4 x 1 inches (50 x 50 x 3 cm)
Courtesy 3D Systems

STUDIO DANIEL LIBESKIND

Are we still able to found a city?

The core of the *Futuropolis* installation lies in a trial made to show if we still have a lively idea, an idea that can be a proof of our reality, an idea about how to represent our lifestyle in this age in a creative manner. This is how these wooden structure came about, 98 elements, absolutely useless and vain, and absolutely inevitable. Like a city that has always to use its origin to create something meaningful, this structure reflects its memories and amnesias in a self-referential, hierarchic, and autonomous way. Its apparent chaos hides new and quite precise forms of order;

it is not a real city in the physical sense, with streets, houses, parks, but a scenario for the urban society of the future. It's an open model to transcribe in the vision of *Futuropolis*. The public city spaces are not formed by concrete and glass only, but also by people and residents, material and spiritual realities, that drive to the development of what men really need. Cities and buildings aren't stylized objects, like cars or machineries, they are part of life going on; to watch the limits of the built-up city, but also to consider the creative power of each single person is part of the creative process to build *Futuropolis* now.

Studio Daniel Libeskind

Futuropolis (detail), 2005
Birch plywood; computer numerical
control (CNC) milling
Courtesy Studio Daniel Libeskind

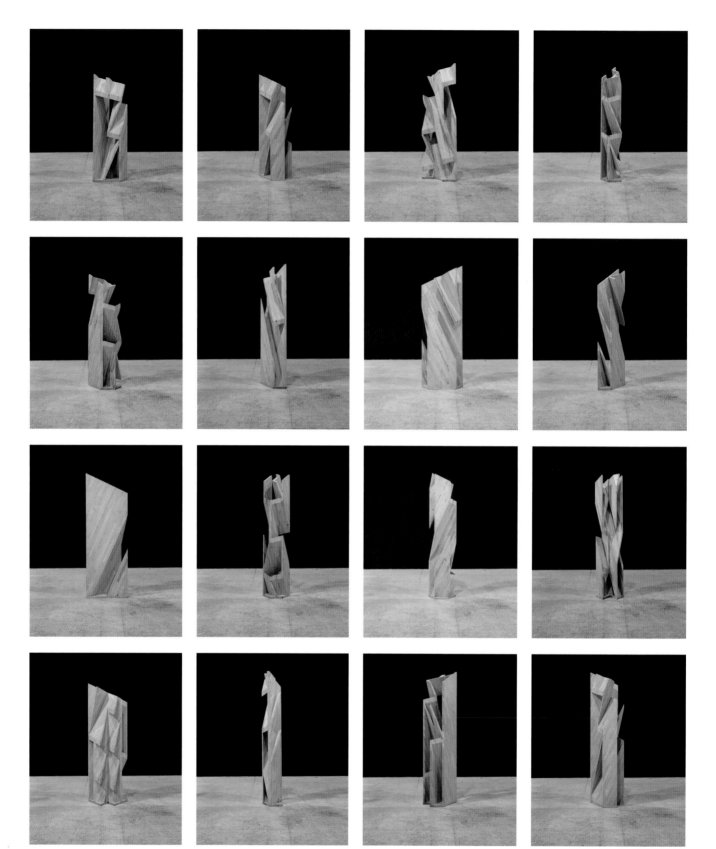

1. *Futuropolis* (detail), 2010
   Installation at Spazio CityLife,
   Milan, Italy
   Selection from 98 unique
   CNC-milled sculptures
   Photography Paolo Rosselli
2. *Futuropolis*, 2005
   Installation at University of
   St. Gallen, Switzerland
3. *Futuropolis*, 2005
   Installation at University of
   St. Gallen, Switzerland

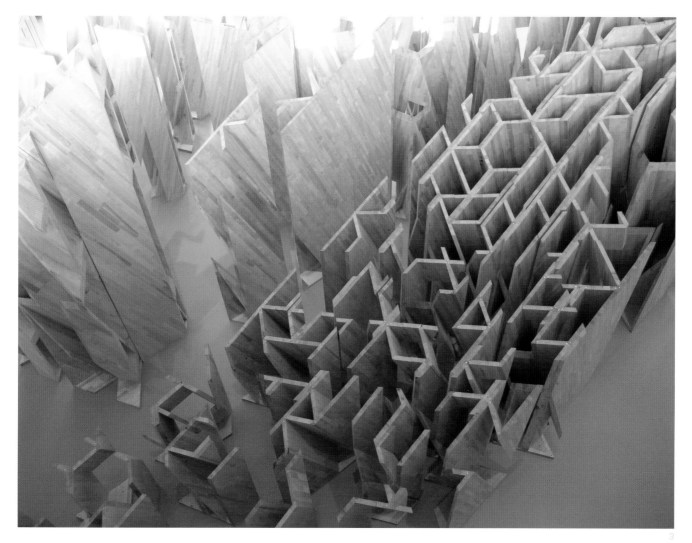

HIROSHI SUGIMOTO

In the spring of 2002, I paid a visit to the University of Tokyo's Graduate School of Mathematical Sciences to see the University's collection of plaster mathematical models, all made in Germany at the end of the nineteenth century and imported to Japan as teaching aids. The beauty of these pure mathematical forms was a wonder to behold, far outshining abstract sculpture. While considering the function of models I realized that the very act of photographing transfigures everything into models, and thus I decided to photographically remodel the mathematical models.

In the course of photographing, I noticed that one model, entitled *Surface of Revolution with Constant Negative Curvature*, looked like a vertically drawn-out Mt. Fuji, its twin equation-curved slopes asymptotically approaching an infinite vanishing point. The peak of this plaster Mt. Fuji was broken, but I thought, just maybe I could use today's high-end technology to create a model with a tip that would extend to infinity. I searched out the highest precision metalworking team in Japan and through much trial and error we managed to get the tip down to a mere 1mm diameter—any less than that, the material itself wouldn't hold up.

I set about modeling each successive cubic function in solid aluminum and stainless steel. I am not a sculptor; I am a model-maker, though when my oil-smeared creations emerged from the multi-axial automated machining lathe I knew the joy a sculptor must feel. In 2006, my first three finished mathematical models were exhibited at the Atelier Brancusi beside the Centre Pompidou.

Not unlike Brancusi's famous *Endless Column*, the very ends of my mathematical model intersect at infinity. In my mind's eye I can see two fine lines extend from either side of the 1mm tip and meet at an infinite vanishing point. Brancusi's *Endless Column* likewise manifests but a sampled portion of the infinite—which is also a model of the artist's imagination.

Courtesy Pace Gallery

Mathematical Model 009: Surface of revolution with constant negative curvature, 2006

$x = \dfrac{\cos u}{\cosh v}$

$y = \dfrac{\sin u}{\cosh v}$

$z = v - \tanh v$

$(0 \leq u < 2\pi , 0 \leq v < \infty)$

Aluminum, glass

Model and glass: 76 (high) x 70 13/16 (diameter) inches/ (160 x 179.9 cm); Base: 30 (high) x 70 13/16 (diameter) inches/ (76.2 x 179.9 cm)

Courtesy the artist and Pace Gallery, New York

Photography Ryan McFate, courtesy Pace Gallery

© Hiroshi Sugimoto, courtesy Pace Gallery

REBOOTING REVIVALS

In the past decade various artists and designers have taken a postmodern approach, using the tools of digital design and manufacture to create works that reference or reproduce historical artworks and past decorative styles. Some take advantage of advancements in 3D laser scanning—in which real objects are scanned optically and converted into digital, three-dimensional models—allowing for the accurate re-creation or dramatic reconfiguration of the original on the computer. Forms and decoration associated with Neoclassicism, Gothic Revival, Rococo Revival, Machine Aesthetic, Organic Modernism, and other styles are digitally reworked with a contemporary twist into sculptural objects that seem at once familiar and new.

MICHAEL EDEN

For over 20 years I ran a ceramics business with Vicky Eden. Work was designed, handmade, and supplied to galleries and stores internationally. During that period we researched and wrote a book on contemporary ceramics and were the co-curators of a large touring exhibition of international ceramics.

Between 2006 and 2008 I undertook an MPhil research project at the Royal College of Art to see how my interest in digital design and manufacturing could be developed and combined with my previous experience. One of the practical outcomes of the project was *The Wedgwoodn't Tureen*, an award-winning series of unique pieces that won an RSA Design Directions competition. In collaboration with the French company Axiatec, the original piece was produced on a ZCorp 3D printing machine and then coated in a unique ceramic material that does not require firing. It was the first time that these materials and processes had been used for commercial production.

Since then I have continued to design and produce a series of pieces, inspired by historical objects and contemporary themes.

The work further explores the relationship between hand and digital tools, investigating experimental manufacturing technology and materials. My working methods have enabled me to create a body of work that can, to some small extent be used to address the future of craft.

I am particularly interested in how the tacit knowledge and sensibility to the three dimensional object developed through extended practice can affect and influence the approach to the creation of objects using digital technology.

As a member of a unique generation that has bridged the digital divide, I firmly believe that this particular perspective has enabled us to contrast and compare life before and after the invention of the personal computer. For me it is not a matter of evolution, I feel very lucky that life at the beginning of the twenty-first century has furnished me with a wider choice of tools in my toolbox. All have their place, the new does not replace the old; the key is to make appropriate use of them.

Michael Eden

À Rebours, 2009
High quality nylon with unique non-fired
ceramic coating, liquid gold leaf; additive
layer manufacturing
15 3/8 x 11 7/8 x 11 inches (39 x 30 x 28 cm)
Private Collection
Photography courtesy Adrian Sassoon

BARRY
X BALL

There is a long history of artists making works "after" those of their forebears. Although employing an advanced technological armamentarium, I am also working in that ancient tradition, harkening to a time centuries before the Modernist Revolution, searching for a way to make something equally revolutionary. New in my art is the utilization of 3D digital scans of specific existing historical sculpture as my point of origin. The Baroque masterworks *La Invidia* (envy) by Giusto le Court and and *La Purità* (purity) by Antonio Corradini serve as specific endpoints to my beginnings. I am no longer content to have my work be "reminiscent of" or "inspired" by historical antecedents. Therefore I set for myself the task of making new Masterpieces—*Envy* and *Purity*—that are "more perfect". Here is a partial list of how I seek to achieve this goal:

1. The substantial additions I effect and the manner in which I carve and polish my works make them true sculptures-in-the-round. The backs, sides, fronts, and tops are treated with equal fastidiousness, not antique frontal portraits intended for niche placement. I also design and create the pedestals for a seamless totality.

2. I choose to work with unusual, exotic hardstones, not traditional white Italian marble. Translucent Golden Honeycomb Calcite renders the veil, shawls, drapery, and figures diaphanous; when externally lit, it appears to radiate inner light.

3. My sculptures are mirror images of their sources. Mirroring adds strangeness and unfamiliarity, especially for those who may be familiar with the historical forebears.

4. I eliminated the Christian Latin cross from the bodice area of *Purity*'s veil. This makes the subject one of rich mystery, more than a relic of religious devotion, penitence, or modesty.

5. I eliminated the lace border from *Purity*'s veil to enhance its smooth, sensual liquidity.

6. My sculptural treatment is intentionally softer, more fluid than the Baroque works. The body has departed and left behind a misty, swirling, dematerialized surrogate.

7. I corrected several of Le Court's and Corradini's confused or poorly executed details.

8. I subtly enlarged *Purity*'s breasts. For a sculpture with chaste devotion as its subject, there is undeniable eroticism in the way her body is concealed and revealed.

9. I have selectively polished various surfaces—backs, the lower frontal regions, exposed flesh. For contrast, matte passages are attained using a fine, non-directional satin finish so that their surfaces softly "disappear."

10. Le Court's *La Invidia* and Corradini's *La Purità* have significant roughly-carved, unfinished portions and have suffered damage over time. *Envy* and *Purity* are precisely finished and pristine.

I want these works to pose questions, not dictate answers. While striving to induce a type of refined viewing, of connoisseurship, I also hope that my sculptures seduce. In an internet-linked world where almost everything from every period is available to everyone, my aim has been to build a new type of sculpture, redolent of its sources, but very much of our time.

Barry X Ball

Envy, 2008–2010
Golden Honeycomb Calcite, stainless steel
22 x 17 1/4 x 9 1/2 inches (55.9 x 43.8 x 24.1 cm)
Pedestal: Macedonian Marble, stainless steel, wood, acrylic lacquer,
steel, nylon, plastic; 46 x 14 x 12 inches (116.8 x 35.6 x 30.5 cm)
Private Collection, Basel
Photography courtesy Barry X Ball Studio

1

2

3

4

5

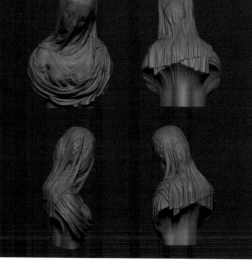

6

1. Antonio Corradini
   La Purità (purity), 1720–1725
   Ca' Rezzonico, Venice
2. 3D digital scanning of La Purità at
   Ca' Rezzonico, Venice
3. Scan data of *La Purità*
4. Digital sculpting *Purity* back drapery
   extensions
5, 6. *Purity* digital model
7. Selecting Calcite at quarry, Utah
8. Cut Calcite slab
9, 10. Rough-sawing *Purity* on CNC lathe
11. Finish-sawn *Purity* on CNC lathe

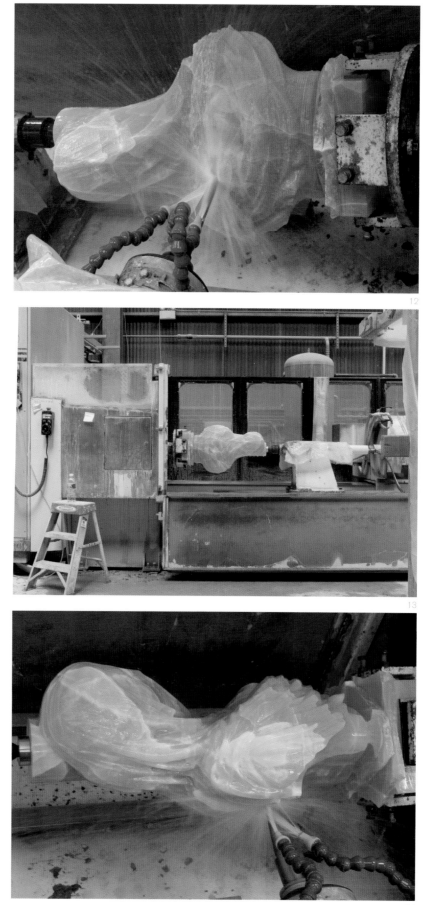

12

13

14

15

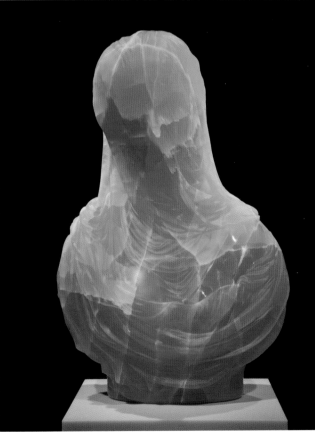

12, 13. Rough-milling *Purity* on CNC lathe

14. Final-milling *Purity* on CNC lathe

15. Hand-finishing *Purity* at artist's studio

16. Barry X Ball

Purity, 2008-2009

Golden Honeycomb Calcite

16

VIVIAN MELLER & LAURA ALVARADO

What excited us about working with new technologies is that it opens completely new fields in the way we design. We like to integrate in our work different disciplines and combine low-tech, high-tech, and craftsmanship in an extraordinary and playful way.

We are inspired by imperfection, spontaneity, and coincidence and aim to break new ground by experimenting systematically with the functional and dysfunctional use of software and hardware tools. We use modeling techniques and design tools intuitively and freely. Scanning freehand with a 3D scanner like drawing with a pencil, following patterns with a Micro-Scribe like drawing a picture, and using the body as a canvas to create new forms.

We met during our design studies in Dusseldorf. Soon our mutual fascination for exploring the relationship between the body and traditional jewelry with a personal, intimate, and individual character, led us to collaborate in a multimedia project that seeks for objects where past and present meet. We think of digitizing technologies as an artistic creation tool with a performative and participative character, which enables us to obtain new and unique forms with a sketchy quality, where one can still recognize the creation process in the material.

Vivian Meller and Laura Alvarado

Portrait me: Baroness from Baroque Series,
2011–2012
Polyamide, acrylic, silk, silver; laser sintering
3 1/2 x 2 3/4 x 1 inches (9 x 7 x 3 cm)
Courtesy Laura Alvarado
and Vivian Meller
Photography Mats Kubiak

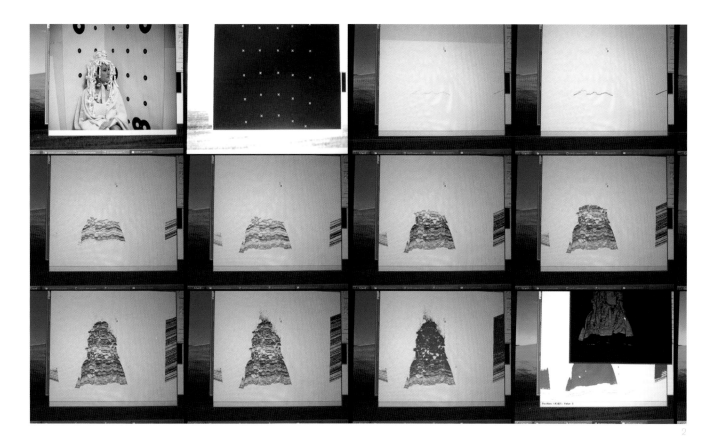

1. Artists styling model Maria's hair,
   costume, and makeup as Baroness
   Photography Valerie Schmidt
2. Screenshots of process of 3D
   scanning Maria as Baroness
3. *Portrait me: Maria and Baroness
   from Baroque Series*, 2011–2012
   Photography Mats Kubiak

DOUG
BUCCI

As an individual with diabetes, my work is inspired by my own health and risk of medical complications. For *Sweetmeat*, I have drawn additional social context from eighteenth-century dining and the intricate service ware used at the time.

Dining for the aristocracy was more about ostentation, display, and consumption of wealth than it was about the necessity of eating in the 1700s. Wealth and status of the owner was conveyed through platters, tureens, and distinct forms such as epergnes. Expensive and rare ingredients were elaborately prepared and served in elaborate tableware, which was placed precisely at the table for full impact during each course. Multiple delicacies were served at each course, from platters of rabbit or game meats in their entire form (today a gruesome image), exotic soups and vegetables forced to grow in winter, to sugarcoated fruits and exotic sweetmeats. The display of each course was abundant and gluttonous. A dinner service could last five hours or more.

When looking back at dining in the eighteenth century and placing it in a social context, it was clearly a display of wealth, power and status. In the present day, such over-indulgences can have deadly consequences, leading to obesity, diabetes, and diabetic complications. I drew from the beauty of the table service to recreate an intricate vessel, but now the gruesome image is the shrouded human consequence of such action.

Doug Bucci

Sweetmeat, 2013
Basket: bronze infiltrated stainless steel;
powder bed and inkjet head printing
Brooch: photopolymer, polychrome, 18K gold
16 1/2 x 21 1/2 x 21 1/2 inches
(41.9 x 54.6 x 54.6 cm)
Courtesy Doug Bucci

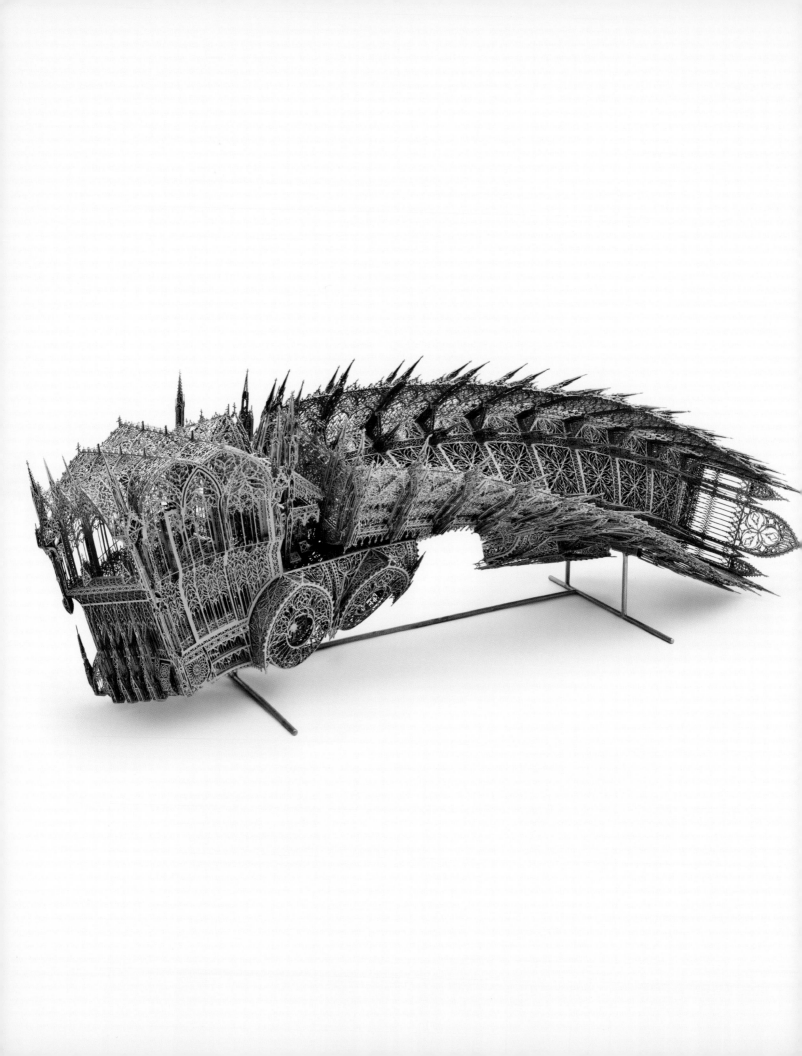

WIM DELVOYE

Gothic has been called many things: the epitome of grotesque, the essence of spirituality, the embodiment of liturgy, the abandonment of classical, the clarification of a structural problem, and the French style subsequent to the Romanesque, which rose in the twelfth and thirteenth centuries. Starting in 2001, a contemporary Belgian artist, Wim Delvoye, began to call Gothic his own. With works ranging from small-scale cathedrals, painted ironing boards, and uncanny stained-glass windows to imposing freestanding metal towers, Delvoye has added his own definition to a style that has eluded and entranced scholars for centuries.

Prominent within Delvoye's Gothic oeuvre are his life-size construction machines adorned in Gothic decoration made out of laser-cut steel. In these works, he marries small and large-scale pieces to create monuments of everyday objects.

Gothic is employed as the raw material, the substance from which the sculptures are made. Thus, unlike the "decorated" machines where it is the truck that is first evident, in these steel machines, one perceives the historicizing decoration along with the object itself. "Functional, industrial machines that are not supposed to be ornamented, 'become spiritual' and dissolve into highly detailed replicas, but ones in which only the outlines, the articulation of the parts and the silhouette of the machine are true to reality, while inside it is not the machine that is presented,

but the logic of the graphical system itself, unfolding freely and completely." In these objects, it is not the truck, or model that dominates the senses, it is the "Gothic." The object has evolved from a utilitarian object into shimmering lattice in space.

In Delvoye's metal machines, "materiality dissolves into structure, decoration dissolved into the substance: the structure becomes geometry—a regular play of lines, and the substance becomes intangible—glass, light." Delvoye is parodying the Gothic in a more profound way with these sculptures than with the earlier set. He is perverting the style in a complex way, instead of simply decorating the surface of the object. It is also evident in these machines that he is looking directly at Gothic examples.

With its mathematical symmetry and skeletal tracery, Delvoye's stainless steel *Twisted Dump Truck* is a hybrid vehicle combining the architectural and mechanical, the divine and secular, the feminine and masculine. Deriving its composite parts from cathedrals, the work evokes the representation of divine harmony and cosmological order in Gothic architecture and conveys both lightness and density. At the same time the work suggests a struggle between the greater glory and power of God and the unrelenting (and destructive) potential of mortal ingenuity, might, and godly ambition.

Courtesy Patricia Low Contemporary

Twisted Dump Truck (Counterclockwise,
Scale Model 1:5), 2011
Nickel-plated steel; laser-cutting
27 9/16 x 78 3/4 x 31 1/2 inches (27 x 200 x 80 cm)
Courtesy Patricia Low Contemporary, Gstaad/St. Moritz
Photography Studio Wim Delvoye

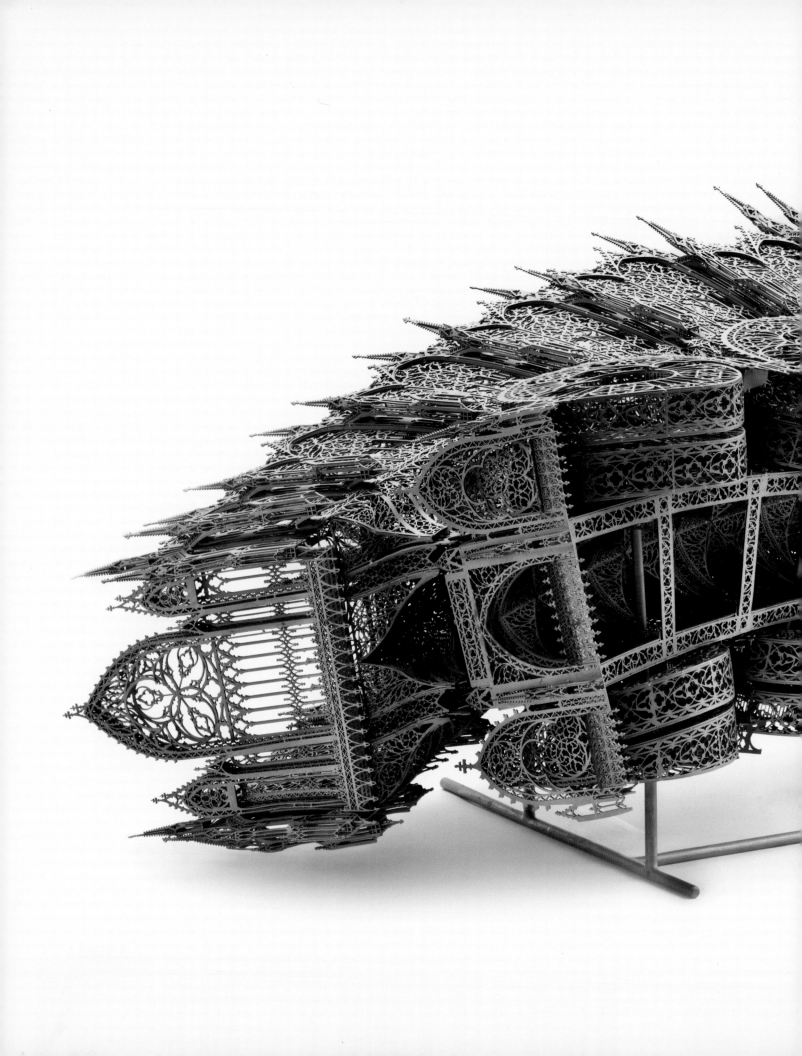

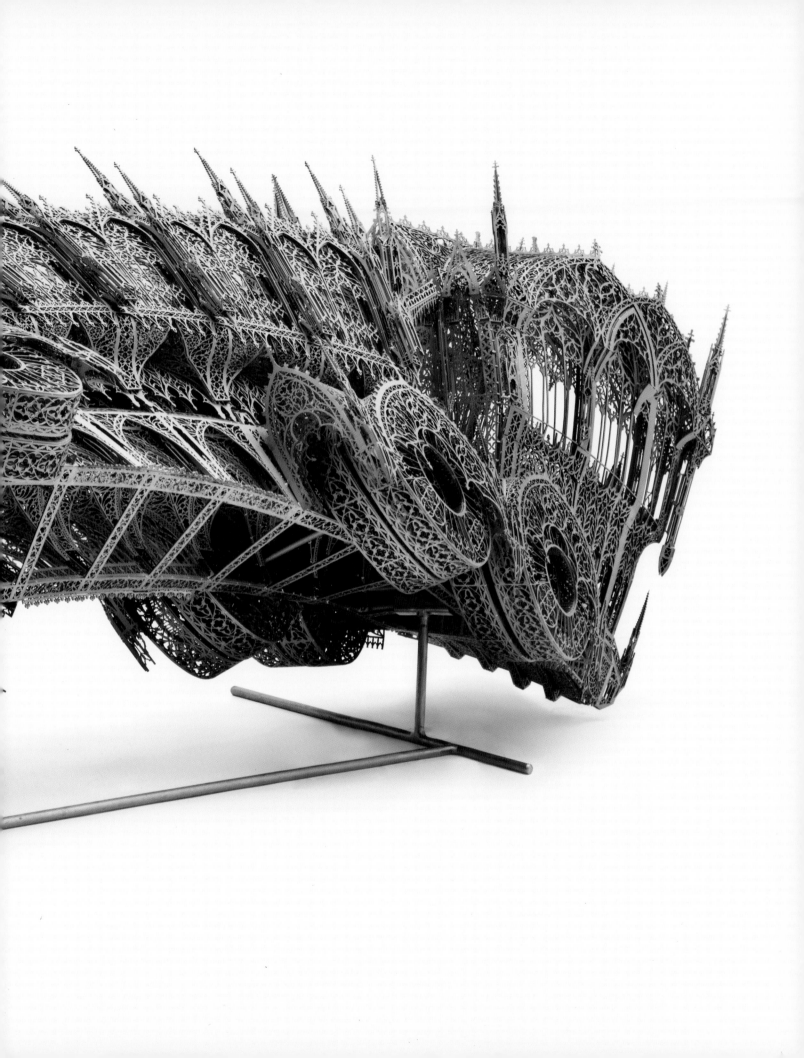

JOSHUA DEMONTE

Architecture has always surrounded the body. Man-made structures not only alter our perception of the space they enclose but also alter our perception of the qualities of their owners. Gargantuan stone cathedrals dwarf the figure and emanate piety and the strength of God. High overhanging balconies send a message of glamor and wealth to the observers far below. The language of architecture and the space it creates is part of every person's visual vocabulary.

My jewelry objects mimic ancient architectural elements, activating the space surrounding the body and altering the viewer's perception of the wearer. Being that the objects are large-scale for jewelry but small-scale for architecture, the wearer becomes a landscape in which my work has been positioned. My choice of ancient forms is a simple one. The details and complex structures of ancient works such as coughers and cornices begin to parallel the details of traditional jewelry objects such as pavé and granulation. My work has replaced the traditional embellishments of jewelry objects with the details of traditional architectural form. The objects have become jewelry that have defined architectural space around the body, altering our perception of the figure.

Joshua Demonte

Cathedral Collar, 2009
Gypsum, cyanoacrylate; power bed fusion
12 x 13 x 11 inches (30.5 x 33 x 27.9 cm)
Courtesy Joshua DeMonte

1, 2. Screen capture of *Cathedral Collar*
3D file in progress

3. Rendering of final collar

4, 5. Extracting 3D-printed section of
collar from bed of plaster powder
in printer

6. Removing excess powder

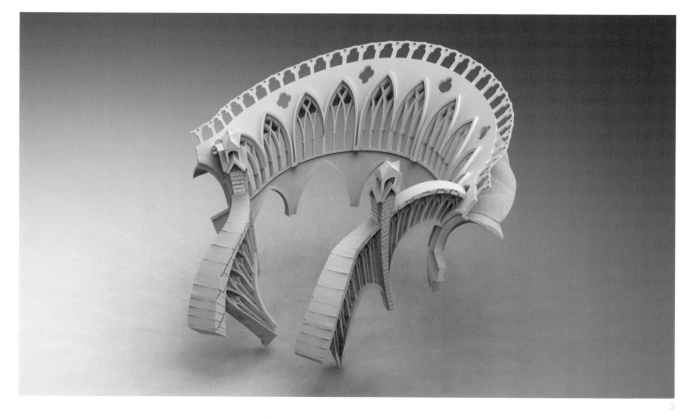

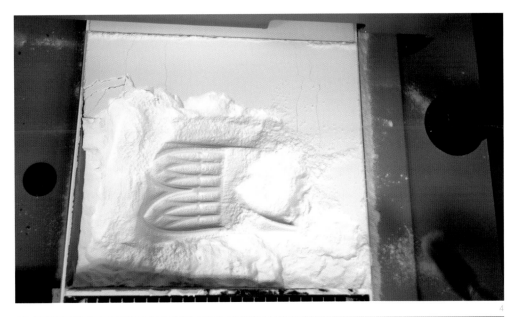

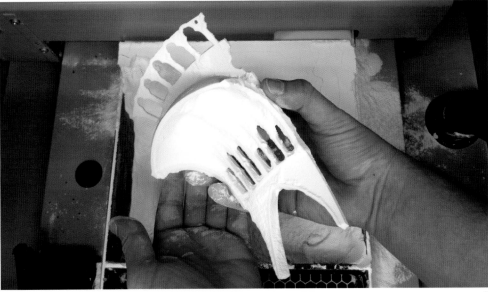

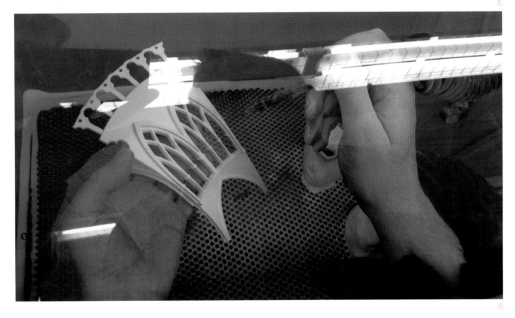

JULIAN MAYOR

The idea of this chair was to explore the boundaries between an original and an identical copy of an object. The chair was based on a Queen Anne chair from the collection of the Metropolitan Museum in New York that has been sampled, digitized, and recreated. It was modeled on a computer from detailed plans, and then cut from sheets of plywood using a numerical router.

Although the piece keeps an appreciation of the form and formality of the original, it has been transformed into something that is more about the idea of possibility. It requires some kind of relationship with the viewer to make it work, and seems to create a question mark rather than a full stop.

Courtesy 21st twenty first Gallery

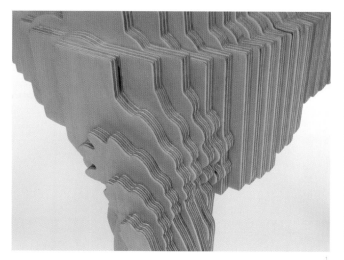

1

2

Clone Chair, 2005

Plywood; computer numerical control (CNC) routing

37 3/18 x 19 11/16 x 23 3/16 inches (95 x 50 x 58.9 cm)

Courtesy 21st twenty first Gallery

Photography © Julian Mayor and Topaz Leung

1. Detail of front knee

2. Detail of back side

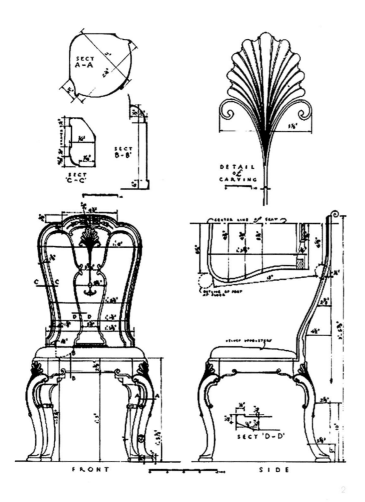

1. CNC milled cross-sections glued together and clamped to set
2. Plate from *Masterpieces of Furniture Design* by Verna Cook Salomonsky, 1931
3. Details of wireframe modeling

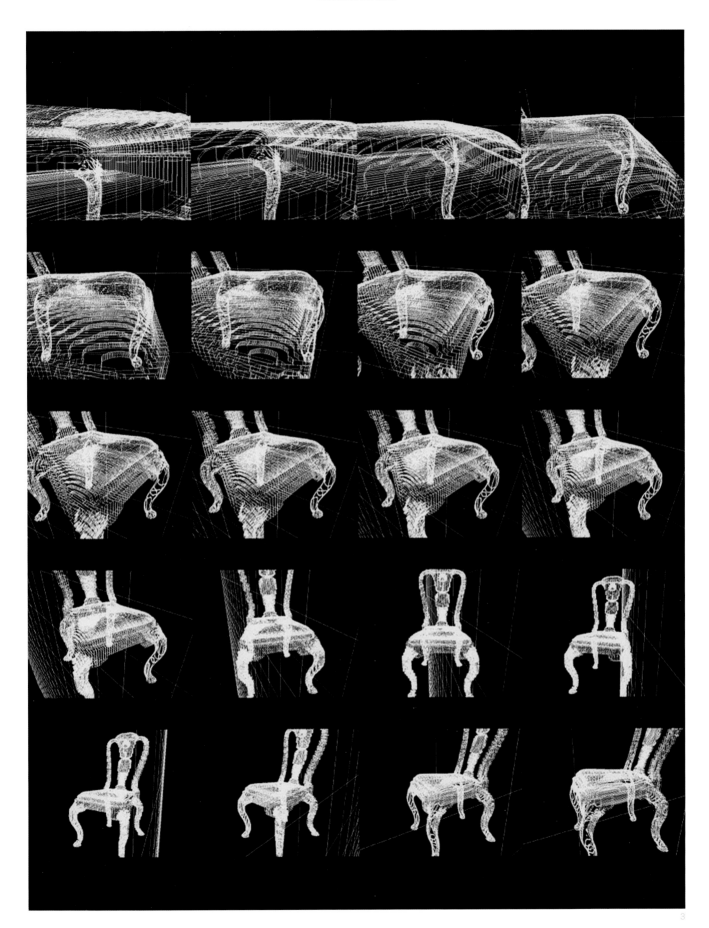

DEMAKERSVAN

The Carrara marble *Cinderella Table* was designed by Demakersvan exclusively for the Carpenters Workshop Gallery. A continuation of Jeroen Verhoeven's plywood version, this piece can be seen as having returned to the issues of the initial project *From Fantasy to Factory.*

Jeroen's rediscovery of craftsmanship within an industrial process has been resolved: "We took as samples seventeenth-century tables, because that period was just before furniture was being made industrially. We obtained hand-sketched working drawings and started designing with them by the computer. The combination of 2D sketches and 3D drawings made really amazing results. This way, we crossed the borderline between craft and high-tech."

Cinderella Table both references and contorts two historical furniture models as it combines the outlines of a Baroque table and a bombé commode at 90 degrees to one another. The result is a highly contemporary object which references historic design and the ancient material of Carrera marble, a medium which was highly prized during the Renaissance period.

A striking testimony to the capability of machinery, the table creates a conversation between light and shadow, forming grand silhouettes from the negative and positive spaces. A fairy tale piece, *Cinderella Table* is an object of fantasy, transformation and metamorphosis befitting its name. Jeroen achieved his "final dream without making any concessions."

Demakersvan

Joep Verhoeven, Jeroen Verhoeven
& Judith de Graauw
Cinderella Table, 2008
Carrara marble
31 7/8 x 52 x 39 3/8 inches (81 x 132.1 x 100 cm)
Courtesy Carpenters Workshop Gallery

CHRIS BATHGATE

As a metal sculptor and self-taught machinist, I use an array of homemade and modified CNC tools built from repurposed and salvaged equipment. Not only do I create intricate works of art, but I also construct new custom machines that increase the range and diversity of fabrication methods at my disposal. In doing so, I find visual inspiration through an ever-expanding mechanical palette of techniques I explore for their aesthetic possibilities. This process-oriented evolution is the main catalyst for my creative concepts. Each new sculpture is a technical challenge that involves weaving together the unique visual and logistical demands of its design in such a way that they complement one another, rather than compete. Balancing this duality of form and engineering imparts to each piece an internal logic, highlighting the symbiotic relationship between artistic vision and the medium through which it is realized.

For many artists, a CNC system can simply function as an output device, rendering digital forms into physical matter, efficiently replacing methods like carving and casting. Owing to their material complexity, my sculptures cannot be realized in such a perfunctory way. Structured much like the machines used to make them, the designs are broken down into various components and assemblages. Their fabrication is carefully planned around the physical limitations of the tools and processes used to create them. Each component is meticulously designed in advance, along with any custom equipment and fixtures that the design may require.

The individual parts are then precisely turned and milled, with margins of error of just thousandths of an inch. Finally, they are polished, finished, and assembled, leaving no trace of their mechanical fasteners or hardware.

My designs often take shape amidst the push and pull between formal ideas and material constraints. For *ML622254434732323*, I utilized several unique fastening systems to realize my initial design. This work incorporates multiple repeating forms within a single wall-mounted composition, posing unique engineering challenges. Since my natural inclination is biased towards using symmetry, I thought it would be interesting to set up a symmetrical system of repeating shapes and components that, although arranged in a logically consistent way, would yield an asymmetrical composition. This sculpture's radial interlocking forms are designed to be displayed in multiple configurations. To achieve this versatility, I employed turnbuckle-style fasteners of my own design. I concealed the fasteners within the bronze bushings on the ends of each of the spoke-like elements, so that they could be secured without requiring openings for conventional fasteners that would disturb the continuity of the form. I also experimented with a new magnetic fastening system, where the center protrusions were attached using a series of strong magnets and alignment pins. These types of design solutions, born out of necessity, consistently give rise to new concepts for future works. Thus problem solving is a powerful source of inspiration throughout my work.

Chris Bathgate

ML6222544347323232, 2012
Aluminum, stainless steel, bronze, brass; computer
numerical control (CNC) machining
64 1/2 x 67 x 10 1/2 inches (163.8 x 170.2 x 26.7 cm)
Courtesy Chris Bathgate
Photography © Chris Bathgate

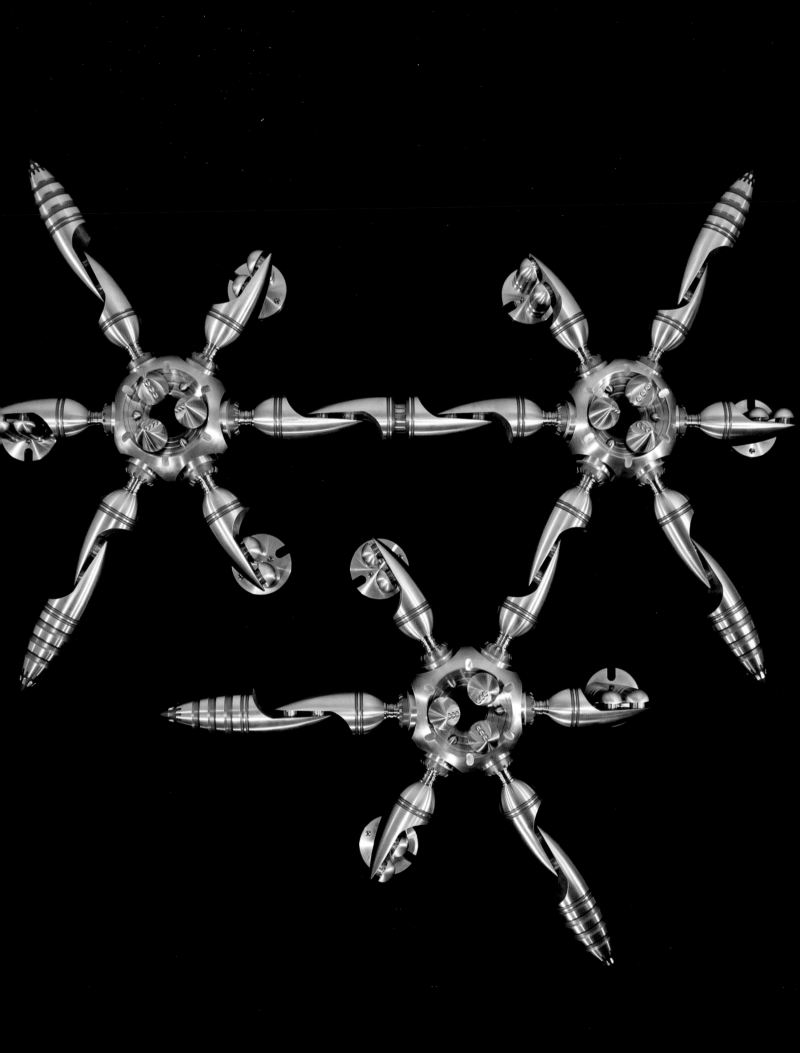

1. Performing rotary milling operation on CNC milling machine
2. Diagram for *ML622254434732323* CAD drawing used as digital reference for programing machinery to create various components of sculpture
3. Milled components being fitted for assembly

RON
ARAD

In a slightly tongue-in-cheek press release for *Not Made By Hand, Not Made in China*, an exhibition of objects made by stereolithography and selective laser sintering (Milan 2000), I claimed that until recently there had been only four ways of making things. The process of making any object could be broken down into one or more of the following steps: WASTE (chip, carve, turn, mill, chisel—i.e. removal of excess material), MOLD (injection molding, casting, rotation molding, extruding etc—i.e. pouring liquid material to take the form of its vessel when hardened), FORM (bending, pressing, hammering, folding, vacuum forming, etc.—i.e. forcing a sheet material into a shape), ASSEMBLE (bolting, gluing, riveting, soldering, welding etc.—i.e. joining parts together by any means), and, I went on to claim,

there is now a fifth way—GROW, an object can be grown in a tank, layer by layer, by computer controlled laser beams. Now I think all this can be reduced further—an object can be made by either ADDING or SUBTRACTING. Computers, with their ZEROS and ONES, love it.

With CNC (Computer Numeric Control), RP (Rapid Prototyping), GM materials, and a little help from robotic friends, virtual can easily become actual; an image on screen rapidly transforms to a solid mass. Anything can be drawn, modeled, and made…. There are virtually no limits. Smart materials, sharp tools, sci-fi production, it's all here. Now. The present is too fascinating to stop and worry too much about the future. If you look at the present deeply enough, the future will become discernible.

Ron Arad (quote taken from *Designing the 21st Century*. Editors Charlotte and Peter Fiell (Taschen: köln, 2001) pp. 39–41.

Oh Void 1, 2006

Acrylic

45 3/4 x 18 1/2 x 78 1/2 inches(116.2 x 47 x 199.4) cm

Edition 5 of 6

Courtesy Friedman Benda

Photography Erik and Petra Hesmerg

GOLDNER GEVA

Wood-Carbon Bracelet, the first piece of jewelry designed and crafted by Goldner Geva in 2012, emerged from a series of furniture entitled *Inside Out*. The pieces of furniture in this series, as with the jewelry itself, are innovative in the unique way they manifest materials beyond their boundaries. They combine not only two materials typically perceived as opposites—the traditional wood and the cutting-edge carbon fiber—but they are also constructed in two contradictory processes: handcraftsmanship together with aviation/computer technology. The marriage between the two materials results in an extraordinary configuration of flexibility paired with great structural strength.

It is this blend of olive-wood and the carbon fiber that gives the bracelet its identity. Each contributes its distinctive character to making the whole; while the wood attains its natural beauty, the carbon brings flexibility and strength to the equation.

The process of making the bracelet begins with a sculptural removal of surface of a block of wood using a computer-controlled milling machine. It is this first step that reveals the natural beauty of the organic material. The inner part of the bracelet is then lined with carbon fiber in an integration of manmade technology and nature.

Gal Goldner

Wood-Carbon Bracelet, 2012
Olive wood, carbon fiber; computer
numerical control (CNC) milling
2 3/4 x 6 x 4 inches (7 x 15 x 10 cm)
Museum of Arts and Design,
gift of Modern Gallery, 2012

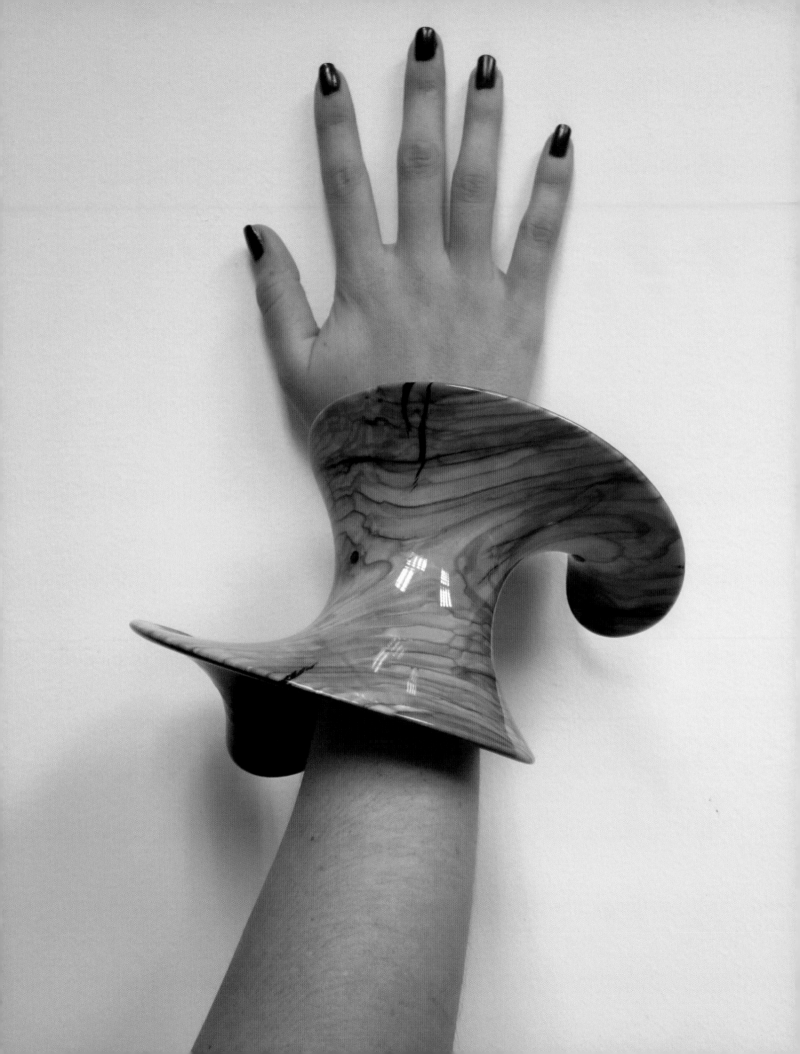

1. Raw block of olive wood
2. CNC-milled interior surface
   of bracelet
3. Woven carbon fiber cloth applied to
   interior and
   infused with resin
4–7. CNC milling preparation
   and progression
8. Finished bracelet

ALISSIA MELKA-TEICHROEW

"I try to find the fine line between aesthetics and functionality," says New York-based industrial designer Alissia Melka-Teichroew. This sentiment articulates the motivation behind Alissia's multifaceted body of design work.

The daughter of a French mother and an American father, Alissia was born and raised in The Netherlands. An early appreciation of Dutch design led to Alissia to complete an undergraduate degree at the Design Academy Eindhoven in The Netherlands, before crossing the continents to be awarded a Masters of Industrial Design at the Rhode Island School of Design in the US.

After gaining experience at IDEO and working with leading brand Puma International, Alissia founded her first design studio in the USA, AlissiaMT Design, in 2005 before launching byAMT in 2007 to fill what she saw as a gap in the American design landscape. While producing and distributing her own designs under byAMT, Alissia's reputation for creating simple but innovative designs have led to collaborations with Van Esch, Palau, Functionals, Y'A Pas Le Feu Au Lac, Blik Surface Graphics, and Charles & Marie.

Alissia considers design an avenue to improve everyday life, the objective for her designs being to create enjoyment from products and their use. With a desire to design items people will want to keep for a long time, Alissia will continue to push boundaries across design, production technique, and the context of products within society.

Alissia Melka-Teichroew

Cut Beauty Large Black Necklace from *Jointed Jewels 2011 Collection*
Polyamide; laser sintering
15 x 8 x 2 inches, approx. (38.1 x 20.3 x 5 cm)
Courtesy Alissia Melka-Teichroew —byAMT Inc.

JAN
HABRAKEN

Intentional genetic tinkering of living species has been around for centuries, ever since the first human mated two individual animals with desirable traits or grafted together two different plants with complementary features. Our greater understanding of genetics has only sped up the process and made it more targeted. What is it that we are ultimately striving for? Perfection? What does perfection even mean? Doesn't it shift over time and between cultures? And can perfection be quantified?

In contemplating these messy questions, FormNation has turned to the chair, that universal touchstone of design. What if we apply the science of genetic engineering to an inanimate object? By crossbreeding individual chairs with desirable traits do we eventually end up with the ultimate chair? Can there even be a perfect chair, given our always-changing demands as users? To find out, we developed *Chairgenics*: a continually evolving modeling experiment.

To begin, we had to quantify the desirability of existing chair types. We enumerated a set of traits and assigned a value to each trait on a scale of 1 to 10 (10 being best). Most of these characteristics —ergonomics, cost, durability, and construction—could be objectively assessed. But aesthetics are subjective. So, for our purposes, we relied on a mix of FormNation's own opinions and popular opinion

(based on Google and Yahoo rankings). We also decided to limit the number of times we could mate a particular chair model. This was our way of maintaining genetic diversity.

Armed with our variables, we were ready to begin breeding chairs—or, more accurately, morphing chair forms. We began by exploring traditional morphing software. We were frustrated with the results until we happened upon Symvol, a new 3D software by the U.S.-Norwegian company of Uformia. Symvol morphs complex objects using mathematical volumes, and produces more logical, usable outcomes.

After our initial efforts yielded some weird (but beautiful) results, we customized the software to more accurately mimic genetics. The new results were interesting enough to be included in a scientific paper about morphosis.

What *Chairgenics* has shown us is that, while perfection remains as elusive as ever, the experimentation itself has been perfectly inspiring. Our exploration has produced exciting new forms and ideas. As we continue with *Chairgenics*, we might introduce whole new species into the mix. What would result from "breeding" a light and a chair? Or a chair and table? Or a chair and something even weirder? We are at the threshold of a brave new world.

Quote from *Chairgenetics by FormNation*, March 21 2013, courtesy Jan Habraken

Jan Habraken/FormNation in
collaboration with Uformia and
Mathieu Sanchez
Chairgenics, 2011-13
30 x 24 x 24 inches (76.2 x 61 x 61 cm)
Courtesy Jan Habraken

1. Overview of different chair morphs
2. Morph of 3% archetypical chair, 27%
   Bertoia Chair and 70% Monobloc
   plastic garden chair
3. Various morphs with more or less
   recognizable design classics

2

3

PETER TING

Peter Ting first visited the Centre for Fine Print Research (CFPR), University of the West of England, in January 2012, when he was introduced to the Centre's research in ceramic 3D printing, funded by the UK Arts and Humanities Research Council. Peter expressed a strong interest in working with the CFPR team on the development of one or more ceramic pieces which would be designed specifically to explore the potential of 3D printed ceramics. He proposed several design concepts including the pierced, double walled teacup.

The teacup is a challenging piece with design features which would be extremely difficult to reproduce by conventional ceramic forming techniques. In the development of the 3D printed ceramic teacup, 2D drawings provided by Peter Ting were translated into a 3D CAD model, using the 3D software Rhinoceros. A wall thickness was assigned to the teacup model and internal ribs were added connecting the inner and outer walls to add strength and to help the structure hold its shape during firing. As well as creating the

teacup itself, the CAD software was used to generate a solid support structure which would support the piece during firing. The teacup and support were built alongside one another in the 3D printer. In the first attempt at firing the teacup, the overall shape was maintained reasonably well, however some distortion which occurred during firing, was clearly visible. In order to overcome these problems, the wall thickness of the teacup was increased, as was the number of ribs connecting the internal and external walls of the piece. These modifications proved to be successful in maintaining the shape of the piece during firing, as can be seen in the biscuit fired piece. The overall shape of the teacup has been maintained and the distortion has been reduced to a minimum.

Peter Ting's *Bristol Teacup* is a demonstration that the ceramic 3D printing process can be exploited to reproduce design features that would be difficult to create using conventionally formed ceramics.

Stephen Hoskins, Centre for Fine Print Research, University of West England, Bristol UK.

Bristol Teacup, 2012
Ceramic composite; 3D printed
2.5 x 4 x 4 inches (6.5 x 10 x 10 cm)
Courtesy Centre for Fine Print Research,
University of the West of England

NENDO

Lacquered Paper-Objects for Nilufar are small containers created using a 3D printer that cuts, stacks, and pastes sheets of paper one by one. We finished the surfaces with lacquer that adhered thickly to the edges of the accumulated paper, and pulled at the paper's surface, resulting in a mysterious texture like wood grain.

Nendo

Lacquered Paper-Objects, 2012
3D-printed paper, urushi lacquer
Six containers, largest:
2 15/16 x 4 3/4 x 4 3/4 inches (7.5 x 12.1 x 12.1 cm)
Courtesy Nilufar Gallery Unlimited
Photography Masayuki Hayashi

1. Surface of 3D-printed paper
   containers sanded smooth
2. Rolls of paper at 3D printing company
3. Build chamber showing 3D printer
   cutting and applying adhesive to
   successive layers of paper
4. Completed 3D printing process showing
   stack of internally-cut sheets of paper
5. "Weeding" or removal of excess paper
6. Weeding complete revealing 3D-printed
   container top and bottom halves
7. Containers sent to *urushi* lacquer studio
8. Lacquer applied to surface of containers
9. Lacquer-coated containers on drying shelves

7

8

9

PATTERN AS STRUCTURE

Patterns, whether repeating or chaotic, commonly recur in nature, but not all are visible to the naked eye. Computer applications, in association with other devices, allow for the transcription of data such as sound, light, motion, and electrical activity, which may then be translated into three-dimensional objects. Sound waves, brain waves, and light reflections take the form of vases, furniture, and sculpture, allowing us to see and touch what we could not before. Decorative motifs and shapes cut into sheets of metal or wood yield light and airy large-scale constructions. Advancements in digital knitting and winding allow for controlled fiber placement, generating structurally inherent designs ranging from footwear to architecture.

SAKURAKO SHIMIZU

Japanese designer and conceptual artist Sakurako Shimizu creates jewelry primarily from gold and silver. For her *Waveform Series* she created wedding rings by recording parts of ceremony and laser cut out the sound wave. Also included in the series are necklaces and brooches created using sounds of people yawning and laughing. It all starts with recording something, be it the "I do," "I'll always love you," or pretty much anything spoken. This sound will generate a waveform when recorded on a digital medium and then played back in a visual form. And Shimizu's idea was to capture that specific waveform, knowing that each sound sequence will produce a different shape. And even more, the same thing, when uttered by different persons will look different as far as waveforms are concerned.

Sakurako Shimizu

Wow Brooch, 2007
Silver, oxidized silver
3 1/2 x 1 1/2 inches (8.9 x 3.8 cm)
Museum of Arts and Design,
gift of the artist, 2012

Yawn Brooch, 2007
Silver, oil paint
4 x 1 1/2 inches (10.2 x 3.8 cm)
Museum of Arts and Design,
gift of the artist, 2012

Sneeze Brooch, 2007
Silver
3 1/2 x 1 3/8 inches (8.9 x 3.5 cm)
Museum of Arts and Design,
gift of the artist, 2012

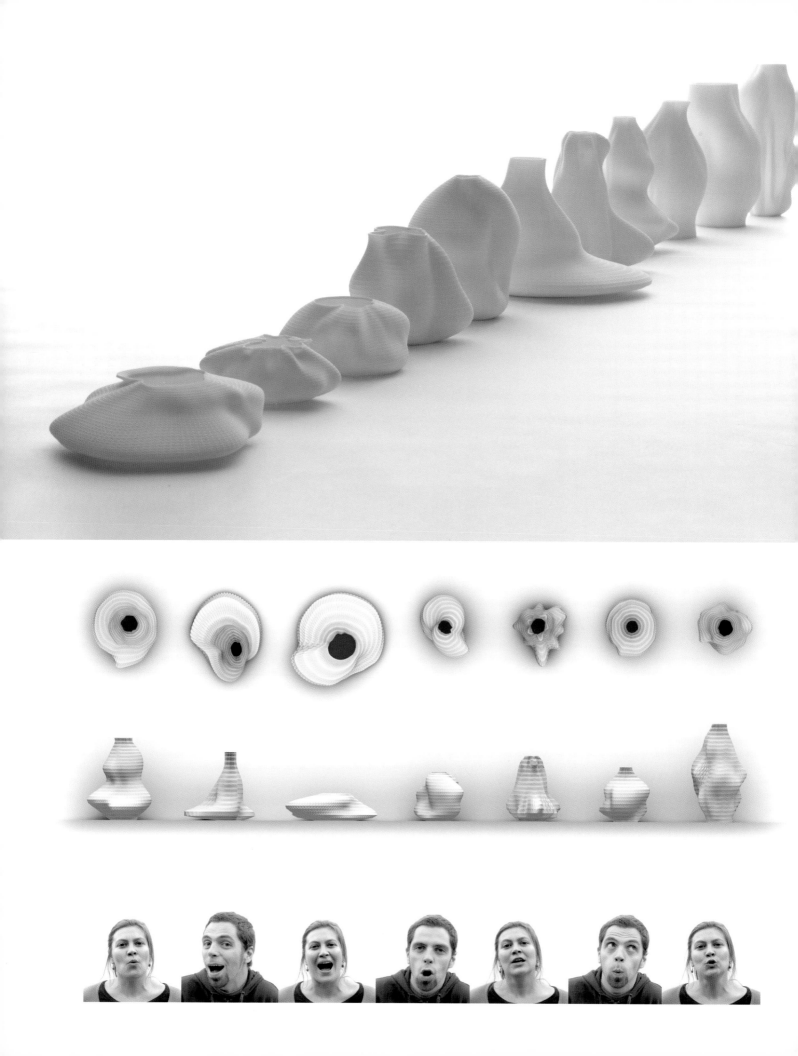

FRANÇOIS BRUMENT

Speak, blow, or whistle. Through a sound-to-volume algorithm, *Vase#44* allows the user to determine the shape of a vase with his or her voice. The shaping rules are easy: the louder one speaks, the wider the vase will be. The longer one speaks, the taller it will be. Modulating one's voice frequency will fold, or undulate, the form.

François Brument

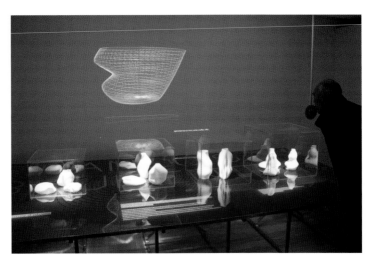

(opposite top) *Vases#44*, 2009
Polyamide; laser sintering Interactive
installation: microphone, computer, projector
Courtesy François Brument
(opposite bottom) concept for *Vase#44*
Photography Véronique Huyghe
(right) Installation showing visitor speaking
into microphone, projection of resultant
digital model of vase, and examples of
previously 3D-printed vases

LUCAS MAASSEN & UNFOLD

The design of the *Brain Wave Sofa* is the result of a brain wave scan measured by means of an electro-encephalogram (EEG), using a set of electrodes connected to the head. A computer application for neuro-feedback displays the data as a 3D landscape image, in which the depth is the frequency of brain-activity in Hertz, the height is the strength of the signal and the length is the progression of time (duration).

In this record and display mechanism, the role of the "designer" is challenged; even by looking at the 3D visuals, you are directly influencing your design. In this case Maassen produced (created) the landscape by opening and closing his eyes while undergoing measurement of a specific wavelength known as the Alpha activity

(8–12 Hertz). The Alpha activity is peculiar because when you close your eyes it strengthens, in contrast to other brain activity that declines. This is to prepare your brain for the large input of signals when you open your eyes.

The resulting three-second computer file is sent to a CNC milling machine that "mills out" the brain wave in soft foam. It is a tongue-in-cheek reference to a futuristic production workflow in which the designer has only to close his eyes and a computer "prints out" (processes) the result as a functional form. The materials, warm grey felt and buttoned facings, are applied by hand to the foam, honoring the traditional character of a sofa.

Quote taken from http://www.lucasmaassen.nl/projects/.index:php?4

Brain Wave Sofa, 2010
Polyurethane foam, felt, wood; computer
numerical controlled (CNC) milling
27 9/16 x 95 1/4 x 27 9/16 inches
(70 x 242 x 70 cm)
Courtesy Lucas Maassen and Unfold
Photography © Lucas Maassen and Unfold

1

2

3

4

5

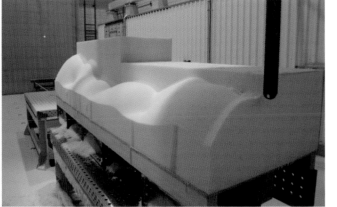

6

7

8

9

10

11

1. Designer wearing quantitative
   electroencephalography (QEEG) headset to
   measure electrical activity of brain
2. 3D point cloud visualization of Alpha
   brainwaves
3. Wood mock-up of Alpha brainwave pattern
4. Final 3-second brainwave mesh
5. 3D data for CNC mill
6—10. CNC milling polyurethane foam for sofa
11. Detail of felt upholstery

GEOFFREY MANN

My fascination with transposing the ephemeral nature of time and motion has created a studio practice that challenges the existing divides between art, craft and design.

Shine investigates the reflective properties of a metallic object; in this case the subject was a Victorian candelabrum. The reference information was generated through documenting the reflection by using raw data via a planar 3D scanner. When scanning a metallic object the laser beam is unable to distinguish between the surface and the reflection. The spikes represent the intensity of the reflection.

Shine is a project that considers an object, its interpretation, misinterpretation and reproduction back to object. When we look at *Shine*, we need to consider the notion of what is a 'correct' reproduction. Sculptors and artists have had the opportunity to explore interpretation and abstraction and *Shine* carries on this tradition in the digital world where high resolution precision has been disrupted using the nature of the materials and processes themselves.

The resulting artifact transpired from an interest in representing the materialization of the beauty that exists above and apart from the material world. *Shine* no longer exists in terms of its known form or matter but rather to those objects or histories of the object located or referenced in time as a temporal modulation between two time events or two form events.

Geoffrey Mann

Shine from *Natural Occurrence Series*, 2010

Cast bronze, silver plating

13 3/4 x 10 5/8 x 11 7/8 inches (35 x 27 x 30 cm)

Courtesy the artist, represented by Joanna Bird

Contemporary Collections, London

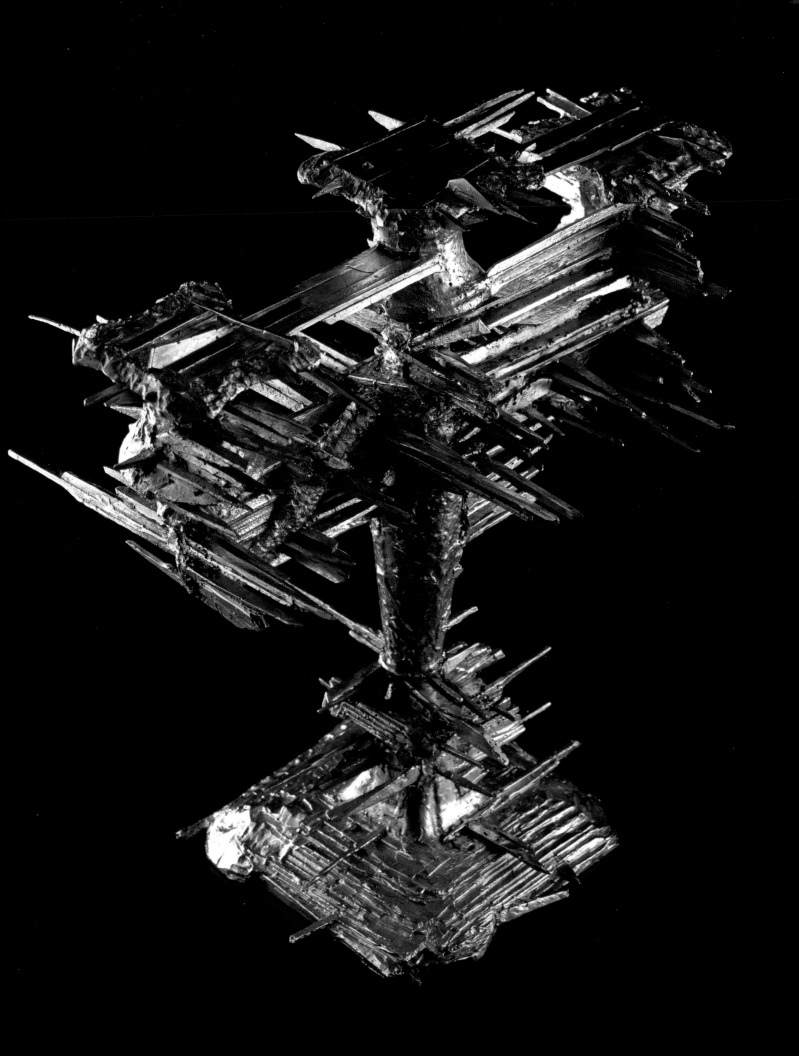

1. Wax model from fiberglass/silicon
   mold as part of ceramic shell
   lost wax process; wooden splints
   support thin wax protrusions
2. Pouring silicon bronze into
   ceramic shell mold
3. Cast bronze processed and
   prepared for final silver plating
4. Silver-plated *Shine*
5. 3D-printed nylon piece was created
   in 2005, here displayed alongside
   original source candelabrum

4

5

ANTONIO PIO SARACINO

The *Ray* sofa and chair are an exploration of the structural components found in the natural world and the ways in which they can find expression in design. Each unit is constructed with a cellular assemblage of "rays" of closed-cell foam. These assembled rays create a comfortable seat in the shape of an uncomfortable chair. The chair, when viewed from above, is reminiscent of an array of pixels or likewise the way that crystals can be formed.

Antonio Pio Saracino

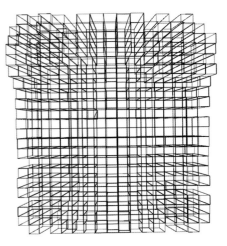

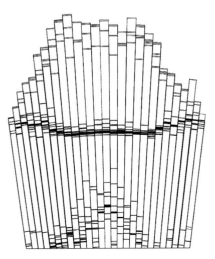

Ray Sofa Prototype, 2010
Foam rubber, latex paint; computer numerical
control (CNC) milling
Made by FoamTek
35 1/4 x 34 x 25 inches (89.5 x 86.4 x 63.5 cm)
Museum of Arts and Design, gift of the artist
and the manufacturer, 2012

MASS STUDIES

The World Expo 2010, held in Shanghai, China, was the largest World Expo to date, 192 countries participated and 73 million visitors attended. With the theme "Better City, Better Life," it took place from May 1 to October 31, 2010. The Korea Pavilion was situated in Zone A, directly neighboring the Japan and the Saudi Arabia Pavilions, and in close proximity to the China Pavilion. The site is around 6,000 m², and was one of the largest lots within the Expo compound. Given its geographical advantage of peninsula, under the influence of both land culture (China) and sea culture (Japan) surrounding the peninsula, Korea has been permeable to imported cultures and global influences, whose progressive mix defines contemporary Korean society. Using "convergence" as the main theme, the Korea Pavilion was conceived as an amalgamation of "sign" (symbol) and "space": Signs become spaces, and spaces become signs.

Han-geul, the Korean alphabet, was the prime element of "signs" used to design the pavilion. The surfaces of the pavilion are clad in two types of pixels: Han-geul Pixels and Art Pixels. Han-geul Pixels were 6mm thick white aluminum panels, CNC cut to achieve a texture-heavy relief of letters and different font sizes, whose combination forms the vertical, outer most, exterior surfaces, defining the overall footprint and volume of the pavilion. CNC was a useful and efficient method in the large production of 962 panel types, each unique, and in achieving combinations of four different font sizes with precision. Sequential lighting was installed behind the Han-geul Pixels to highlight the individual letters on the exterior facade at night, further animating the pavilion as a sign (similar to a text message) on a larger scale.

The rest of the inner bound (non-peripheral) surfaces were composed of Art Pixels, color-heavy printed aluminum panels created by Korean artist Ik-Joong Kang. Various digital processes were used to achieve a mass reproduction of the artist's work initially drawn by hand with crayons. These original works were then scanned and digitized, allowing for him to digitally arrange, compose, and edit the Art Pixels on the facade of the Korea Pavilion. The artist's final composition was then digitally printed on the aluminum composite panels to install. About 40,000 of these panels repeat a poem titled *What I Know* throughout the Art Pixel surfaces, expressing the artist's message of hope and unity.

As a map is a type of sign that depicts space, the ground level piloti space was itself a sign, which was an abstract 1/300 scale 3D map of a characteristic Korean city. To create a semi-exterior landscape, the piloti space, at 86 m x 37 m, slightly larger than half the size of a soccer field, represents the convergence of mountains, water, and a dense metropolitan area, as exemplified by Seoul, the national capital. The main exhibition space, elevated 7 m above the ground, provided shade, and an artificial river modeled after Seoul's Han River flowed from one corner to the other.

Betty Bo Ra Kim, Mass Studies

Korea Pavilion, Shanghai World Expo, 2010

Aluminum panels; computer numerical control

(CNC) milling

Courtesy Mass Studies

Photography © Yong-Kwan Kim

1–4. Korea Pavilion, Shanghai World
Expo, 2010
Aluminum panels; computer
numerical control (CNC) milling
Courtesy of Mass Studies
Photography © Yong-Kwan Kim
(overleaf) Photography © Iwan Baan

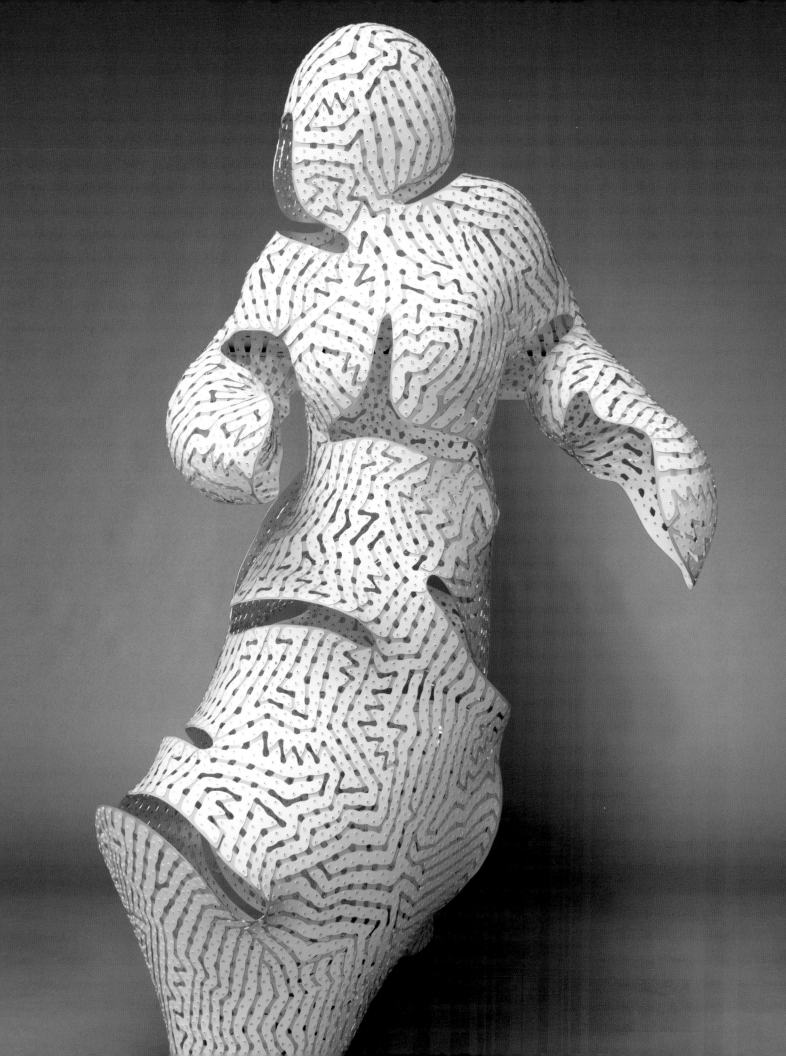

MARC FORNES

THEVERYMANY is a New York based art/architecture studio committed to the design and construction of prototypical architecture via custom computational methods. Practice is structured through the process of rigorous serial experimentation.

This methodology delineates a research trajectory of continuously developable processes with internal differentiation per project through case-specific constraints and conditions. Thus, the body of work becomes a continuous investigation, with intensive focus on architecture's relation to structure, form description, information modeling, and digital fabrication.

Within the terms of research, structure pertains to rigidity of form through structural skins and form-finding methods. Form description explores the means through which a single overall geometry is segmented into multiple sub-elements. Information modeling is the means through which logistical information is integrated into computational models. While digital fabrication examines the process of physical production from computational schemes.

This method of experimentation necessitates the definition of explicit and encoded parameters through which the research methodology is refined. An explicit process entails describing a given phenomenon as a series of discrete steps, forming a hierarchically ordered set of basic logical operations, also known as a protocol. Encoding is the act of then translating ordered protocols into the syntax readable by a computer in order to execute a particular task. The control made available through explicit processes enables the research to continually be informed by prior investigations.

The desire is not to generate models, nor installations, but rather 1:1 scale prototypical structures. The methodology continually pushes constraints at larger scales to engage fundamental questions of stability and efficiency. The construction of a prototype is the construction of a system in formation; not yet achieving the status of architecture, but continually developing towards it.

The notion of a prototypical structure engages a diverse range of morphologies, and works to advance formal complexity and structural efficiency simultaneously. This may manifest within the logic of non-linear network topologies or differentiated skins/shells. Central to the research process is the input of logistical factors which define the process of physical production. Geometry is optimized for efficiency in digital fabrication as well as in assembly sequence.

Within studio practice, design and research through built prototypes constitute a feedback loop between the digital and physical domains. At work is the implementation of custom state-of-the-art computational techniques to interrogate the physical ramifications of digital design. The effect is an atmosphere of rich formal interplay and perceptual complexity driven by an attitude of rigorous exploration.

Marc Fornes

BODY PARTS, 2013
Aluminum sheet, aluminum rivets;
computer numerical control (CNC) cut
Design & computation: Marc Fornes &
THEVERYMANY
72 inches (182.9 cm) high
Courtesy Marc Fornes

SOFTKILL DESIGN

Softkill Design investigated the architectural potential of the latest Selective Laser Sintering technologies, testing the boundaries of large-scale 3D printing by designing with computer algorithms that micro-organize the printed material itself. With the support of Materialise, Softkill Design produced a high-resolution prototype of a 3D-printed house at 1:33 scale.

The model consists of 30 detailed fibrous pieces which can be assembled into one continuous cantilevering structure, without need for any adhesive material. The arrangement of 0.7 mm radius fibers displays a range of flexible textures and the ability to produce in-built architectural elements, such as structure, furniture, stairs, and facade, all in one instance. The Softkill house moves away from heavy, compression based 3D printing of on-site buildings, instead proposing lightweight, high-resolution, optimized structures which, at full-scale, are manageable truck-sized pieces that can be printed off site and later assembled on site.

Softkill Design is a London based team of architects (Nicholette Chan, Gilles Retsin, Aaron Silver and Sophia Tang) researching new methods of generative design for additive manufacturing. The unique workflow aims to produce intelligent designs which intuitively utilize 3D print technology. Softkill Design specialize in 3D-printed design and provide design consultancy for architecture, furniture, product design, and fashion.

ProtoHouse 1.0 research was founded at the Design Research Lab from the Architectural Association School of Architecture. Research prototypes of 1.0 were generously supported by Materialise, with additional support from VoxelJet and Sirris. Currently Softkill Design is working on the development of *ProtoHouse 2.0*—a much more market-friendly version.

Softkill Design

Concept for *ProtoHouse* 1.0: *Prototype for a 3D Printed House*, 2012
Laser sintered powder
Courtesy Softkill Design
Photo credit: © Softkill Design

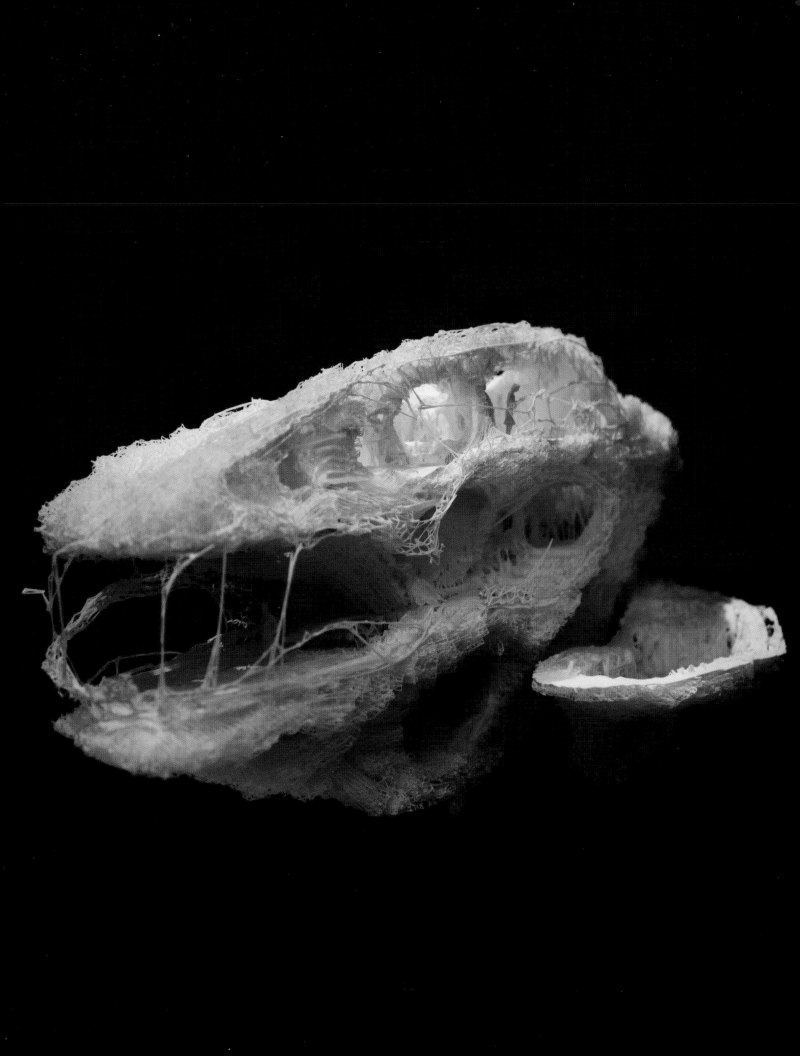

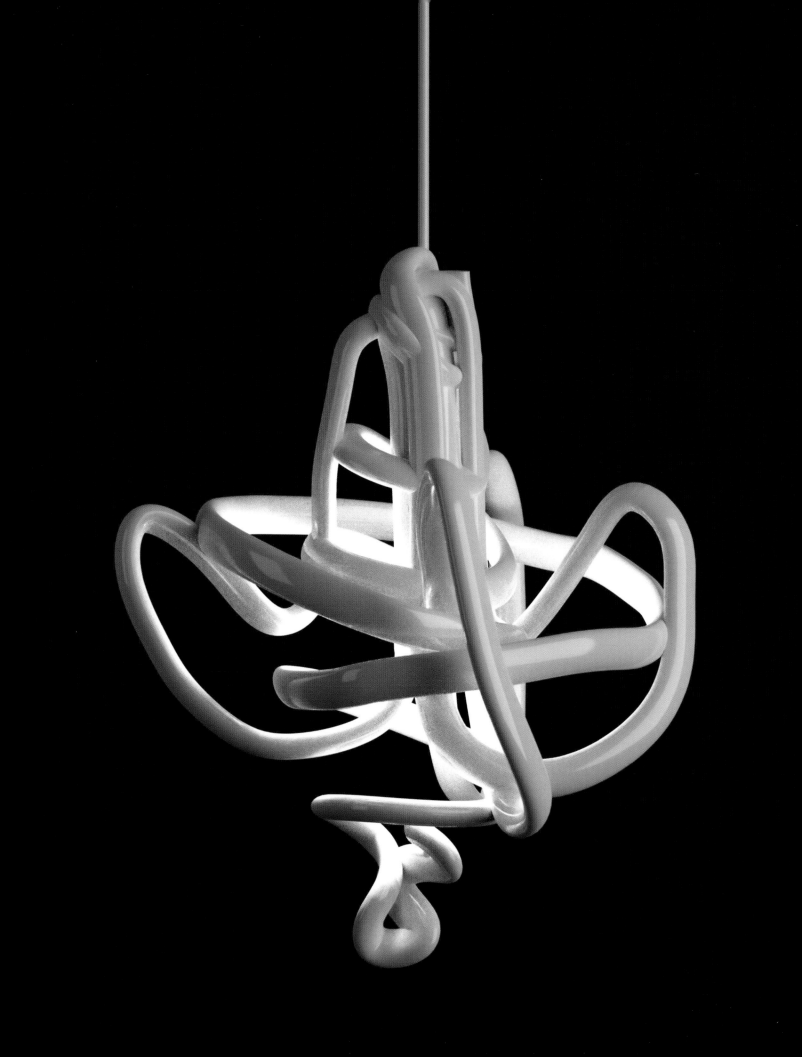

FRONT
DESIGN

Is it possible to let a first sketch become an object, to design directly onto space? The four FRONT members have developed a method to materialize freehand sketches. They make it possible by using a unique method where two advanced techniques are combined. Pen strokes made in the air are recorded with Motion Capture and become 3D digital files; these are then materialized through Rapid Prototyping into real pieces of furniture.

http:www.designfront.org/category.php?id=818product=191

Prototype for *Materialized Sketch*

of a Chandelier, 2005

Thermoplastic powder

Edition of 3, 2 AP

33 7/8 x 31 1/8 x 27 11/16 inches (86 x 79 x 70.3 cm)

Courtesy Friedman Benda and the artists

THE T\SHIRT
ISSUE

"After hearing a story about a boy brought up by a wolf, I wanted this more than anything else. The wolf would have accompanied my nocturnal wanderings, would have eagerly shared my reconnaissance and sometimes my thunderous sighs."

For *Digital Portraits*, people are portrayed digitally by scanning their bodies. The output of this scan is a 3D file, of which the resolution is defined by the amount of polygons — similar to pixels in a bitmap graphic. Linked with biographical memories, a digital twin of the body is created, extending the garment a formal-poetic character.

The 3D data is turned into 2D sewing patterns by using the unfolding function, which is a common tool used for paper models. The fabric and the inner interface, which defines the edges, are cut out with a laser cutter. Using strictly jersey as fabric, the perceived complexity of the garments is reduced to an approachable and basic level.

The *Muybridge* installation is a study set out to capture temporal change in 3D. A three-step sequence of a bird changing its position and spreading its wings is reconstructed and sculpted into sweatshirts. As the change in the wings' position is a function of time, each wing's plumage is reduced to polygonal form, modeled and rigged into successive arrangements to portray the spreading motion.

This study leans on Eadweard Muybridge's photography work in the late 1800s, with which he pioneered in the field of capturing animal and human locomotion. Challenged by a bet whether all four horse's hooves are off the ground at the same time during gallop, he conceived stop-motion photography and later on the Zoöpractiscope, which turned still photographs into dynamic projections.

With the *Muybridge* installation, shape and fractional motion are interpreted through jersey garments. The T-shirts capture a movement that happens in the bat of an eye and perpetuate it by material augmentation.

The T\shirt Issue

No.419, 2008
Jersey, iron-on interface; laser cutting
27 9/16 x 15 3/4 x 9 13/16 inches
(20 x 40 x 24.9 cm)
Courtesy of the T\shirt Issue

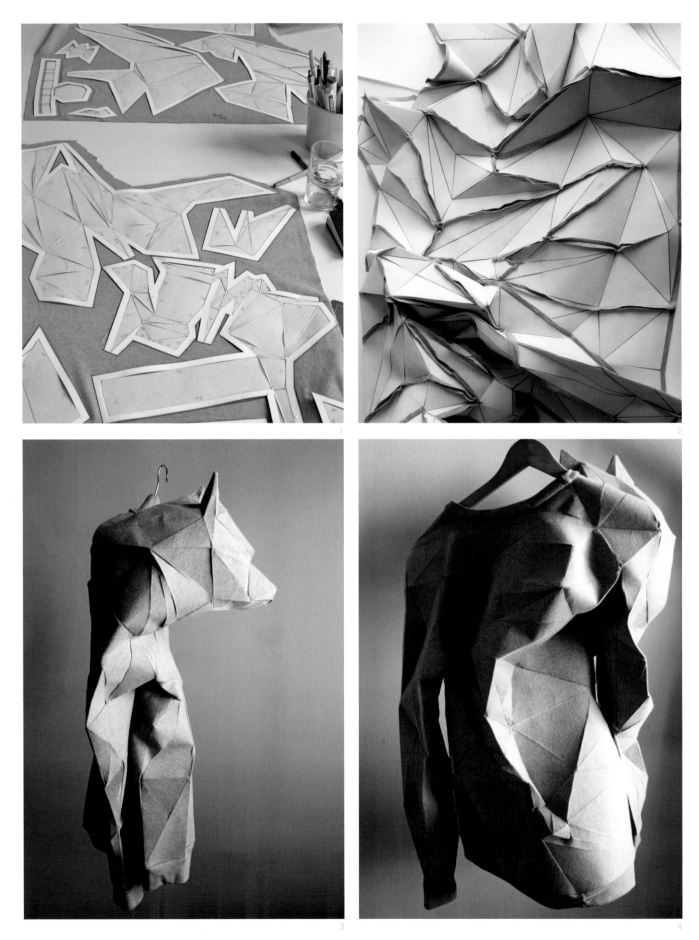

1

2

3

4

5

6

7

1. Laying out laser-cut interface
   pattern on jersey
2. Interior view of *No. 419* showing
   iron-on interface applied to Jersey
3–4. Side and back views of *No. 419*:
   interface pattern determines faceted
   folds of garnments
5–7. *Muybridge*, 2013
   Jersey iron-on interface; laser cutting
   Each 29 1/2 x 23 5/8 x 11 13/16 inches
   (75 x 60 x 30 cm)
   Courtesy of The T\Shirt Issue

BEN SHAFFER

NIKE has engineered knit for performance to create running footwear that features only the essentials. Employing a new technology called Nike *Flyknit*, yarns and fabric variations are precisely engineered for a featherweight, formfitting, and virtually seamless upper.

With all the structure and support knitted in, the Nike *Flyknit Racer*'s upper and tongue weigh just 34 grams (1.2 ounces). The whole shoe weighs a mere 160g (5.6 ounces) for a size 9, which is 19% lighter than the Nike *Zoom Streak 3*, a shoe worn by first, second and third place athletes in the men's marathon at the 2011 World Championships.

While reducing shoe weight is one aspect of helping runners, the Nike *Flyknit* upper is also engineered for a more precise fit, creating a feeling of a second skin.

An additional environmentally sustainable benefit to Nike *Flyknit* is that it reduces waste because the one-piece upper does not use the multiple materials and material cuts used in traditional sports footwear manufacture. Nike *Flyknit* is truly a minimalist design with maximum return.

The inspiration for Nike *Flyknit* was born from the common runner feedback, craving a shoe with the qualities of a sock: a snug fit that goes virtually unnoticed to the wearer.

But all the features that make a sock desirable have proven to make them a bad choice for a running upper. An inherently dynamic material like yarn generally has no structure or durability.

NIKE embarked on a four-year mission of micro-engineering static properties into pliable materials. It required teams of programmers, engineers and designers to create the proprietary technology needed to create the knit upper.

The next steps were to map out where the specific yarn and knit structures were needed. Applying 40 years of knowledge from working with runners, NIKE refined the precise placement of support, flexibility and breathability – all in one layer.

The result is precision engineering in its purest form, performance on display. Every element has a purpose: resulting in one of the lightest, best fitting running shoes NIKE has ever made.

Courtesy Nike

Flyknit Racer, 2009-2012
Various polyester yarns with dynamic
Flywire upper, ethylene vinyl acetate
foam midsole with Zoom Air sole unit,
rubber outsole
Made by Nike
Courtesy Nike

ACHIM MENGES
& JAN KNIPPERS

In 2012 the architectural and engineering researchers of ICD and ITKE with students and in collaboration with biologists of the University of Tubingen, investigated the possible interrelation between biomimetic design strategies and novel processes of robotic production. The research focused on the material and morphological principles of arthropods' exoskeletons as a source of exploration for a new composite construction paradigm in architecture.

The exoskeleton of the lobster (*Homarus americanus*) was analyzed in greater detail for its local material differentiation,

which finally served as the biological role model of the project. The resulting isotropic fiber structure allows a uniform load distribution in every direction. On the other hand, areas which are subject to directional stress distributions exhibit a unidirectional layer structure, displaying an anisotropic fiber assembly which is optimized for a directed load transfer. Due to this local material differentiation, the shell creates a highly adapted and efficient structure. The abstracted morphological principles of locally adapted fiber orientation constitute the basic for the computational form generation, material design, and manufacturing process of the pavilion.

Achim Menges

ICD/ITKE Research Pavilion, 2012

University of Stuttgart

Carbon and glass fiber composites;

robotic filament winding

Courtesy Achim Menges

Photography Roland Halbe

(overleaf) KUKA robot arm executing

controlled fiber placement

Photography ICD/ITKE Stuttgart University

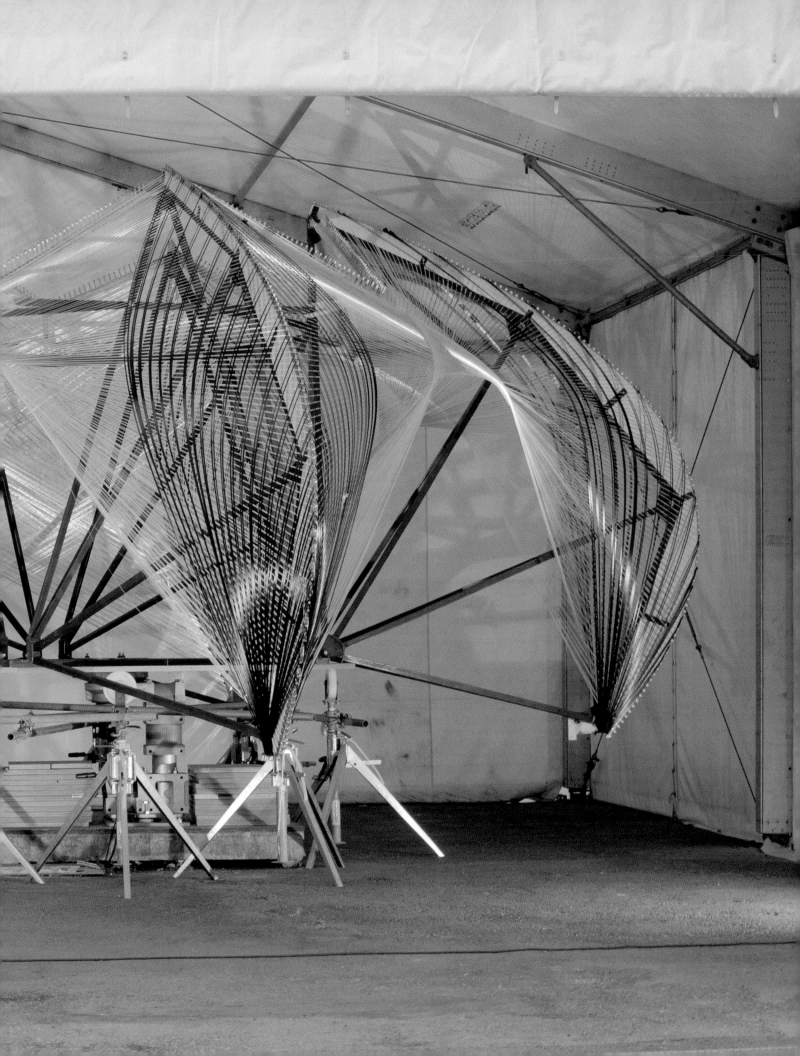

J. MAYER H. ARCHITECTS

Metropol Parasol, the redevelopment of the Plaza de la Encarnacíon in Seville, designed by J. MAYER H., became the new icon for Seville—a place of identification—and to articulate Seville's role as one of the world's most fascinating cultural destinations. *Metropol Parasol* explores the potential of the Plaza de la Encarnacíon to become the new contemporary urban center. Its role as a unique urban space within the dense fabric of the Medieval inner city of Seville allows for a great variety of activities such as memory, leisure, and commerce. A highly developed infrastructure helps to activate the square, making it an attractive destination for tourists and locals alike.

The *Metropol Parasol* scheme with its impressive timber structures offers an archaeological museum, a farmers market, an elevated plaza, multiple bars and restaurants underneath and inside the parasols, as well as a panorama terrace on the very top of the parasols. Realized as one of the largest and most innovative bonded timber-constructions with a polyurethane coating, the parasols grow out of the archaeological excavation site into a contemporary landmark, defining a unique relationship between the historical and the contemporary city. *Metropol Parasol*'s mixed-used character initiates a dynamic development for culture and commerce in the heart of Seville and beyond.

J. Mayer H. Architects

Metropol Parasol, 2004–2011
Seville, Spain
Adhesively-bonded timber, polyurethane;
computer numerical control (CNC) milling
Photography Fernando Alda

Metropol Parasol, 2004–2011
Seville, Spain
Adhesively-bonded timber,
polyurethane; computer numerical
control (CNC) milling
Photography Fernando Alda

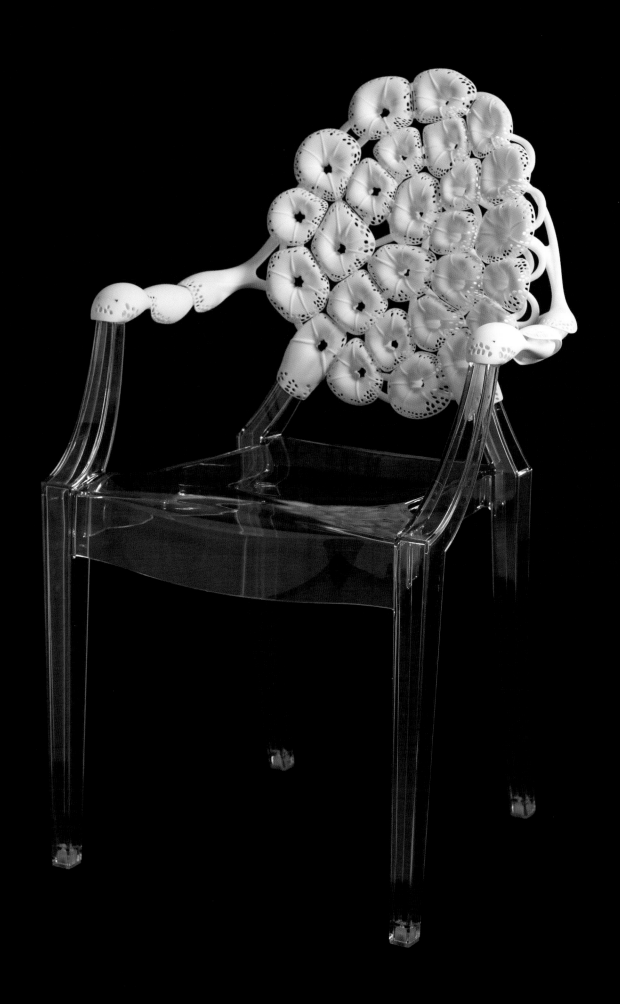

LIONEL
T. DEAN

Product artist Lionel T. Dean's practice is focused exclusively on direct digital manufacturing; physical artifacts generated direct from computer data. In 2002 Dean proposed a blue skies research project exploring the use of 3D printing, or what was then termed Rapid Prototyping (RP), in the end-use manufacture of decorative products. The premise was that in 3D printing there is little economic advantage in producing multiples. Given this and the flexibility of digital design tools, serially produced works could be varied with every artifact produced. The project and the principle of individualization proved an immediate success and developed quickly to a practice-based PhD study and from there to form the central tenet of Dean's work.

From the beginning of the project the aim had been "living" designs evolving and mutating in real-time without repetition. Early designs exploring the principles were based on fixed length animations with every movie clip frame providing a discreet design solution. These offered "proof of concept" but fell short of the project's aspirations for infinite variety.

Holy Ghost was originally an Arts Council England funded commission in 2006. With this design the computational research behind the project caught up with the 3D design work allowing a computational design approach that combines parametric Computer Aided Design (CAD) with computer programming. The computer script creates a unique iteration every time it is run using carefully controlled random variables.

The generative script runs in phases:

1. The number of mushroom-like button forms (so-called because they are deliberately reminiscent of button leather) that make up the back is defined. This is a random variable between 24 and 28. The buttons are then arbitrarily positioned on a virtual 3D surface that defines, structurally and ergonomically, where the chair back should be. The buttons are not allowed to clash, if they do they are re-positioned.
2. The buttons expand in a uniform manner (i.e. they remain circular) until they touch one another. This is done sequentially in small steps to prevent the first features in the cycle from dominating the form.
3. A non-uniform expansion of the buttons allowing the forms to distort and fill the gaps.
4. A matrix of curved links is formed between the buttons.

The design is limited to an edition of ten pieces. Two chairs where produced for the original commission and a total of six have been produced to-date.

Lionel T. Dean/Future Factories

Holy Ghost Chair, 2006
Polyamide, polycarbonate Kartell *Louis Ghost*
chair base; laser sintering
37 3/8 x 21 5/8 x 21 5/8 inches (95 x 55 x 55 cm)
Courtesy Lionel T. Dean

REMIXING THE FIGURE

Digital advancements have inspired a re-examination of the
body and figural representation in art and design. Appropriated
forms pay homage to past masterworks while the ability to
capture the true likeness of a live sitter brings the venerable
tradition of portrait sculpture into the twenty first century,
both made possible by 3D scanning. Visceral works, created
by splicing together digital figures into grotesque creatures,
allude to hybridity and metamorphosis in a fast-changing world.
In the fashion industry, designers build fabric and clothing
mathematically on the computer, permitting a more sculptural
approach through improvised alterations to the virtual model,
for production by 3D printing or whole-garment knitting.

NICK HORNBY

Nick Hornby's sculptures cite multiple specific sources taken directly from art history and rearticulated as single shifting structures. In the eight-foot marble-dusted sculpture, *I never wanted to weigh more heavily on a man than a bird* (Coco Chanel), Brancusi's *Bird in Space* is glimpsed from one perspective, and Rodin's *Striding Man* is caught from another.

Carved from a single solid by a computer controlled hotwire, each line drawing is cut out without error in a continuous gesture. Through both its production process and archetypal subject matter, Hornby's work creates a nuanced historical take on a contemporary penchant to complicate authorship and dematerialize the objects of art.

Courtesy Churner and Churner

I never wanted to weigh more heavily on a man than a bird (Coco Chanel), 2010
Marble resin composite
94 x 51 x 18 inches (238.8 x 129.5 x 45.7 cm)
Edition of 3
Courtesy the artist and Churner and Churner, New York

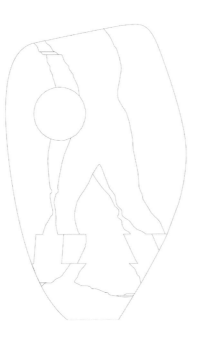
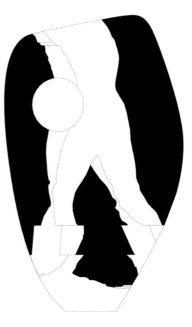

BARRY
X BALL

My sculpture is inspired by Umberto Boccioni's 1913 Futurist work, *Unique Forms of Continuity in Space*. The original Boccioni plaster, much damaged and restored, is in Sao Paolo, Brazil. All the *Unique Forms* bronzes were cast many years after Boccioni's death. They vary widely. Multiple generations have been produced with a range of patinas, polishes, and details. They are often surprisingly crudely finished—all bear evidence of the speed with which Boccioni and his assistants hand-sculpted the plaster model. Bronze casting is a millennia-old process. The rough, hand-hewn character of the *Unique Forms* bronzes stands in inelegant opposition to their advanced conceptual genesis. Boccioni's Modern Man has heretofore been realized with ancient methods in an antique material.

The challenge I set for myself was to transform Boccioni's extremely familiar artwork, a Modernist icon, into something completely new—to bring together form, material, technique, and concept. Employing a state-of-the-art Breuckmann white-light scanner, I began my work by 3D digital scanning one of the *Unique Forms* bronzes. My studio team and I then proceeded to alter every curve, line, and edge of the virtual model. The post-scanning digital 3D sculpting alone took almost three years of exacting labor. I believe the cumulative impact of those thousands of subtle changes yields a work simultaneously familiar and fresh. The final alteration was to digitally "flip" my model so that it formally mirrors the Boccioni.

Perfect Forms is reminiscent of its historical antecedent, yet it is thoroughly re-sculpted, with hyper-refined edges and surfaces, smoothly sweeping curves, the precision of a car body.

Perfect Forms will receive its public debut in 2013 at the Museum of Arts and Design, exactly 100 years after Boccioni created his 1913 plaster. For its physical realization, I chose mirror-finished 24K gold. In contrast to the traditional bronze casting of the Boccionis, my work was "grown" by an advanced large-format "Viper Pro" SLA machine. The resultant hollow plastic rapid prototype was filled with resin. The sculpture and its integral CNC-milled solid brass base plate were then plated with nickel and a heavy layer of copper. At each stage of the elaborate, multi-step process, the piece was extensively hand refined. The final step was to coat the work in an appropriately perfect metal, 24K gold. *Perfect Forms* painstakingly polished mirrored surfaces glow in the daylight and scintillate with the movement of viewers around it. The dance of reflections across and around its surfaces renders it ethereal, melting its crisp contours. Light reflected from the sculpture plays across walls, floor, and ceiling. The work both affects and is affected by its environment. Boccioni strove to depict a striding figure, at one with its surroundings and the forces released by its movement. My intention is that *Perfect Forms* radically expand and complete the unification of form, space, and action my Futurist forebear initiated a century ago.

Barry X Ball

Perfect Forms, 2010-2013
Mirror-polished 24K gold on
nickel on copper on polymer
21 x 16 3/8 x 7 inches (53.4 x 41.7 x 17.8 cm)
Courtesy the artist and Sperone
Westwater, New York

RICHARD DUPONT

In 2001 I began to turn my body into data. At first, it was hard to find body scanners. I located a video game company on Long Island that was producing the game *Doom*. At that time they were still using motion capture to animate the characters, and they had a massive black room filled with trampolines, with all kinds of acrobats wired up all over their bodies doing impossible tricks. They also had a small head scanner which you could rent cheaply and use for a half hour.

Scanning the rest of the body proved more difficult. I ended up flying to Dayton, OH and did a full body scan with General Dynamics on the Wright-Patterson Air Force Base. This was very cheap to do because I agreed to participate in an anthropometry study being conducted by the military. It took me some time to work up the nerve to go to the base, but the experience ended up being more banal than sinister. At the end I got my body scan data and spliced that together with the head data and also the data from scans of plaster casts of my feet, hands, and torso. These days, it's possible to use machines and technology in a more unconscious freestyle process.

Untitled (#5) is an extreme sculpture because of the level of its distortion. When I made the piece I had just installed a large installation, *Terminal Stage*, at Lever House in New York. The installation consisted of nine 80-inch-tall figures. Each of the figures had been manipulated in a single axis to appear thinner or wider. These distortions created a phenomenological effect. As the viewer moved around the environment, all the figures were subtly shifting and changing. The effect was prosaic but also metaphysical.

These sculptural transformations were compounded by the dynamics of the site and the architecture. All of the large glass windows further distorted the sculptures and the city around them into a watery series of fractures and reflections. These distortions were the basis for the distortion of *Untitled (#5)*. Like the figures in *Terminal Stage*, *Untitled (#5)* is distorted on a single axis. The effect can only be seen when one is not standing on that same axis as the distortion of the sculpture.

The "watery" or "melting" effect was achieved through a combination of several digital modeling programs. The piece was then both rapid prototyped and CNC milled in sections. The sections were assembled and connected by hand, patched sanded, primed and then painted. That figure was then molded and cast in archival polyurethane resin. Once the piece was removed from the mold, weeks of patching and sanding followed to achieve the monochromatic flawless surface.

It was always important to me that the pieces not be painted, and that the color of the piece is the color of the material itself. Although these works make use of a type of 3D photography, I consider them abstractions based in Body and Process Art.

Richard Dupont

In Direction, 2008
Installation at Carolina Nitsch
Project Room, 2008
Pigmented cast-polyurethane resin, mirror
Photography courtesy Richard Dupont

Hutton Award, 2008
Created for the *Medals of Dishonour*, 2009
exhibition, British Museum
Commissioned by the British Art Medal Trust
Cast bronze
2 3/4 inches (7 cm) diameter
Courtesy Stephen Hoskins, Centre for
Fine Print Research, University of the West
of England
Photography courtesy Rita Hamilton, Richard
Hamilton Studio

RICHARD HAMILTON

Richard Hamilton was commissioned by the British Art Medal Trust to create the Hutton Award to be included as part of the exhibition *Medals of Dishonour*, held at the British Museum in 2009. The University of the West of England's Centre for Fine Print Research (CFPR) was invited by Hamilton to contribute to the creation of the medal.

Hamilton was a member of the Independent Group, founded in 1952, and a pioneer of the British Pop Art movement. His collage *Just what is it that makes today's homes so different, so appealing?*, for the Independent group's 1956 exhibition *This is Tomorrow*, became a defining image of twentieth century. He trained as an engineering draughtsman, before furthering his studies in fine art at Royal Academy and Slade School of Art, in London. In the late 1950s Hamilton visited the Hochschule fur Gestaltung in Ulm, Germany's radical "New Bauhaus." The über rational "Ulm Style" is evident in Hamilton's minimalist design for the sleeve of the Beatles *White Album* (1968). Hamilton had previously collaborated with the CFPR for his prints *Typo/Topography*, the translation of Marcel Duchamp's *Large Glass*, 2003; and *Shock and Awe*, 2007–2008, an image of former British Prime Minister Tony Blair, portrayed as a wild west gunslinger.

The medal refers to the enquiry into the circumstances surrounding the death of the UK government weapons advisor Dr. David Kelly. Kelly had been exposed as the source of a BBC journalist's statement that the Blair government had exaggerated evidence on Iraq's weapons of mass destruction—evidence which was used in support of the case for war. The enquiry, chaired by Baron Hutton of Bresagh, concluded that the BBC's claims were unfounded. However, critical media reports described the enquiry as a "whitewash." The obverse face of the medal is a portrait in relief of Tony Blair, accompanied by the Latin text CONFIDIMVS DEO DE ABSOLVTIONE: MMIV (trusting in God for absolution: 2004). The text refers to Blair's statements relating to his faith and the decision to go to war in Iraq. The reverse shows a portrait of Alastair Campbell, Government Director of Communications at the time, and the text HUTTON AWARD and DIALBATI (whitewash).

The portraits of Blair and Campbell were generated from greyscale 2D image files, using the "emboss" function within Geomagic software. The lightest tones of the grayscale image produce the areas of highest relief, and the darkest tones recede as the background. Hamilton prepared the original artwork images in Adobe Photoshop, working from press photographs to remodel the images. He adjusted the greyscale tones to suit the relief generation process, and exaggerated certain features of his subjects—in Hamilton's rendering, Blair's smile becomes a menacing grin.

In order to ensure production of the highest quality of image, the development models were produced by 3D printing using a wide range of 3D print processes and CNC milling, with the final master patterns being CNC milled. Working from the master patterns, the Royal College of Art, London produced wax master copies for casting into silver and bronze.

Stephen Hoskins, Centre for Fine Print Research, University of West England, Bristol UK

STEPHEN JONES

Lady Belhaven's passions of music and millinery are
rendered floating through her head and into the ether.

Stephen Jones

Bust of Lady Belhaven
(after Samuel Joseph), 2011
Epoxy resin, nylon; stereolithography,
laser sintering
Made by .MGX by Materialise
36 1/4 x 22 x 10 1/4 inches (92.1 x 55.9 x 26 cm)
Museum of Arts and Design, Museum
purchase with funds provided by Marcia
and Alan Docter, 2012
Photography Kent Pell, courtesy Phillips de Pury
and Company
(right) Sketch for *Bust of Lady Belhaven*

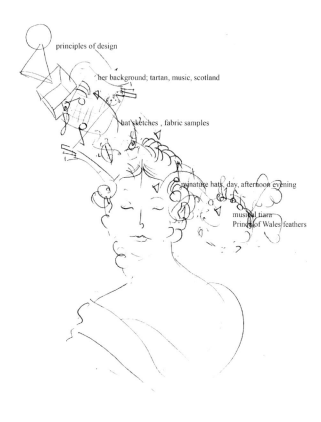

principles of design

her background; tartan, music, scotland

hat sketches , fabric samples

miniature hats, day, afternoon evening

musical tiara
Prince of Wales feathers

CHUCK CLOSE

For almost four decades, Chuck Close has created portraits from tonal grids of fingerprints, pointillist dots, brushstrokes, paper pulp, and countless other media. It was only natural that the artist's ambitions led him to tapestry, a classical and difficult medium possessing Close's signature tension between abstracted units (woven thread combinations) and a legible, unified surface. A series of daguerrotypes begun in the mid-1990s provided a uniquely suited pool of images for transformation into tapestry: each daguerreotype plate contains an enormous wealth of visual information in the tiny grains of its silver surface. This level of detail and intimacy is amplified by Close's use of the large-scale tapestry medium, as every line, freckle, twinkle in the eye, or slight tonal variation in his subjects' faces are faithfully transmitted via thousands of colored threads.

To create his woven editions, Close works with Magnolia Editions' Donald Farnsworth to develop a digital instruction set, called a weave file, translating the daguerreotype image into data which can be read by an electronic Jacquard loom in Belgium. This customized Dornier loom uses 17,800 Italian dyed cotton warp threads woven at 75 shots per cm, generating colors via different combinations of eight warp thread colors and the ten weft thread colors selected by Close and Farnsworth. A color palette must be developed for each tapestry edition containing all of the necessary values. A weave file is then constructed based on this palette. "There is more raw data in a single weave file". explains Farnsworth, "than if you digitally combined the text of all of Shakespeare's plays."

With *Self-Portrait/Five Part*, Chuck Close sets a new standard for fine art tapestries. In this technically virtuosic work, a near-panoramic series of five daguerreotype portraits have been woven together into a single tapestry. Close and Farnsworth have been working to refine and perfect *Self-Portrait/Five Part* since 2007, weaving nearly a dozen proofs using different color palettes until the desired level of clarity was achieved. By including multiple views, Close again makes his medium and process central to the viewer's experience of the image. As the translation of human topography into warp and weft takes precedence over any one particular expression or view of the artist, the capacity for mere colored threads to capture the extraordinary play of light on the artist's face emerges as the work's focal point.

Nick Stone, Magnolia Editions, Inc. *Chuck Close: Self Portrait/Five Part* [press release] 2009.

Self-Portrait/Five Part, 2009
Jacquard tapestry; digital weaving
State II: 79 x 229 inches (200.7 x 581.7 cm)
Edition of 6
Courtesy the artist and Magnolia Editions
Photography Magnolia Editions

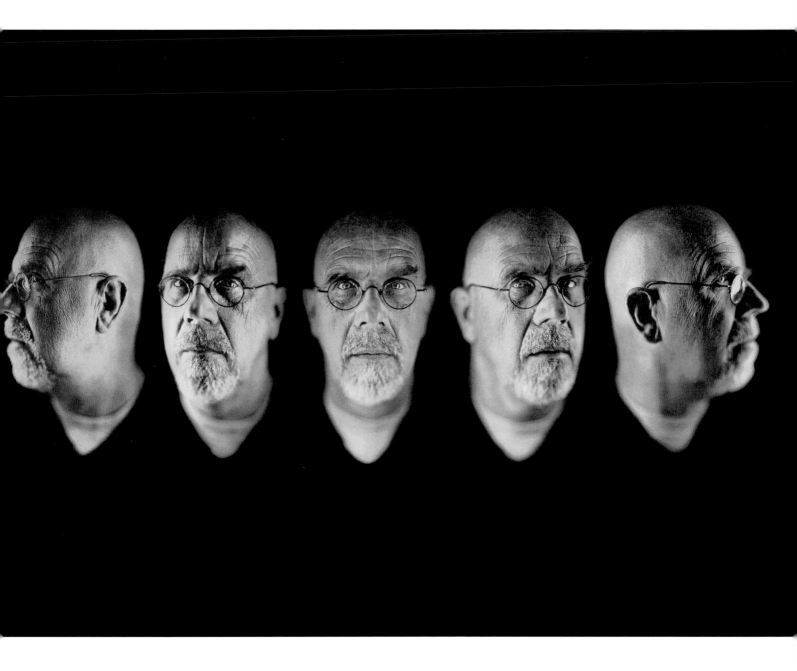

IRIS VAN HERPEN
& NERI OXMAN

The 3D-printed skirt and cape were produced using Stratasys' unique Objet Connex multi-material 3D printing technology, which allows a variety of material properties to be printed in a single build. This allowed both hard and soft materials to be incorporated within the design, crucial to the movement and texture of the piece.

"The ability to vary softness and elasticity inspired us to design a 'second skin' for the body acting as armor-in-motion; in this way we were able to design not only the garment's form but also its motion. The incredible possibilities afforded by these new technologies allowed us to reinterpret the tradition of couture as 'tech-couture' where delicate hand-made embroidery and needlework is replaced by code."

This project has taken *Imaginary Beings* [featured in the *Multiversités Créatives* exhibition at the Centre Pompidou in 2012] to *Wearable Beings*, myths that one can wear. The original collection includes eighteen Stratasys 3D-printed prototypes for the human body inspired by Jorge Luis Borges' *Book of Imaginary Beings*. They are human augmentations inspired by nature; but not all wearable. For Iris' collection at Paris Fashion Week it was important to take the series to the next level, thinking not only about form and materials, but also about movement and wearability. This was a new challenge for me and my colleagues—Prof. W. Craig Carter (Department of Materials Science and Engineering) and Keren Oxman. It inspired us to design algorithms that could map physical movement and material behavior to geometrical form and morphological variation in a seamless and continuous wearable surface."

Neri Oxman

Cape and Skirt, 2013
Iris Van Herpen and Neri Oxman in collaboration
with Prof. W. Craig Carter and Keren Oxman
Multiple materials; 3D-printed
Made by Stratasys
Museum purchase with funds donated by the
Fashion Council, Museum of Fine Arts Boston
Photography courtesy Stratasys

TAMAE HIROKAWA

The SOMARTA Skin series is a line of high quality bodywear based on the concept of a "Second Skin." The non-sewn seamless production method uses a whole garment knitting machine to achieve a fabric of artistic beauty that is free from the stress of stitches and fits perfectly over the entire body.

While the precise computer programming and manufacturing process deserve special attention, the detailed design executed through highly skilled craftsmanship gives SOMARTA's *Skin* series appeal beyond technology.

Due to the high density fabric and production method, minute, elegant tattoo-like patterns can be seen in each piece when worn. This new level of sophistication sees the patronage of global creators such as Lady Gaga and Madonna.

SOMARTA has also applied this innovative technique in furniture design. While their bodywear focuses on "skin," the chair consists of materials corresponding to skin (knit cover), bone (iron frame), and a new form like muscle (the air between skin and bone).

SOMARTA

PROTEAN Bodywear from *Skin* Series, 2007
Seamless nylon-polyurethane knit, Swarovski
crystal; digital whole garment knitting
60 inches (152.4 cm) high, 34 inches (86.4 cm) bust
Courtesy of the artist and SOMARTA
Photography Mitsuaki Koshizuka (MOREVISION);
art direction: SOMA DESIGN

1. *Skin and Bone Chair* from
Skin Series, 2008
Seamless nylon-
polyurethane knit, steel

2. *Frost Mehndi Bodywear* from
Skin Series, 2007
Seamless nylon-polyurethane
knit, pigment paint, foil print
Photography Mitsuaki Koshizuka
(MOREVISION); art direction:
SOMA DESIGN

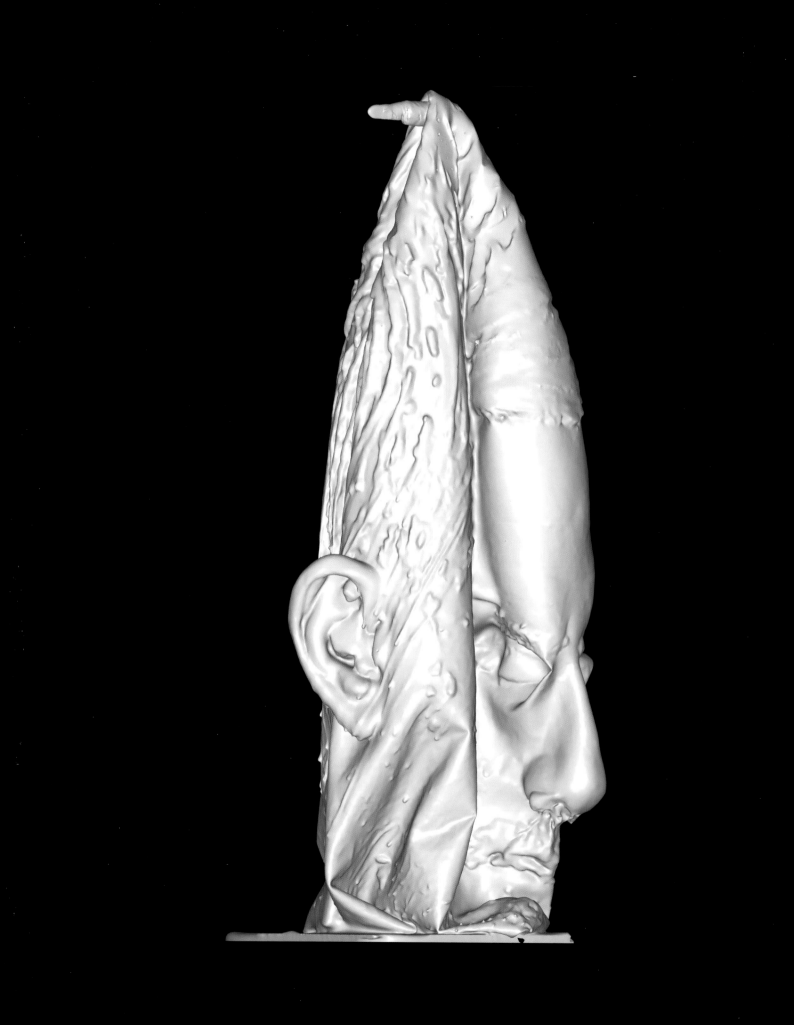

RICHARD DUPONT

I have always been much more interested in physical material— residue—than information, but technology is a great tool as long as you disrespect it. I often think of Chris Burden's willful misuse of machines and technology as subversive in just the right way. Using things, whether ideologies, machines or materials, in ways that they were not meant to be used, can be a good way to work.

The Process and Body Art that evolved in the late 1960s was varied in intention and effect. In general though, it visualized both the behavior of materials and the behavior of artists—rendering transparent the interconnectedness of thought, feeling, action, and the overarching framework of social systems.

Anthropologically speaking, Process Art engages the ritual origins of art and the metaphysical, transformative and alchemical potentialities of art. This artistic approach has only gained momentum since then—particularly considering today's collapse of the psychic and social landscapes into a single entropic black hole.

The more we are dehumanized by the tyranny of technology, the more artists are returning to the visceral.

Richard Dupont

Going Around By Passing Through, 2013
Cast aluminum
180 x 81 5/8 x 75 inches
(457.2 x 207.3 x 190.5 cm)
Courtesy of the artist and Chad Loweth

SANDRA BACKLUND

For me knitting is freedom but at the same time the ultimate challenge. I like that you are building the fabric while working and the way it's both mathematical and yet permits improvisation. With the human body as the main starting point I improvise on a mannequin to discover ideas of shapes and silhouettes that I could never come to think about otherwise. I don't sketch, but invent the pieces while doing them. I work with a three-dimensional collage method where I develop some basic bricks that I multiply and attach to each other until they become a garment. In that sense I guess you can say that I approach fashion more like a sculptor, than a tailor.

The Collection *Control-C* for Fall/Winter 2009–2010 could be described both as an ending and a new beginning.

Up until that point I had been doing everything myself by hand. In 2008 I was introduced to Italian top knitwear producer Maglificio Miles and together we decided to try a collaboration. The challenge was to make some unique pieces inspired by my hand made collections that could require only a limited amount of manual work. It was of course a big step for me to go from working alone in my studio, to suddenly be a part of a team of experts within a field of knitwear that I never before have had the chance to get to know. I was overwhelmed by all the possibilities I saw and even though I will always be doing my hand knitted signature pieces, I now see how to develop my collections in ways that I never thought was possible.

Sandra Backlund

Knitted Wool Top
from *Control-C Collection*,
Fall/Winter 2009-2010
Wool, cashmere; machine knit
Made by Maglificio Miles
Courtesy Sandra Backlund

MICHAEL SCHMIDT

I am a clothing and jewelry designer working primarily in the entertainment industry. I was approached by my friends at Ace Hotel NY to create a finale ensemble for a symposium they were hosting on 3D printing and its ramifications for the fashion industry. I've been fascinated by this technology for many years and was eager to accept the challenge.

I suggested that we not create just a dress but a piece of fantasy, something that would entice people and hold their attention while demonstrating my understanding of what this technology can do. Since this was never going to be an ordinary gown, we needed an extraordinary girl to pull it off. Dita Von Teese is the world's foremost burlesque star and a style icon by anyone's definition, and is also a great friend with whom I've collaborated in the past, so I felt she was perfect to bring this fantasy to life.

I'm accustomed to doing everything in my studio; I have a wonderful team and we can handle most any request. This dress, however, required a great deal of expertise which I don't possess, such as writing the computer code necessary for communicating with the printers. For this I turned to a young architect named Francis Bitonti and his team. They were able to take my designs for the gown and its articulated joints and import them into the software programs Maya and Rhino. He's located in NY and I'm based in LA, so we worked it all out via Skype, essentially draping the mesh over a rendering of Dita's body in his computer. He sent the files to the 3D printing company Shapeways and they printed them out. It took roughly three months to design, encode, and print the 17 separate pieces and then another month to join them together, to color the gown, and finally to embellish it with thousands of Swarovski crystals.

I'm not only interested in seeing how this technology can build more refined fabrics for the modern consumer but I also intend to stretch people's expectations by imagining some exciting things for my clientele of entertainers. They, after all, have both the verve to wear inventive things and the stage to wear them upon.

Michael Schmidt

Michael Schmidt with Francis Bitonti
Fully Articulated 3D Printed Gown
(as worn by Dita Von Teese), 2013
Nylon, Swarovski crystal; laser sintering
Courtesy Michael Schmidt
Photography Albert Sanchez/courtesy
Michael Schmidt Studios

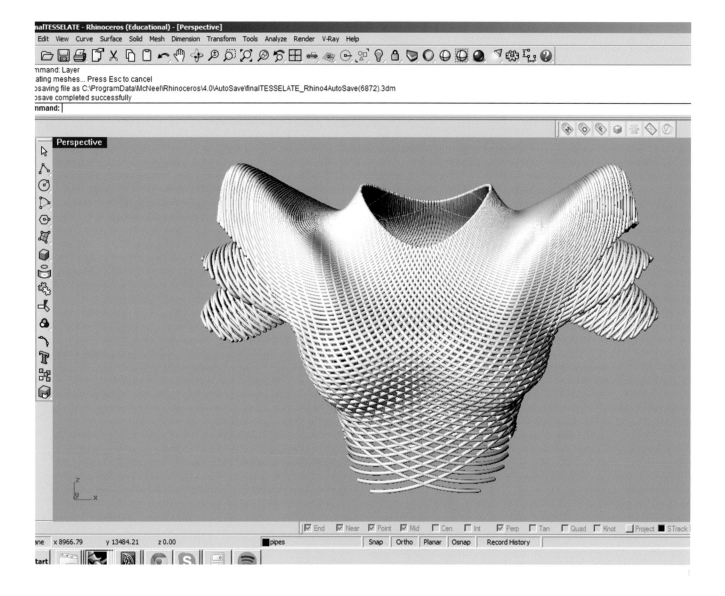

1. Screenshot of final coded bodice form
2. Forming shoulder lattice
3. Fully rendered gown draped over exact virtual model of Dita Von Teese, ready for 3D printing with nearly 3000 unique articulated joints
4. Left shoulder structure of gown emerging from 3D printer still encased in nylon powder
5. Screenshot of color coded assembly pattern showing 17 different formfitting sections of 3D-printed mesh
6. Section emerging from black dye bath, prior to lacquer finish
7. Hand application of 12,000 Swarovski Elements crystals

CONTINUUM FASHION

The *N12 Bikini* is the world's first first ready-to-wear, completely 3D-printed article of clothing. All of the pieces, closures included, are made directly by 3D printing, and snap together without any sewing. Designed by Jenna Fizel and Mary Huang of Continuum Fashion, *N12* represents the beginning of what is possible for the near future.

N12 is named for the material it's made out of: Nylon 12. This solid nylon is created by the SLS 3D printing process. SLS stands for Selective Laser Sintering, in which a laser melts plastic together layer by layer with extreme precision. With a minimum wall thickness of 0.7 mm, it is possible to make working springs and almost thread-like connections. For a bikini, the nylon is additionally appropriate because it is waterproof.

The bikini's design fundamentally reflects the beautiful intricacy possible with 3D printing, as well as the technical challenges of creating a flexible surface out of the solid nylon. Thousands of circular plates are connected by thin strings, creating a wholly new material that holds its form as well as being flexible. It works well for a bikini in balancing support and flexibility, creating a design that is comfortably wearable, even when wet. The layout of the circle pattern was achieved through custom written code that lays out the circles according to the curvature of the surface. In this way, the aesthetic design is completely derived from the structural design.

The bikini is a starting point. It is possible to make a complete 3D-printed dress, zipper included, in a similar way. As the technology develops, it is conceivable that we can make any range of clothing directly from digital designs, without any sewing and on one machine. The combination of accessible rapid fabrication and direct interaction with consumers presents many exciting possibilities for the future of fashion, and the future of products in general.

Continuum Fashion

N12 Bikini, 2011
Nylon 12; laser sintering
Courtesy Mary Huang and
Jenna Fizel
Photography ©Continuum
Fashion Inc, Mary Huang

SCOTT SUMMIT

Bespoke Fairings are specialized coverings that surround an existing prosthetic leg, accurately recreating the body form through a process that uses three-dimensional scanning to capture the unique leg shape. But *Fairings* not only return the lost contour, they invite an expression of personality and individuality that has never before been possible.

Fairings infuse the individual's lifestyle and taste into the design from the start. But to make this an even more personal part of the prosthetic leg, *Fairings* can be enhanced with patterns, graphics, and materials—including leather, ballistic nylon fabric, chrome plating, and even tattoos. By creating a unique custom form that presents the individual, we hope to change the way the world thinks of prostheses.

Courtesy 3D Systems

Bespoke Fairings, 2011
3D-printed nylon custom-tailored
prosthetic leg covers
Made by Bespoke Innovations
Courtesy 3D Systems

MICHAEL
REES

Converge: Graib Bag is connected to a series of sculptures from 2003–2010. Located within the grotesque and the uncanny, I experimented and developed a method of working that used animations and industrial forms of manufacture to create large scale sculptures and media experiences that engaged political realities. The ideas grew out of art historical antecedents but were extended to address our new political reality, a nation at war willing to stretch legalities and to engage in torture. *Converge* recalled Hans Bellmer sculptures, Calder's large modernist plaza installations, and Nauman's linguistic constructions but then also the photographs from the prison at Abu Graib. The body is a conglomeration of many bodies: the sense of multiple consciousnesses occupying the same corporeal body, or the valences of an object containing various layers of the political, the aesthetic, the historical and so on. As such, they begged questions about our technologies, our desires, and our moralities. They put the viewer in the cockpit view of a train wreck of tendencies. They reflected a concern about war and our divided culture.

Michael Rees

Converge: Graib Bag, 2008
Installation at Fields Sculpture Park, Omi
International Arts Center, Ghent, New York
Steel, expanded polystyrene, epoxy, fiberglass, paint
132 x 72 x 72 inches (335.3 x 182.9 x 182.9 cm)
Courtesy Michael Rees
Photography Michael Rees

ELONA
VAN GENT

On a typical day in the studio, I use digital technologies to design and animate monstrous morphologies. The term "monster" can bring to mind many things—Grendel, giant squid, Sullivan, extremophiles, bahamut, dragons, or Hannibal Lecter. This breadth of association points to the rich historical lineage of monstrous beings and to the many layers of personal and cultural significance they convey.

Despite a tendency to dismiss them as too common and childish to be taken seriously, monsters endure. Their ancestry goes back nearly as far as our own and permeates every culture on the globe. Humans have left traces of their beasts—real and imagined—everywhere: on cave walls and around cathedral columns, as ornamentation on tea sets and along the margins of books, in countless stories of adventure and adversity, and on television, computer, and movie screens worldwide.

Along with their historical and cultural prevalence, what keeps me engaged with monsters is their conceptual reach. Monsters bring together threads of a wondrous range of disciplines, entangling together what would otherwise be disparate areas of inquiry. A discussion of monstrous matters will likely include reference to mythical archetypes, morphological variation, fairy tales, and developmental biology. The distorted and hybridized anatomies of monstrous creatures might engage a designer's interest in form and visual composition, while similarly occupying the attention of a philosopher delving into the ontological implications of shape shifting and metamorphosis.

I approach monster-making as a challenge of embodiment, of visualizing and giving morphological form to the tangle of ideas, imaginings, facts and fears associated with things we don't entirely understand. Three-dimensional computer technologies— modeling, animation, simulation, and fabrication—provide the perfect environment for this endeavor. Through the portal of the computer screen, we see a familiar world of 3D objects in 3D space. We can look at things from various points of view, position them next to each other or stack them on top of each other. In the digital 3D world, however, we also find aspects that are quite unlike our physical reality: two objects can occupy the same space, gravity is not a factor therefore things do not fall down (unless we consciously turn gravity on), scale is entirely relative, things can change size infinitely, and there are no material limitations. Equally significant, digital fabrication processes like 3D printing, stereolithography, fused deposition modeling, and laminated object manufacturing enable fabrication of highly convoluted forms in materials with visual characteristics that are unfamiliar and other-worldly.

WheelClawsTeeth is an ambiguous hybrid form similar to a flower, or perhaps a wheel, or a crustacean, or a giant frog… with a copious number of human teeth. Its fragmented, partially assembled state suggests the sculpture is either falling apart or, having fallen apart, is now struggling to pull itself together. It is the largest 3D print I have made and was built using a LOM (laminated object manufacturing) machine that cuts and layers paper to build shapes. The varying brown tones on the sculpture's surface are the result of each sheet of paper being slightly burned as it is cut with a laser.

Elona Van Gent

WheelsClawsTeeth, 2006
Laminated paper; laminated object
manufacturing (LOM)
30 x 50 x 60 inches (76.2 x 127 x 152.4 cm)
Courtesy Elona Van Gent

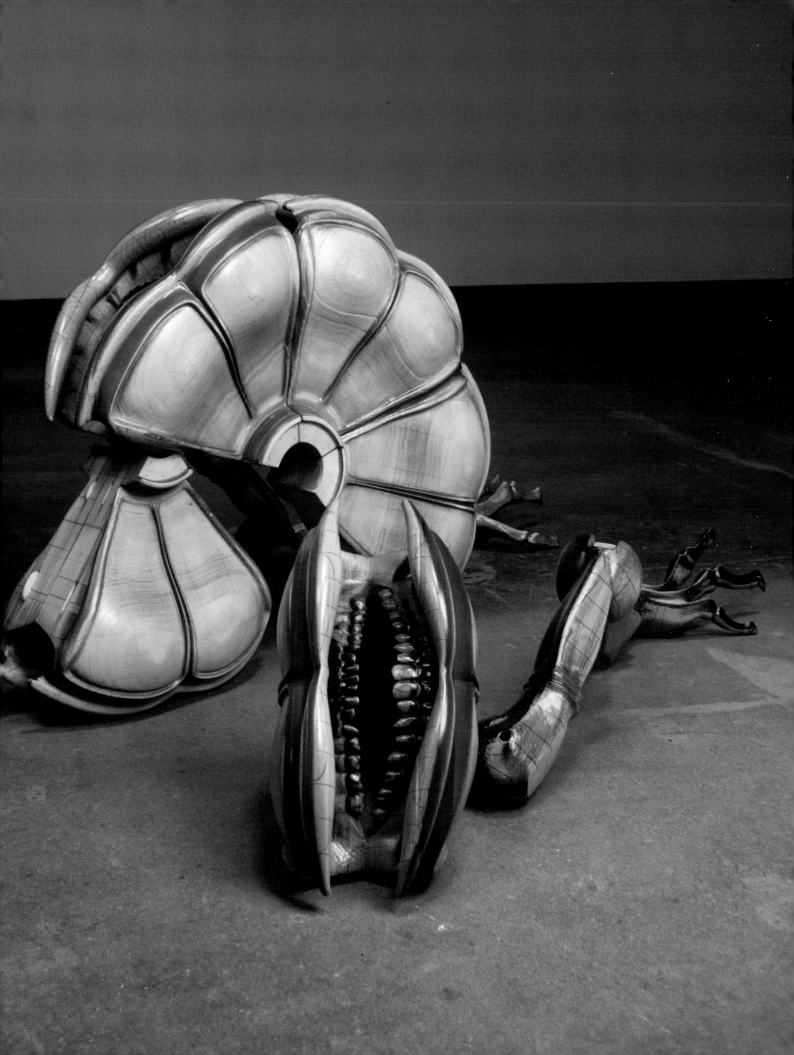

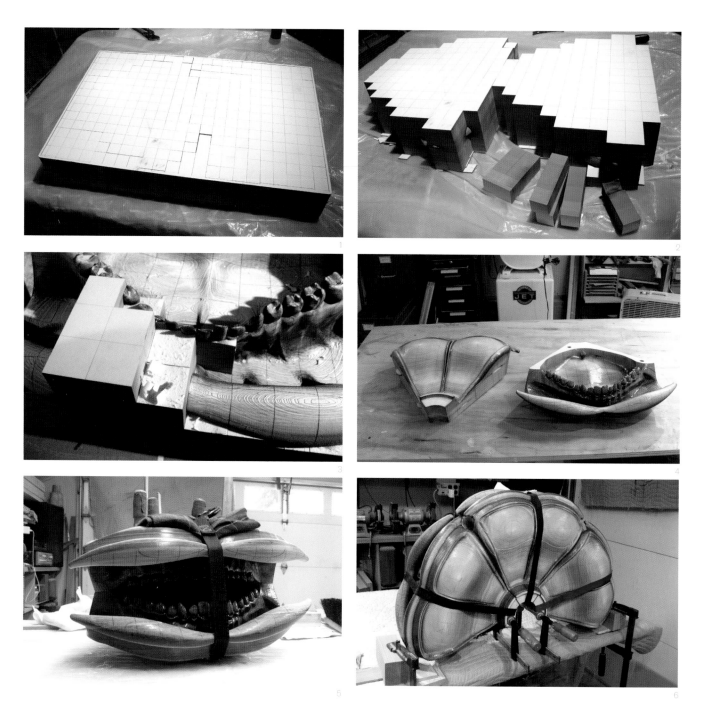

1. Solid block of internally laser-cut,
   stacked, and adhered sheets of
   paper with 3D-printed object
   embedded within
2. Excess areas of each layer of paper
   have been cut by machine into grid
   pattern for easy removal
3. (opposite) Object is carefully excavated,
   revealing scorched brown surface from
   laser cutting

4. Smaller parts and sections are built
   individually and later adhered together
5. Clamps and straps hold parts in place
   as adhesive sets
6. Sections are joined and entire
   sculpture coated with epoxy resin

PROCESSUALITY

For some artists and designers the process of making plays a crucial role in the presentation of the final work. Highlighting a generative approach, the systems they create range from being fully autonomous—in which the formal qualities of the artwork are determined by the computer program—to those that require audience participation or interaction to complete the activity. Installations may include such documentary schema as charts, video, interactive elements, or the machines themselves—3D printers or multiaxial industrial robots—physically fabricating the objects as a multimedia performance.

ALLAN McCOLLUM

To create *The Shapes Project*, Allan McCollum designed a system to create over 31 billion unique two-dimensional shapes: one for every person on the planet when the globe's population peaks in 2050. Not generated, but rather ingenuously formulated using Adobe Illustrator, each shape is created by a series of consecutive actions of first drawing small parts and then cutting and pasting them further into bigger parts.

According to McCollum, "For the time being, around 214,000,000 of the shapes have been set aside for creative experimentation. These can be used for many different purposes—not only for fine art and design projects, but also for various social practices such as: gifts, awards, identity markers, emblems, insignias, logos, toys, souvenirs, educational tools, and so forth. The shapes can be printed graphically as silhouettes or outlines, in any size, color or texture, using all varieties of graphics software; or the files can be used by rapid prototyping machines and computer-numerically-controlled (CNC) equipment—such as routers, laser and water-jet cutter—to build, carve, or cut the shapes from wood, plastic, metal, stone, and other materials."

During the Summer and Fall of 2006, Graphicstudio published a series of 25 sculptural shapes employing the artist's digital files to drive a CNC router to cut a set of eight identical shapes out of birch plywood. To produce each unique sculpture, the layers of wood were glued and clamped together into a solid form, which was then sanded and finished with two coats of satin lacquer.

The Shapes Project is McCollum's latest visualization of his career-long interest in issues related to representation, categorization, symbolic systems, and questions of uniqueness, originality, and mass production. McCollum reflects on his *Shapes Project*: "Instead of looking to one flag and saying 'that's our country,' we now have 31 billion shapes to represent each of us. We need to question the way we use our symbols, because for every reason we have to unify ourselves under a single symbol, there are many more for doing the opposite."

Courtesy Graphicstudio, University of South Florida

Shape, 2006
Laminated birch plywood; computer
numerical control (CNC) milled
12 x 18 x 5 1/2 inches (30.5 x 45.7 x 14 cm)
Courtesy Graphicstudio/USF and artist
Photography Will Lytch, courtesy USF
Graphicstudio

1. Applying wood adhesive with roller before registering and pinning each layer for lamination
2. First stage of sanding process using spindle sander
3. Freshly glued *Shapes* clamped and allowed to cure overnight
4. Testing production procedures on prototype using pneumatic grinder
5. Freshly lacquered *Shapes*
   Photography Will Lytch, Courtesy USF Graphicstudio

DAAN VAN DEN BERG

"From an unknown location, I break into IKEA's computer server. In this nerve center, the CAD files for every IKEA product are stored and downloaded worldwide. By infecting the CAD files with the "Elephantiasis virus" I have just designed, I can hack the entire range of products. The virus causes random deformities, like lumps, cracks and humps, which only show up when the customer prints his product at home with his 3D printer."

The MERRICK originated during a fantasy about the development described above. The MERRICK is a digital file infected with the human "Elephantiasis virus" and then converted into a tangible product by using a 3D printer. Every lamp that is printed will therefore be different.

Three-dimensional printing at home might sound like science fiction. But it is far from unthinkable. Consumer 3D printing is still in its infancy, but is expected to touch off a new revolution.

Daan van den Berg attempts to play with appearances and the expectations these instigate. This results in objects, furniture or products. Furthermore, he works as a freelancer on projects in the field of interior, architecture, visual arts and product design.

Daan van den Berg

Merrick Lamp, 2010
Polyamide; laser sintering
12 5/8 x 7 7/8 x 7 7/8 inches
(32 x 20 x 20 cm)
Courtesy Joanna van der Zanden,
Artistic Director Platform 21, Henk
Buining Consultant/project manager
at TNO Science and Industry
Photography Maarten Willemstein

DIRK VANDER KOOIJ

At Studio Dirk Vander Kooij, developing new techniques for new designs is an ongoing job. We consider ways of developing a new design just as interesting as the new design itself. It requires constant re-adjustment of techniques until the form we have in mind appears. We work on the interface of design, craft, and production. This is the archetype, the first chair that satisfied us. In the beginning the small robot memory presented some limits that caused the geometric and jagged look. The simplicity of the form leaves plenty of room to do full justice to the "Pulse Structure." In the past, the "Pulse Structure" was a given, we had no choice. We do have a choice now. Nevertheless we faithfully left this model as is, a sturdy, heavy chair, made up of thick, wavy lines.

Studio Dirk Vander Kooij

Endless Pulse Low Chair, 2010
Recycled plastics, pigment
31 1/2 x 16 9/16 x 29 15/16 inches
(80 x 42 x 76 cm)
Courtesy Wabnitz Editions Ltd
Photography ©Dirk Vander Kooij

(above) Artist's studio with furniture—
making robot and recently completed
Endless Flow Saloon Table

EZCT

During the summer of 2004, EZCT led a project wherein a series of chairs were computed using genetic algorithms for optimization using a cluster of 12 computers from the École Polytechnique in Paris. They were controlled by Hatem Hamda, from a geographically distinct lab (INRIA), using a Linux platform and open-source libraries and software including Evolving Objects (an evolutionary computation library) and xd3d (a

scientific visualization tool). In this process, first a human collaborative practice was evidently implied in the previous development of the open-source libraries, software and so on, and second a computational and "post-human" collaborative practice became the paradigm since a very limited number of people were able to appropriate a vast amount of computational resources.

Philippe Morel

(opposite) *Computational Chair*
(Best Test 1-400), 2004
Elm
35 3/8 inches (89.9 cm) high
Edition of 25
Private collection Switzerland

(right) *Model T1-M after 860*
genrations (8600 structural evaluations)
Photography Ilse Leenders
© EZCT Architecture and
Design Research

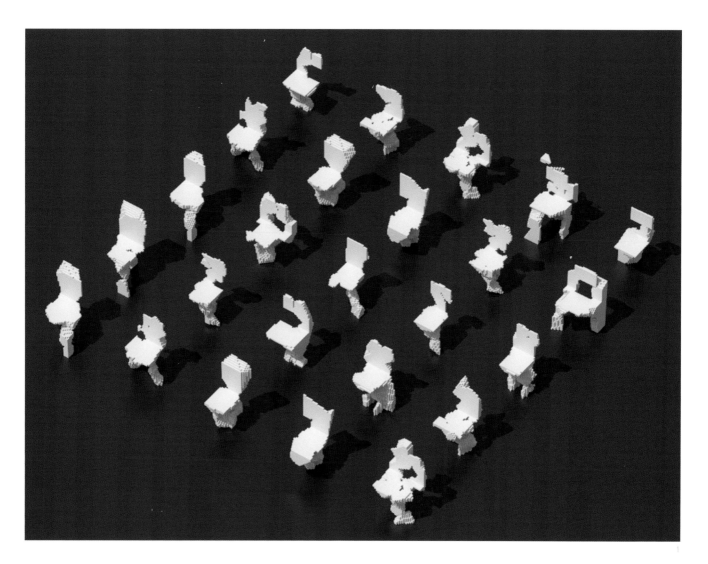

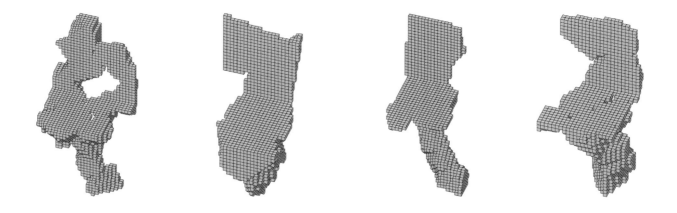

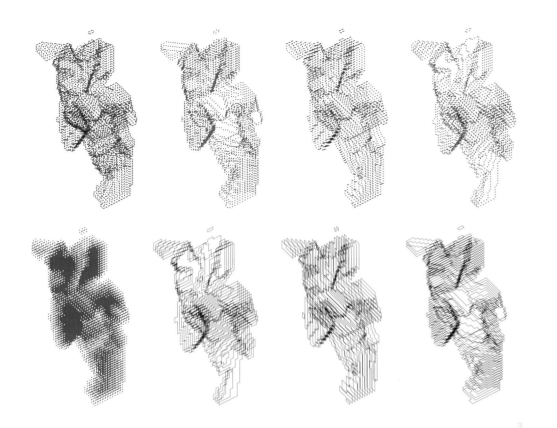

3

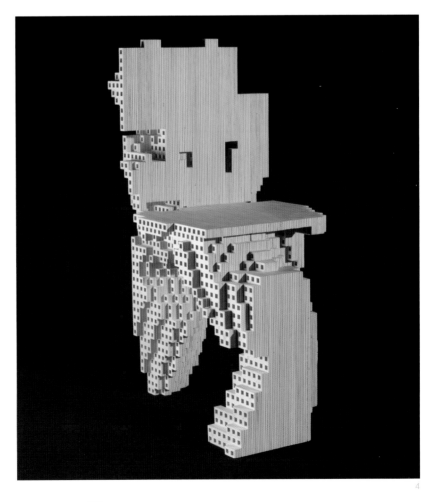

4

1. 25 chairs designed by genetic algorithms
   Photography EZCT Architecture and
   Design Research ©2004
2. Different models of chairs with same
   mechanical performances
   Photo: EZCT Architecture and Design
   Research ©2004
3. Data analysis, *Bolivar* model, Mathematica
   drawings, Centre Pompidou Collection
   Photo: EZCT Architecture and Design
   Research ©2004
4. *Bolivar* Model
   Centre Pompidou Collection
   Photo: Georges Meguerditchian, ©Centre
   Pompidou; courtesy EZCT Architecture
   and Design Research

BEHROKH KHOSHNEVIS

There are nearly one billion homeless people in the world and many live in slums. In the United States alone, nearly 30 million households face cost burdens, overcrowding, and/or space inadequacy. While large cities in developing countries are growing at rates nearing five per cent per year, slums and squatter settlements have been growing nearly twice as fast. At the same time, disasters at home and abroad overstress our ability to respond in a timely manner with the timely construction of a sufficient number of affordable high-quality shelters and homes.

The core of the problem is that building construction is too slow —it currently takes six to nine months to construct an average house in the United States—and costs too much. While in manufacturing, this dual problem has been addressed via automation, resulting in reduced production times and costs that are about twenty five per cent of manual methods, construction has remained largely a manual process.

The University of Southern California has invented automated construction technology—*Contour Crafting*—that has the potential to build housing units in a single day, and at a quarter of the cost of existing manual methods.

Contour Crafting is a hybrid fabrication method that robotically builds up structures layer by layer. The walls are built up by forming their outer surfaces via extrusion of a paste-like material, such as concrete, and the use of robotic trowel to provide a smooth contoured surface. As the layers are built up, gaps in the walls are left for windows and doors, while plumbing and electrical modules are placed robotically into conduits that are created within the walls by leaving portions of their cores unfilled. *Contour Crafting*

is a very flexible technique, capable of constructing aesthetically pleasing "organic" curvilinear shapes as easily as "boxy" rectilinear shapes; and, as such, it has attracted strong interest from leading architects. *Contour Crafting* will achieve automation of tiling of floors and walls, plumbing, electrical and communication line wiring, imbedding of sensors and computational devices, automated insulation, finish work and painting.

The results would be a revolution in construction, enabling large numbers of custom designed structures with wonderful architectural features to be built quickly and at low cost. Simultaneously, construction injuries would be reduced as many of the more hazardous aspects of construction are eliminated. The environmental impact would be reduced due to a reduction of both waste and emissions by reducing the number of days at, thus trips to, the construction site and by the use of a fully electric machine.

Contour Crafting will offer:

- Customer designed houses completed in one day.
- Dignified but affordable housing constructed for low income populations.
- Comfortable and livable emergency shelters (not tents) constructed rapidly for long term usage by disaster victims.
- Construction without waste and without noise, dust and emission pollution
- No accidents and injuries on construction sites—no related litigations.
- New architectural designs giving new appearances to our homes, neighborhoods, and cities.

Dr. Behrokh Khoshnevis

Contour Crafting, 2012

Layered fabrication technology

for automated construction

Image shown: NASA Poster of Lunar Construction

Courtesy Dr. Behrokh Khoshnevis

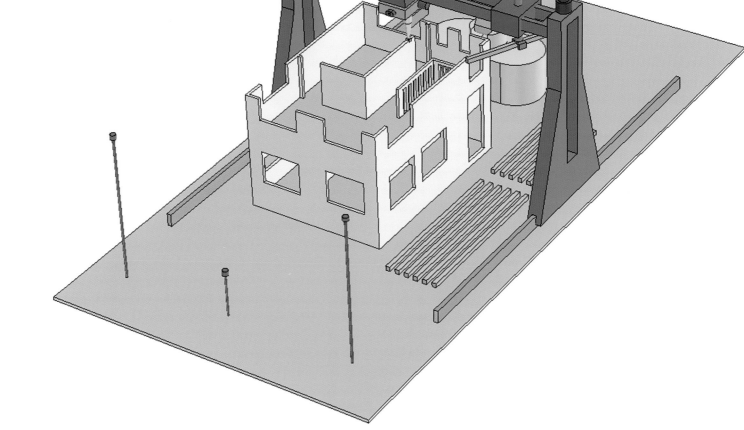

1. Alternative Contour Crafting (CC) Robotic Systems.
   There are several approaches to the robotics system.
   One uses a gantry (crane) robot (pink) to position a
   CC extrusion nozzle (yellow) which is attached to the
   moving platform (purple) of the robot. A laser tracker
   (red) senses the platform position

2. In another approach the body of the building structure
   may be used to anchor the gantry platform. The gantry
   frame climbs the building by means of vertically
   reciprocating legs (green) that extend and retract into
   and out of metal tubing sections robotically imbedded
   into the walls during the layer construction

3. To build large structures such as apartment buildings,
   hospitals, schools and government buildings, the
   overhead gantry platform (yellow) may extend above
   the width of the structures. Two cranes riding on
   tracks laid alongside the structure lift the platform

4. Different Contour CC-Nozzles provide options
   for building solutions

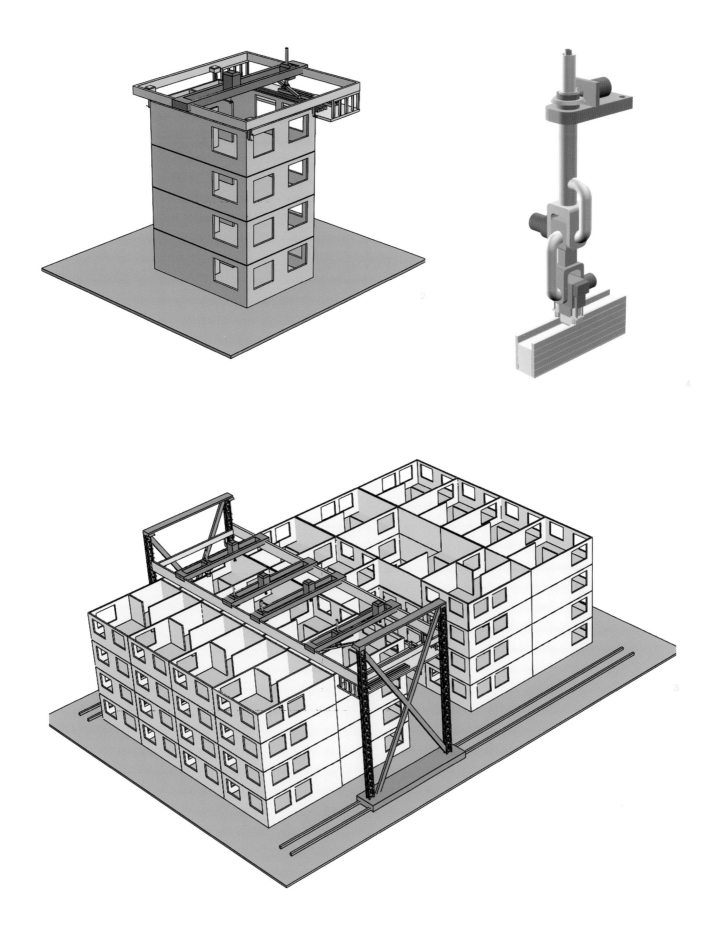

5. CC-Nozzle extruding concrete into
   corrugated wall pattern
6. Corrugated wall showing conservation of
   material to create lighter structures
7. CC-Nozzle forming inner wall of building
8. Completed model for lunar construction
(opposite) Robotic construction technologies
   for Lunar and Martian infrastructures

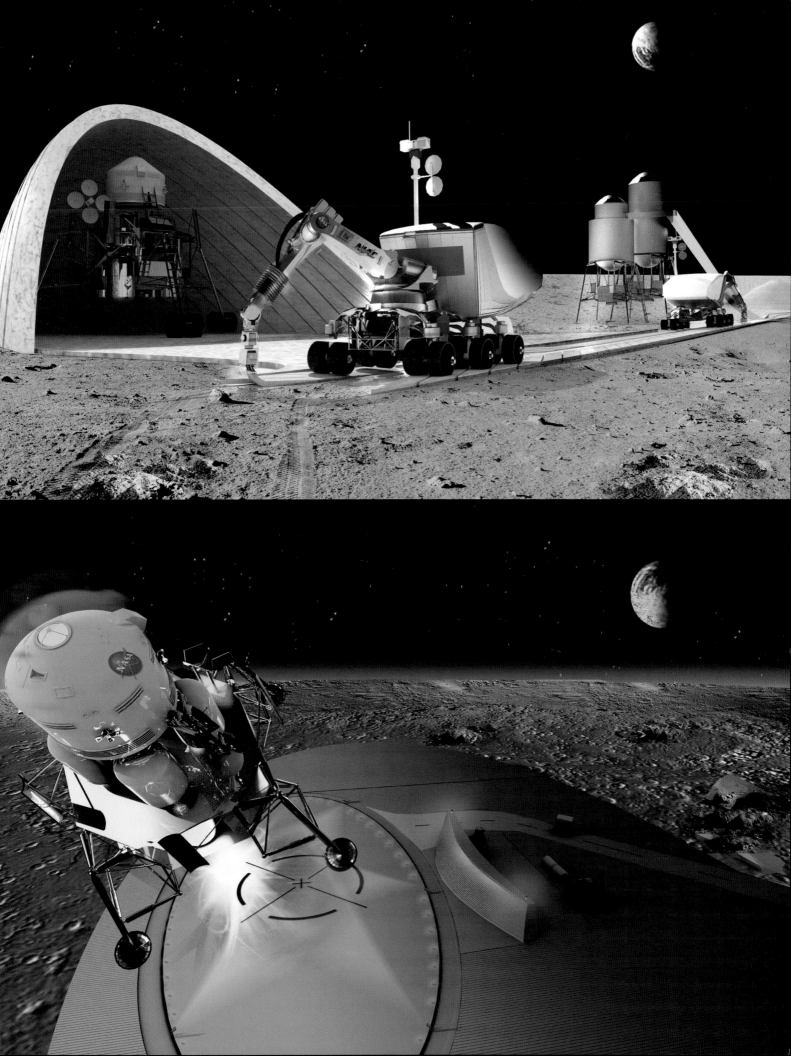

ROXY PAINE

I have always sought alternatives to standard modes of presenting information. My ideas are primary and it is the idea that generates the vehicle. The machines function conceptually on multiple levels. First, the machines are a meditation on control and non-control. Second, they are collisions between the needs and preconditions of factory production and the needs and preconditions of the production of a unique art object. Third, the machines are a study in technology as a mediating force and technology as surrogate, stand-in or perhaps impostor for the artist.

There are two sculpture making machines, *Scumak No.1* and *Scumak No 2*. Scumak stands for "sculpture making." The Scumak machine sets up a language composed of elements and rules by which those elements are utilized. Each of the objects made have 40 layers of polyethylene: consisting of 40 dispensing and 40 cooling. Other elements of the language are the apparatus, the way thermoplastic is dispensed, and the way the computer controls all the motions. Each object can vary within those parameters—the time of each dispensing, the time of each cooling cycle.

Scumak No. 2 operates from a computer program that I write or draw. Each object being made is subject to natural forces and inherent properties of the polyethylene. It is not, as industrial plastic normally is, forced into a mold or extruded through a die to take on a preconceived form. Rather the plastic is allowed to take on a form dictated by gravity, temperature and the essential nature of the material, it is DNA, if you will. Although computer programmed, the machines enlist natural systems, such as thermal dynamics, liquid dynamics, gravity, air currents and temperature, all of which are events removed from human control. Essentially, the Scumak machine can create a nearly infinite variety of forms within these type constraints. It is a complex machine of program and nature that together influence the form of its art objects.

Roxy Paine

S2-P2-MAR1, 2011
Low-density polyethylene, maroon pigment
16 x 30 x 36 inches (40.6 x 76.2 x 91.4 cm)
The Nelson-Atkins Museum of Art, Kansas City, Missouri. Gift of
the artist, 2011.33.1. ©Roxy Paine c/o James Cohan Gallery,
New York
Photography Joshua Ferdinand

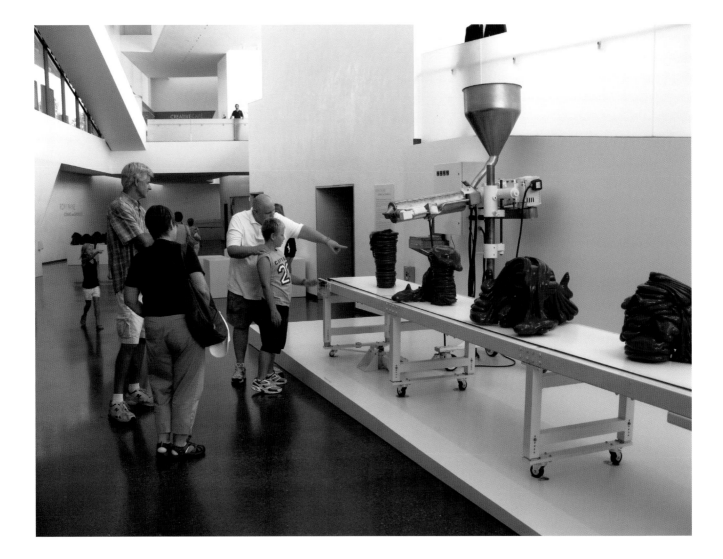

(top) Visitors viewing *Scumak No. 2*
at The Nelson-Atkins Museum of Art,
Kansas City, Missouri, 2011
Aluminum, computer, conveyor,
electronics, extruder, stainless steel,
polyethylene, and Teflon
90 x 276 x 73 inches
(228.6 x 701.04 x 185.42 cm)
Photography Adrianne Russell
adriannerussell.wordpress.com

(opposite) *S2-P2-MAR20*, 2011
Low-density polyethylene
(plastic) and maroon pigment
16 x 30 x 36 inches 55.9 x 22.9 x 45.7 cm
Courtesy the Nelson-Atkins Museum
The Nelson-Atkins Museum of Art, Kansas
City, Missouri. Gift of the artist, 2011.33.2.
© Roxy Paine c/o James Cohan Gallery,
New York
Photography Joshua Ferdinand

GREG LYNN

The *Toy Furniture* project consists of prototypes of high technology scavenging of recycled plastics for furniture. The collection includes four different sized tables with Panelite or glass tops, a low bench, and a storage wall.

I had been preoccupied with recycling my kids toys into walls, furniture, and usable objects; using their toys as bricks. The Recycled Toys do not use the labor or expertise of masonry and the wet forgiving technology of mortar to become level and true. Instead, they are laser scanned and digitized into a computer, they are designed and arrayed like bricks, their intersections are defined as cutting paths, and a robot cuts their joints and connections with precision. They do not rest on mortar joints, they are not even glued; the toy bricks are welded together with a tool used to repair car fenders.

Greg Lynn FORM

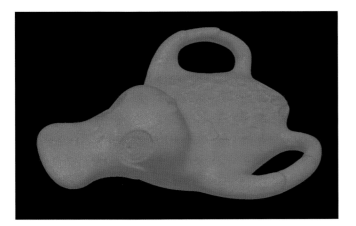

Toy Furniture, 2008
Winner of Golden Lion, Best
Installation, Venice Architecture
Biennale, 2008
Recycled plastic toys; computer
numerical control (CNC) laser cut
Courtesy Greg Lynn FORM

CARABALLO-FARMAN

For most women diagnosed with breast cancer each year, medical imaging is the entry point into the disease. Yet, rarely does a woman get to see her MRI or get a sense of the shape or physicality of the malignancy. *Object Breast Cancer* (OBC) by caraballo-farman is based on the conviction that artistic interventions can have important social and psychological effects. OBC questions and challenges the popular conceptions and visual culture of the disease.

Using collected MRIs, starting with their own, the artists use medical imaging and 3D software to produce accurate models of breast cancer tumors, which are used as the basis for cast sculptures, fetishes, personal pendants, performances and installations. These objects are externalizations of unseen malignancies, surrogates for the extracted tumors that succeed in being simultaneously beautiful and unsettling.

The project has inspired a new research project at Weill Cornell Medical College to investigate 3D features of breast cancer tumors.

caraballo-farman

Object Breast Cancer, 2011
Photography Object Breast Cancer/
courtesy caraballo-farman
(top right) *OBC Amulet-Necklace*
Gold-plated bronze, rubber cord
(top left) *OBC Worry Bead*
Sterling silver
Unique
(bottom) *OBC Extractions 8*, 2011
Cast bronze
Unique

MICHAEL REES
& ROBERT GERO

Intervening Phenomena was developed as part of a Tactical Play Exchange (TPE) by artists Robert Gero and Michael Rees. TPE is a strategy to co-create a series of artworks. These works are forms that generally begin with contextual architectural elements derived from the site of exhibition, for example, the floor plan of a gallery, or other localized features. These become the core structures that are added to, morphed and modified in multiple iterations using 3D modeling software, automatic manufacture and later with physical manual interventions. The digital files are passed back and forth between Gero & Rees creating a networked "ground of play." Using the gallery floor plan to create a series of hundreds of iterations, a number of these forms were then selected to be physically produced by using a combination of 3D printing (rapid prototype), CNC milling and hand working the structures. In the radical multiplication of objects an energetically unique ecosystem has been created.

Developed by combining Play theory with Systems theory, Gero & Rees utilize the concept of operativity; in other words, the operation is the significant systemic constituent. They are play in the sense of a to-and-fro movement that becomes a transformation into structure. The structures or objects are infinitely malleable, producible, and "playable-with," they cannot be attributed to an originator, so no one artist is privileged as author. Intervening Phenomena is the implementation of this operativity.

Michael Rees

Intervening Phenomena, 2012
Polyurethane foam, joint compound,
painted 3D print, video projection
65 x 55 x 30 inches (165.1 x 139.7 x 76.2 cm)
Courtesy Robert Gero and Michael Rees
Photography Jimi Billingsley

UNFOLD &
TIM KNAPEN

In *l'Artisan Electronique*, pottery, one of the oldest artisanal techniques for making utilitarian objects, is combined with new digital media. However, the installation still clearly refers to the artisanal process of working in clay. The printing process imitates the traditional coiling technique used by ceramists, in which the form is built up by stacking coils of clay. The virtual pottery wheel on the other hand, is a digital tool to "turn" forms and objects in thin air.

Unfold

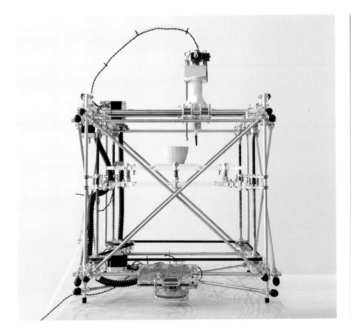

Vases created by *L'Artisan Electronique*, 2010
Interactive installation: 3D scanner, digital design software, modified 3D printer, clay
Courtesy Unfold
Photography Kristof Vrancken

(left) Ceramic 3D printer
Photography Kristof Vrancken
(right) Virtual wheel
Photography Peter Verbruggen

BIOGRAPHIES

BY COLIN FANNING

Laura Alvarado

Laura Alvarado (Germany, b. 1977, Colombia) studied industrial design at Universidad Jorge Tadeo Lozano in Bogotá, Colombia from 1998 to 2003, and subsequently trained as a goldsmith at Escarof Bogotá (2003–2004) and Vassiliou Juwelier GmbH in Bonn, Germany (2005–2006). Between 2006 and 2011, she attended the University of Applied Arts and Design Düsseldorf, receiving a degree in Jewelry design. She is part of the design group Formativ (est. 2009), and she currently collaborates with fellow Formativ member Vivian Meller on the PortraitMe 3D-printed jewelry project, which was selected for Talente 2012 in Munich and honored at the Ritual 21st Silver Festival in Legnica, Poland. *http://www.lauralvarado.com*

Ron Arad

Ron Arad (United Kingdom, b. 1951, Israel) attended the Bezalel Academy of Art and Design in Jerusalem between 1971 to 1973, and the Architectural Association in London from 1974 to 1979. He established his first firm, One Off Ltd., together with Caroline Thorman in London in 1981, and the architecture and design studio Arad Associates (also with Thorman) in 1989. His architectural and industrial design work has been widely featured in design publications and exhibited at major museums and galleries worldwide. His work is included in the collections of the Centre Georges Pompidou, Paris; The Metropolitan Museum of Art, New York; the Victoria and Albert Museum, London; and the Vitra Design Museum, Germany, among others. Arad also taught in the Design Products Department at the Royal College of Art from 1997 to 2009. *http://www.ronarad.co.uk*

Aranda\Lasch
(Benjamin Aranda and Christopher Lasch)

Aranda\Lasch is a New York-based architectural studio established in 2003 by Benjamin Aranda (b. 1973) and Chris Lasch (b. 1972). Aranda\Lasch investigates the realm of structure and space, forming crystalline designs for buildings, installations and objects through computational exploration. The duo's early projects were the subject of the critically acclaimed book, *Tooling*, published by Princeton Architectural Press, and Aranda\Lasch was selected as the 2007 United States Artists Fellow in Architecture & Design. In 2008 they were commissioned by the Museum of Modern Art in New York to produce a large-scale installation for the exhibition *Design and the Elastic Mind*, and participated in the Venice and Seville Biennales in a collaboration with artist Matthew Ritchie and arts institution T-BA21. Objects and furniture designed by Aranda\Lasch are represented by Johnson Trading Gallery in New York. *http://www.arandalasch.com*

Sandra Backlund

Sandra Backlund (Sweden, b. 1979) is a fashion designer with a degree from Beckmans College of Design in Stockholm. She graduated in 2004, founding her own label that same year. Since then, her work has been selected and supported by some of the most important editors and exhibition curators in the world. Her experiments with materials and three-dimensional, sculptural forms for knitwear have incorporated both traditional handcraft techniques and advanced digital knitting technologies. In 2007 Backlund was the Grand Prix winner of the Festival International De Mode et De Photographie in Hyeres, France, and collaborated with Louis Vuitton on the Autumn/Winter collection in the same year. She was also selected by Vogue Italia editor Franca Sozzani for the magazine's Project Protégé in 2008, and received NewGen sponsorship from The British Fashion Council in 2009. *http://www.sandrabacklund.com*

Barry X Ball

Barry X Ball (United States, b. 1955) received his degree from Pomona College in Claremont, California in 1977, and has lived and worked in New York since 1978. His work has been exhibited extensively in international contemporary galleries and art fairs, and is represented in the collections of the Hammer Museum, San Francisco Museum of Modern Art, the Norton Museum of Art, the Maramotti Collection, Le Fonds régional d'art contemporain Bretagne, Magasin 3 Stockholm Konsthall, Museo Cantonale d'Arte, Museo di arte moderna e contemporanea di Trento e Rovereto, the Berlingieri Collection, the Thomas Olbricht Collection, and the Panza Collection. He has had recent solo exhibitions at the Venice Biennale (2011); Galerie Nathalie Obadia, Paris, and the National Museum of Palazzo Mansi, Lucca, Italy (2012); and the Bass Museum of Art, Miami, and the Thomas Olbricht Collection, Berlin (2013), among others. *http://www.barryxball.com/index.php*

Chris Bathgate

Chris Bathgate (United States, b. 1980) is a self-taught machinist sculptor who lives and works in Baltimore, Maryland and has spent more than a decade learning how to build and use a variety of metalworking tools and machinery. He has assembled a machine shop of repurposed and homemade robotic and manual machine tools in a basement studio at his home. Bathgate's work has been featured in *Make Magazine, Popular Mechanics* magazine in Russia, *Sculptures Pacific Magazine*, and *Best of American Sculpture*, Volume II. He was twice awarded grants from the Pollack-Krasner Foundation, in 2007 and most recently in 2011; he has also received hometown recognition through a Creative Baltimore grant in 2008 and a Baltimore "B" grant in 2011. His works have been exhibited at the Baltimore Museum of Art and the Dennis and Phillip Ratner Museum, and are held in numerous private collections throughout the U.S. and abroad. *http://www.chrisbathgate.com*

Dror Benshetrit

Dror Benshetrit (New York, b. 1977, Israel) received his education at the Eindhoven Design Academy in Holland. Since 2002, he has headed a multidisciplinary practice specializing in innovative design projects. Studio Dror works with a range of international clients, including Alessi, Bentley, Boffi, Bombay Sapphire, Cappellini, Kiehl's, Levi's, Lualdi, Material ConneXion, Maya

Romanoff, Marithé + François Girbaud, Puma, Rosenthal, Skins Footwear, Yigal Azrouël, Shvo, Swarovski, Tumi, and Target. Benshetrit has also lectured widely and received numerous awards, including the GE Plastics Competition "Merging Boundaries" 2001, iF Product Design Award 2006, and the Good Design Award 2008, 2010. His work is included in the permanent collections of major museums in North America, Europe, and the Middle East. http://www.studiodror.com

Francis Bitonti

Francis Bitonti (United States, b. 1983) is ushering in a new manufacturing paradigm through his innovative use of computational design techniques and emerging manufacturing technologies. Bitonti's design process is a blend of cutting edge digital design and manufacturing technologies, aimed to transform mass production. Looking instead to the future of manufacturing; mass customization, Bitonti sees computational design, smart materials, and interactive environments as opportunities to create new aesthetic languages for our built environment and he has taken that vision and applied it to a wide range of disciplines ranging from architecture to product design to fashion. Francis holds a Masters of Architecture from Pratt, where he is a researcher at the Digital Arts and Humanities Research Center and professor at Rensselaer Polytechnic Institute School of Architecture. His work has been published internationally in many prestigious institutions including the Smithsonian Cooper-Hewitt National Design Museum has been published in outlets such as the Wall Street Journal, V Magazine, Wired, and The New York Daily News and continues to garner global recognition.

Doug Bucci

Doug Bucci (United States, b. 1971) is a jewelry designer who uses digital processes to explore and display biological systems and the effect of disease on the body. His work has appeared in multiple periodicals and texts, including Metalsmith magazine, American Craft magazine, and Lark Book's 500 series & Darling Publication's The Jewelry Compendium. Bucci is represented in the collections of Windsor Castle, Berkshire, London; the Philadelphia Museum of Art; Pinakothek der Moderne, Munich; the Newark Museum; Deutsche Goldschmiedehaus Hanau, Germany; and Design Museo, Helsinki. Bucci earned his MFA (1998) from the Tyler School of Art at Temple University, and currently teaches in the Metals/Jewelry/CAD-CAM area at Tyler and in the Industrial Design department at The University of the Arts, both in Philadelphia. http://www.dougbucci.com

caraballo-farman
(Leonor Caraballo and Abou Farman)

Abou Farman (b. 1966, Iran/Canada,) and Leonor Caraballo (b. 1971, Argentina) formed caraballo-farman in 2001, a collaborative that works in new media, video, installation and photography. Their work has been supported by several foundations and art centers, including: New York Foundation For the

Arts Fellowship, 2011, Guggenheim Fellowship, 2010, NYFA (SOS), Lower Manhattan Cultural Council, Canada Council for The Arts, the New York Community Trust, Eyebeam Art and Technology Center, and Art Omi. Their work has been exhibited around the world, including at the Tate Modern; Museum of Modern Art's PS1 in New York; the Whitney Museum of American Art's Independent Study Program; Artists Space, New York; El Museo del Barrio, New York; LAXART; the Havana Biennial; and the Yerba Buena Center for the Arts in San Francisco. http://www.caraballofarman.net

Andreia Chaves

Andreia Chaves (Brazil, b. 1980) graduated from Polimoda Fashion Institute in Florence, Italy in 2010, where her work had already attracted attention from the international media. Her first series, the InvisibleShoe, launched in February 2011 and has been featured in leading fashion publications and international exhibitions. Chaves is best known for her innovative and distinctive visual approach, fusing craftsmanship, experimental materials and cutting edge technology to realize her footwear designs. Now working between Europe and Brazil, Chaves is also an international design consultant. http://www.andreiachaves.com/AndreiaChaves

Chuck Close

Charles Thomas "Chuck" Close (United States, b. 1940) is an American painter, photographer, and printmaker who initially found fame through his large-scale photorealist portraits. His work has been exhibited extensively around the world. Close has been the subject of major retrospectives at The Museum of Modern Art and The Metropolitan Museum of Art in New York, the Museo Nacional Centro de Arte Reina Sofía in Madrid, and the State Hermitage Museum in St. Petersburg, Russia. Close received a BA from the University of Washington School of Art in 1962, and a BFA and MFA from the Yale University School of Art and Architecture in 1963 and 1964 respectively. In 1988, he was left severely paralyzed by spinal artery collapse, but he continues to paint and produce work. Close currently lives and works in New York City's West Village and in Bridgehampton, New York. http://chuckclose.com/#/official-galleryry

Continuum Fashion
(Jenna Fizel and Mary Huang)

Continuum (est. 2011) is a fashion label and experimental design lab founded by Jenna Fizel (United States, b.1986) and Mary Huang (United States, b. 1986). Fizel lives in Boston and holds a BSAD in Architecture from MIT. She has previously worked at Small Design Firm in Cambridge, Massachusetts, for clients such as the Metropolitan Museum and the Museum of Fine Arts, Boston. Huang, based in Brooklyn, New York, received her BA in Design, Media Arts from the University of California Los Angeles and an MA from the Copenhagen Institute of Interaction Design. Previously, she worked in product development for Shapeways and interaction design for Local Projects in New

York City. Mary lives in Brooklyn, New York. Together as Continuum, they treat fashion as software, using digital technologies to create bespoke designs. *http://www.continuumfashion.com*

FutureFactories
(Lionel T. Dean)

Lionel Theodore Dean (United Kingdom, b. 1962) graduated from the Royal College of Art, London in 1987. He worked as designer for the automotive company Pininfarina in Italy before forming his own studio in 1989. In 2002, as Designer in Residence at the University of Huddersfield, Dean formed FutureFactories, a studio practice that focuses on digital fabrication and evolutionary and computational design. Initially part of an extended research project, the studio has proved a success and has yielded products ranging from gallery pieces to retail designs. FutureFactories' works have been exhibited in London, Milan, and New York. In 2005, one of Dean's pieces was acquired by The Museum of Modern Art in New York for the permanent collection of the Department of Architecture and Design. *http://www.futurefactories.com*

Wim Delvoye

Wim Delvoye (Belgium, b. 1965) lives and works in Ghent, Belgium. His artistic career is highly varied, but he is best known for his more controversial works, such as *Cloaca* (an installation that turns food into fecal matter, initially unveiled in 2000 at the Museum voor Hedendaagse Kunst, Antwerp) or *Art Farm* (in which live pigs are tattooed with a variety of designs). Important solo exhibitions of Delvoye's work have been held at Castello di Rivoli, 1991; Kunsthalle Nürnberg, 1992; Open Air Museum Middelheim, Antwerp, 1997; Centre Georges Pompidou, Paris, 2000; Migros Museum, Zurich, 2001; Museum Kunst-Palast, Dusseldorf (2002); The Power Plant, Toronto, 2004; and the Peggy Guggenheim Collection, Venice, 2009. *http://www.wimdelvoye.be*

Joshua DeMonte

Joshua DeMonte (United States, b. 1984) is a Philadelphia-based jewelry designer. He holds both a BFA (2007) and an MFA (2009) from the Tyler School of Art at Temple University in Philadelphia, with concentrations in metalsmithing, jewelry design, and computer-aided design and manufacturing. DeMonte is currently an assistant professor at the College of Fine Arts and Communication at Towson University, where he teaches interdisciplinary object design and acts as Associate Director of the Object Lab. He has won several awards for his jewelry objects, including the Tyler School's Albert Paley Award, and an honorable mention in the 2009 juried exhibition *Layers* through the Fredericksburg Center for the Creative Arts in Virginia. He has shown work in both solo and important group exhibitions, including the recent *40 Under 40* exhibition at the Smithsonian's Renwick Gallery. *http://www.joshuademonte.com*

Richard Dupont

Richard Dupont (United States, b. 1968) lives and works in New York City. He received a BA from the Departments of Visual Art, and Art and Archeology at Princeton University (1991), and his artistic practice encompasses installations, sculptures, drawings, reliefs, animations, and prints. His solo exhibitions include The Hudson Valley Center for Contemporary Art (2008), The Middlebury College Museum of Art, 2011, and the Carolina Nitsch Project Room, New York, 2011 and 2013. He has also presented major installations at Lever House, 2008, and The Flag Art Foundation, 2010, both in New York. Dupont's works are represented in the permanent collections of The Museum

of Modern Art, the Whitney Museum of American Art, the Museum of Fine Arts, Boston, the Cleveland Museum of Art, the Brooklyn Museum, the Yale University Art Gallery, the Hammer Museum, and The New York Public Library Print Collection, among others. *http://www.richarddupont.com*

Michael Eden

Michael Eden (United Kingdom, b. 1955) ran a relatively traditional handmade ceramics business for more than two decades, selling work and publishing on contemporary ceramics. Between 2006 and 2008, he undertook an MPhil research project at the Royal College of Art, combining his interest in digital design and manufacturing with his previous experience. This project resulted in his *Wedgwoodn't Tureen* series, which won the RSA (Royal Society of Arts) Design Directions competition. Since then, Michael has continued to design, produce, and exhibit work inspired by both historical objects and contemporary themes, exploring the relationship between hand and digital tools and investigating experimental manufacturing technology and materials. Eden is an Associate Lecturer on Ceramic Design at Central Saint Martins College of Art and Design in London; he also contributes to the MA Industrial Design course, and is a visiting Lecturer at the Royal College of Art. *http://www.edenceramics.co.uk/*

Richard Elaver

Richard Elaver (United States, b. 1980) received his Bachelor's degree from the University of Wisconsin-Madison in 1999, and his MFA from the Cranbrook Academy of Art in 2005. In 2006, he completed a Fulbright Fellowship in the Netherlands, where he worked with the Droog collective and studied design history at the University of Leiden. He has worked as both a jeweler and industrial designer, and now teaches as an Assistant Professor of Industrial Design at Appalachian State University in Boone, North Carolina. Elaver's work has been shown at the National Ornamental Metal Museum, the New York Hall of Sciences, and the Tampa Museum of Science and Industry, among other institutions in the United States and abroad. He is also named on more than 15 design patents and has developed products for companies like Wilson Sports, 3M, and Craftsman. *http://www.designercraftsman.com*

Ammar Eloueini

Ammar Eloueini (French-American, b. 1968, Lebanon) received the degree of Diplômé par le Gouvernement from Paris-Villemin in 1994, and graduated with a Master of Science in Advanced Architectural Design from Columbia University in 1996. The following year, he established Ammar Eloueini Digit-all Studio (AEDS) in Paris, and the office has had locations in both Europe and the United States since 1999. The firm has been recognized with awards such as the New York Architectural League's Emerging Voices, 2007, nine AIA Design Excellence awards, and the French Ministry of Culture Nouveaux Albums des Jeunes Architectes, 2002. Eloueini's work is represented in the collections of The Museum of Modern Art, the Centre Pompidou, the Canadian Centre for Architecture, Disseny Hub Barcelona, and The Ogden Museum of Southern Art in New Orleans. Eloueini also chaired the Digital Media Program at the University of Illinois in Chicago and taught design courses between 1999 and 2005. He is currently a Favrot Professor at Tulane University and a thesis advisor at the ENSCI in Paris. *http://www.digit-all.net*

EZCT

EZCT Architecture & Design Research (est. 2000) is a collaborative practice dealing in research with the current complexity of sciences. Architect and theorist Philippe Morel (France, b. 1979), a cofounder of EZCT with Jelle Feringa (b. 1978) and Felix Agid (b. 1979), is an Associate Professor at the

École nationale superieure d'architecture Paris-Malaquais, where he cofounded the Digital Knowledge program and department. He is also visiting Studio Master at the Bartlett School of Architecture (University College of London). Before teaching at the Bartlett, he taught at the Berlage Institute (seminar and studio) and at the Architectural Association (History & Theory Studies and AADRL studio). Work by EZCT is held in the FRAC Centre and Centre Pompidou permanent collections, as well as by private collectors. *http://www.ezct.net*

Front Design

Sofia Lagerkvist, Charlotte von der Lancken, Anna Lindren, and Katja S'vstr'm form the Stockholm-based collective Front Design (Sweden, est. 2003). The four women each hold masters degrees in industrial design; S'vstr'm also studied as a textile designer, while Lagerkvist has worked in stage design. Front's designs are notable for their narrative aspects, conveying to their users statements about the nature of materials and the design process. Some of their works are partially "designed" by animals, computers, or machines, lending an aspect of accident or ephemerality to the object and the environment; others are reinterpretations of classic or traditional designs. All four members are active participants in each project from conception to realization. *http://www.designfront.org*

Goldner Geva

Goldner Geva is the joint practice of native Israelis Gal Goldner (b. 1977) and Iftah Geva (b. 1977), who live and work in a Kibbutz in Northern Israel, crafting innovative furniture and other objects from wood and carbon fiber. Gal studied mechanical and industrial engineering at Ben-Gurion University; Iftah Geva studied industrial design at Holon Institute of Technology. In addition to their furniture and jewelry work, they cofounded Life Assistant, a company for development and designing solutions for the aging population, and ABA Science Play, where they develop projects for cutting-edge playgrounds. *http://ggi.co.il/index.html*

Bathsheba Grossman

Bathsheba Grossman (United States, b. 1966) is a mathematician artist turned digital designer working in three-dimensional printing. Grossman earned her degree in mathematics from Yale University in 1988 and studied art at the University of Pennsylvania. Her forays in sculpting include lost-wax casting, electroforming, stereolithography, ZCorp printing, Prometal direct steel printing, and subsurface laser-etching. Grossman's contributions to science include a service for imaging protein structures used by pharmaceutical companies. While she found a natural audience among math enthusiasts, Grossman has reached a greater community by making her designs available for sale. Grossman currently lives and works in Santa Cruz, California. *http://www.bathsheba.com*

Jan Habraken

Jan Habraken (United States, b. Netherlands, 1975), the founder and lead designer of FormNation, studied architectural engineering before he pursued industrial design at the Netherlands' prestigious Design Academy Eindhoven. After graduating in 2002, he cofounded WATdesign with Maarten Baptist and spent several years in Europe making and exhibiting products and furniture. In 2008, Habraken moved to New York City, where he founded Studio Jan Habraken, the predecessor of FormNation. Habraken's current enterprise draws upon his diverse experiences in the fields in architecture, interior, furniture, retail, and product design. FormNation shares a studio space and frequently works together with designer Alissia Melka-Teichroew, who is Habraken's wife. *http://www.formnation.com*

Zaha Hadid

Zaha Hadid (United Kingdom, b. 1950, Iraq) initially studied mathematics at the American University in Beirut, and moved to London in 1972 to study architecture, graduating in 1977 from the Architectural Association. She joined the Office of Metropolitan Architecture (OMA) and taught at the Architectural Association before starting her own practice in London in 1980. Her boundary-pushing work has been collected and exhibited worldwide, and many of her built works are well-known, like the Vitra Fire Station, Weil am Rhein, Germany, 1993; the Mind Zone at the Millennium Dome, Greenwich, UK,1999; and the Rosenthal Center for Contemporary Art in Cincinnati, Ohio, 2003. Hadid continues to be active in academia, holding chairs and guest professorships at Harvard University, Yale University, the University of Illinois at Chicago, Columbia University, the University of Visual Arts in Hamburg, and the University of Applied Arts in Vienna. *http://www.zaha-hadid.com*

Richard Hamilton

Richard Hamilton (United Kingdom, 1922–2011), considered one of the figureheads of British pop art, studied painting at the Royal Academy School from 1938 to 1940, and worked as an industrial designer until 1945. In 1946, he resumed his studies of painting at the Royal Academy School, but was expelled and conscripted into UK national service. From 1948 to 1951, he studied at the Slade School of Art in London, concentrating mainly on etching. Hamilton cofounded the Independent Group in 1952 at the Institute of Contemporary Arts in London, which would become central to the development of pop art in the UK. He also taught at the Central School of Arts and Crafts and at the Royal College of Art from 1957 to 1961. Over the subsequent decades, Hamilton increasingly combined the mediums of photography and painting in his work, and in the 1980s he began to explore the effects of digital media on image perception and their ramifications for fine art. Major retrospective exhibitions of his work have been organized by the Tate Gallery, London, 1970 and 1992; the Solomon R. Guggenheim Museum, New York, 1973; the Neue Nationalgalerie, Berlin, 1974; Museum Ludwig, Cologne, 2003; Dublin City Gallery and the Minneapolis Institute of Arts, both in 2011; and London's National Gallery in 2012.

Michael Hansmeyer

Michael Hansmeyer (Germany, b. 1973) is an architect and programmer who explores the use of algorithms and computation to generate architectural forms. He is currently based in the Computer Aided Architectural Design group of the architecture department at the Eidgenössische Technische Hochschule (Swiss Federal Institute of Technology) in Zurich. Recent projects include The Sixth Order at the Gwangju Design Biennale 2011 and Digital Grotesque for Archilab 2013. He holds an M.B.A degree from Insead Fontainebleau as well as a Master of Architecture degree from Columbia University. He previously worked with J.P. Morgan, McKinsey & Company, and at Herzog & de Meuron architects. *http://www.michael-hansmeyer.com*

HAWK

(Hochschule für Angewandte Wissenschaft und Kunst (HAWK) – Barbara Kotte, Andreas Schulz, Nikolas Eggert, Johannes Zäuner, and Rebecca Wilting) Professor Andreas Schulz (b. 1958) and Professor Barbara Kotte (b. 1971) teach at the Faculty of Design of the Hochschule für Angewandte Wissenschaft und Kunst (University of Applied Sciences and Arts) in Hildesheim, Germany. In 2013 they organized the 8.Akkuschrauberrennen (Cordless Screwdriver Race), the eighth iteration of an event in which their Rapid Racer took part in 2011. Their students and collaborators Nikolas Eggert (b. 1988) and Johannes Zäuner (b. 1981) have finished their studies

and currently work as designers; Rebecca Wilting (b. 1988) is currently completing a master's degree.
www.hawk-hhg.de/en/index.phpmaster's degree.

Nick Hornby

Nick Hornby (United Kingdom, b. 1980) lives and works in London. He received his BA in Fine Art from the Slade School of Art in 2003, and his MA from the Chelsea College of Art in 2007. In 2011, he was an Artist in Residence at Eyebeam in New York; he has also been a resident at the Institute of Contemporary Indian Art in Mumbai and the Fleischmann Foundation in Slovakia. He has exhibited at the Tate Britain, the Southbank Centre, Fitzwilliam Museum in Cambridge, The Hub in Athens, and the 2012 Polish Biennale. Hornby's work has been awarded the Clifford Chance Sculpture Prize, RBKC Artists' Professional Development Bursary, the Deidre Hubbard Sculpture Award, and the BlindArt Prize; he was also shortlisted for the inaugural Spitalfields Sculpture prize and Mark Tanner Sculpture Prize. *http://www.nickhornby.com/slideshow.htm*

Impossible Productions Ink LLC
(Veronika Schmid and Alistair Gill)

Impossible Productions Ink LLC (est. 2009) is a New York-based design studio led by Alistair Gill (b. 1971, United Kingdom) and Veronika Schmid (b. 1973, Austria). The multidisciplinary practice specializes in yacht design, architecture, and product design. Gill previously worked at Francisdesign, Grimshaw Architects, and Urban Research Laboratory London, among other architecture practices. Schmid has worked as project architect at Arup AGU with Cecil Balmond, Richard Meier & Partners, Francisdesign, and done ongoing work with artist Frank Stella. Both directors have also taught advanced architectural design for more than 15 years. *http://impossible-productions-ink.com*

François Brument and Sonia Laugier

Based in Bagnolet, France, In-Flexions is the collaboration between independent Parisian designer François Brument (France, b. 1977), a graduate of ENSCI-Les Ateliers, and Sonia Laugier (France, b. 1974), a graduate from the École Centrale de Nantes and ENSCI-Les Ateliers. Brument researches the potential of digital creation in the field of design; swapping computer programming for design, he has developed a perpetually mutating design style, showcased through creations that oscillate between digital objects and industrial productions. Since 2005 Brument's works have been exhibited in France and abroad, appearing in the collections of the Fonds national d'art contemporain, the Centre Pompidou, the Musée des arts Décoratifs, the Canadian Centre for Architecture, and VIA. Laugier is an engineer and designer whose work involves graphics, programming and design in the development of interfaces and digital objects. *http://in-flexions.com*

J. Mayer H.

Jürgen Mayer Hermann (Germany, b. 1965) is the founder and principal of the Berlin-based firm J. Mayer H. Architects (est. 1966). He studied at Stuttgart University, The Cooper Union, and Princeton University, and his work has been published and exhibited worldwide. He is represented in several permanent collections, including The Museum of Modern Art, New York and the San Francisco Museum of Modern Art. His national and international awards include the Mies van der Rohe Award for Emerging Architect, Special Mention, (2003); the Holcim Award Bronze, 2005 for the Metropol Parasol in Seville, featured in the *Out of Hand* exhibition; and the Audi Urban Future Award (2010). Jürgen Mayer H. has taught at Princeton University, University of the Arts Berlin, Harvard University, Kunsthochschule Berlin, the Architectural Association in London, Columbia University, New York and at the University of Toronto, Canada. *http://www.jmayerh.de*

Stephen Jones

Stephen Jones (United Kingdom, b. 1957) entered the High Wycombe Art School in Buckinghamshire in 1975, and in 1976 attended Saint Martin's School of Art (now Central Saint Martins) in London, graduating in 1979 with a BA in fashion design. During the late 1970s, he was an active participant in the growing street-style fashion scene; by 1980, he opened his own millinery salon in Covent Garden. Jones quickly attracted a high-profile clientele, and has made hats for celebrities ranging from Boy George and Lady Diana to Marilyn Manson and Beyoncé Knowles. He also designed a hat collection for Fiorruci and has made hats for the Theatre Royal Windsor. His prolific millinery career was the subject of a 2009 major retrospective organized by the Victoria and Albert Museum, London, shown both there and at the Bard Graduate Center: Decorative Arts, Design History, Material Culture in New York. *http://www.stephenjonesmillinery.com*

Naim Josefi

Naim Josefi (b. 1980) studied at Beckmans College of Design in Stockholm, Sweden. He currently lives and works in Stockholm. The Melonia Shoe, featured in *Out of Hand*, was nominated for the Brit Insurance Designs of the Year Fashion Award in 2011. In 2012, he was also a winner in the reality television show *Project Runway Sweden*. In addition to his education in tailoring and fashion design, Josefi has studied elementary medicine and microbiology, and draws inspiration from the sciences and mathematics for his organic designs. *http://naimjosefi.com/*

Anish Kapoor

Anish Kapoor (United Kingdom, b. 1954, India) lives and works in London. He moved there in 1973 to study art at the Hornsey College of Art and later at the Chelsea School of Art and Design, taking part in the notable 1978 *New Sculpture* exhibition at London's Hayward Gallery in 1978. He taught at Wolverhampton Polytechnic (now Wolverhampton Universtiy) in 1979, mounted his first solo exhibition at Patrice Alexandra in Paris in 1980, and in 1982 was an Artist in Residence at the Walker Art Gallery in Liverpool. Kapoor's work has been exhibited, collected, and celebrated worldwide, and he has garnered numerous honors throughout his career. He represented Britain at the 1990 Venice Biennale, winning the Premio Duemila award. The following year, he won the prestigious Turner Prize, organized by the Tate. Kapoor was elected a Royal Academician in 1999 and made a Commander of the British Empire in 2003; in 2011, he was made a Commander in the French Ordre des Arts et des Lettres and was awarded the Japanese Praemium Imperiale. *http://anishkapoor.com*

Markus Kayser

Markus Kayser (Germany, b. 1983) studied 3D Furniture and Product Design at London Metropolitan University between 2004 and 2008, and received his master's degree in Product Design from the Royal College of Art in 2011. He established Markus Kayser Studio in London that same year. In his practice, he has focused on linking technology and natural processes in manufacturing, and production processes. Kayser currently holds a research assistantship at the MIT Media Lab (Cambridge, Massachusetts) as part of the Mediated Matter Group. His work has been included in recent exhibitions at The Museum of Modern Art, New York; Museum of Contemporary Art, Krakow, Poland; the Royal Danish Academy, School of Design, Bornholm, Denmark; Design Museum, London; Centre Pompidou, Paris; and Salone del Mobile, Milan. *http://www.markuskayser.com*

Behrokh Khoshnevis

Behrokh Khoshnevis (United States, b. Iran) is Professor of Industrial & Systems Engineering and Civil & Environmental Engineering at the University of Southern California. He also directs the Center for Rapid Automated Fabrication Technologies (CRAFT) and the Manufacturing Engineering Graduate Program at USC. His research encompasses computer-aided design and manufacturing, robotics and mechatronics, and rapid-prototyping processes for both medical and construction application. He is a Fellow of the Institute of Industrial Engineers and the Society for Computer Simulation, and a senior member of the Society of Manufacturing Engineering. Dr. Khoshnevis received his BS in Industrial Engineering from Sharif University of Technology, Iran, in 1974, and his MS (1975) and PhD (1979) in Industrial Engineering and Management from Oklahoma State University. *http://www.bkhoshnevis.com*

Shane Kohatsu

Shane Kohatsu (United States, b. 1975, Japan) is an industrial designer and innovation leader at Nike. Born in Tokyo to musician parents, Shane emigrated to Southern California and as a teenager became immersed in sports. In 2002, with a degree in industrial design from California State University Long Beach, Shane's passion for design and sports, combined with his entrepreneurial spirit landed him as a founding member of Nike's innovation group. Shane has driven some of Nike's key innovations such as the LeBron Air Max and Zoom Air sole technologies, the transformational Hyperfuse technology, the now-ubiquitous Dynamic Flywire technology, and the revolutionary 3D-printed Vapor Laser Talon cleat. *www.skcollab.com*

Janne Kyttanen

Janne Kyttanen (Finland, b. 1974) began his studies in industrial design in 1996 at the Escola De Disseny, Elisave in Barcelona, later attending and graduating from the Gerrit Rietveld Academy in Amsterdam, where he currently lives and works. In 2000, he founded the Helsinki-based company Freedom Of Creation to continue his early experiments with 3D printing technology, partnering with the Belgian company Materialise, which specialized in both 3D printing and software development. Kyttanen collaborated with Materialize from 2000 to 2004, and Kyttanen re-formed Freedom Of Creation in Amsterdam in 2006, in partnership with Michiel Dekkers and Han Oey. In 2011, the New York-based company 3D Systems acquired Freedom Of Creation, where Kyttanen continues to act as Creative Director. *http://www.jannekyttanen.com*

Joris Laarman

Laarman (Netherlands, b. 1979) studied at the ArtEZ Institute of the Arts in Arnhem, The Netherlands, and graduated from the Design Academy Eindhoven in 2003. He established the Joris Laarman Studio and Lab in Amsterdam the following year. He quickly gained recognition and has received several honors, including the Wallpaper Magazine Young Designer of the Year, 2004, the Woon Award, 2007 and 2009, International Elle Decoration Award, 2008, and Innovator of the Year by the *Wall Street Journal,* 2011. Laarman has exhibited extensively at design shows and museums, and his work is held in permanent design collections around the world. He has lectured at institutions including the Israel Museum, the National University of Singapore, the Stedelijk Museum Amsterdam, and the High Museum of Art, Atlanta. *http://www.jorislaarman.com/about.html*

Daniel Libeskind

Daniel Libeskind (United States, b. 1946, Poland), B.Arch. MA BDA AIA, is an international architect and designer. His practice extends worldwide from museums and concert halls to convention centers, universities, hotels, shopping centers, and residential projects. Born in Łód'z, Poland in 1946, Libeskind was a virtuoso musician at a young age before giving up music to become an architect. He has received numerous awards and designed world-renowned projects including: the Jewish Museum in Berlin, the Denver Art Museum, the Royal Ontario Museum in Toronto, the Military History Museum in Dresden, and the masterplan for the World Trade Center site in New York. Daniel Libeskind's commitment to expanding the scope of architecture reflects his profound interest and involvement in philosophy, art, literature and music. Fundamental to Libeskind's philosophy is the notion that buildings are crafted with the perceptible human energy, and that they address the greater cultural context in which they are built. Daniel teaches and lectures at universities across the world. He resides in New York City with his wife and business partner, Nina Libeskind. *http://daniel-libeskind.com*

Maya Lin

Maya Lin (United States, b. 1959) received her Master of Architecture from Yale University in 1986, and has maintained a professional studio in New York City since then. She has maintained a careful balance between art and architecture throughout her career, creating a body of work that includes large-scale site-specific installations, intimate studio artworks, architectural works and memorials. Maya Lin has been drawn to important social and historical issues of the time, addressing them in her numerous memorial projects (the Vietnam Veteran's Memorial in Washington, D.C. the most famous among them). The environment features prominently in her work and informs her design. Utilizing technological methods to study and visualize the natural world, Lin translates data into sculptures, drawings and environmental installations. She is the recipient of numerous prizes, awards, and honorary degrees, and her work has been exhibited in galleries and museums worldwide. She is a member of the American Academy of Arts and Letters, the American Academy of Arts and Sciences, and in 2005 she was inducted into the National Women's Hall of Fame. Lin is represented by The Pace Gallery in New York City. *http://www.mayalin.com*

Greg Lynn

Greg Lynn (United States, b. 1964) graduated from Miami University of Ohio with a Bachelor of Environmental Design and Bachelor of Philosophy; he later obtained a Master of Architecture from Princeton University and founded his studio, Greg Lynn FORM. He taught as the Professor of Spatial Conception and Exploration at the ETHZ (Swiss Federal Institute of Technology Zurich) until 2002, when he became an Ordentlicher University Professor at the University of Applied Arts in Vienna. He is also a Studio Professor at UCLA's school of Architecture and Urban Design and the Davenport Visiting Professor at Yale University. He has received numerous awards and honors, including the American Academy of Arts & Letters Architecture Award, 2003, the Golden Lion at the Venice Biennale of Architecture, 2008, a fellowship from United States Artist, 2001. His work is held in the permanent collections of the Los Angeles County Museum of Art, the San Francisco Museum of Modern Art, the Art Institute of Chicago, The Museum of Modern Art, and the Canadian Centre for Architecture. *http://glform.com*

Lucas Maassen

Lucas Maassen (Netherlands, b. 1975) studied design at the Design Academy Eindhoven between 1997 and 2002, working as an independent designer since then. His clients have included the Nederlands Architectuurinstituut in Rotterdam; the Grand Palais, Paris; Charles & Marie; Unilever, Rotterdam; Droog Design; Barbara Visser, Amsterdam; and Philips Design. He has also worked as a curator for exhibitions on digital design, including *Bits 'n Pieces* (with Alissia Melka-Teichroew) at Material Connexion in New York, 2009, and *After the Bit Rush* at MU Eindhoven, 2009. Maassen's work has been shown in numerous galleries and design fairs, as well as museum exhibitions including the Indianapolis Museum of Art, 2008, The Museum of Modern Art, 2011, and the Vitra Design Museum, 2012. *http://www.lucasmaassen.nl*

Geoffrey Mann

Geoffrey Mann (United Kingdom, b. 1980) is a Scottish artist, designer, and lecturer particularly interested in exploring the ephemerality of time and motion, bridging the categories of art, craft, and design in his studio practice. He has exhibited work at varied venues, including The Museum of Modern Art, New York; the International Bombay Sapphire Awards, London and Milan; the Jerwood Contemporary Makers exhibition; and the European Glass Context in Denmark. Mann has received prestigious awards in the field of contemporary craft, including the World Craft Council Prize for Glass in 2008 and the Jerwood Contemporary Makers Prize in 2009. His work is represented in the permanent collections of the Design, and Architecture and Design departments of The Museum of Modern Art and the Museum of Arts and Design, New York. *http://www.mrmann.co.uk*

Mass Studies
(Minsuk Cho)

Seoul-based firm Mass Studies (est. 2003) was founded by Minsuk Cho (Korea, b. 1966). Cho received degrees from the Architectural Engineering Department of Yonsei University in Seoul and the Graduate School of Architecture at Columbia University. He has worked for Kolatan/MacDonald Studio and Polshek and Partners in New York, OMA in the Netherlands, and previously established the firm Cho Slade Architecture in 1998 with James Slade in New York. His work has received numerous awards, including first prize in the 1994 Shinkenchiku International Residential Architecture Competition, the Architectural League of New York's "Young Architects Award" in 2000, and two U.S. Progressive Architecture Awards (Citations) in 1999 and 2003. The Korea Pavilion, exhibited in *Out of Hand*, was awarded the Silver Medal by the Bureau International des Expositions, as well as a Presidential Citation from Korea. Most recently, Minsuk Cho was appointed Commissioner of the Korean Pavilion for the 14th International Architecture Exhibition for the 2014 Venice Biennale. *http://www.massstudies.com*

Julian Mayor

Julian Mayor (United Kingdom, b. 1976) is an artist and designer based in East London. His work is inspired by the sculptural possibilities of computers combined with industrial and craft making processes. After graduating with an MA from the Royal College of Art in 2000, he worked in California as a designer for IDEO design consultancy. On returning to London in 2002, he worked for Pentagram and other design studios before teaching 3D modeling at the London College of Communication and beginning to exhibit his own work. Julian's work has been exhibited at the Victoria and Albert Museum in London, Rossana Orlandi in Milan, FAT Galerie in Paris and 21st twenty-first Gallery in New York. *http://www.julianmayor.com*

Allan McCollum

Allan McCollum (United States, b. 1944) was born in Los Angeles, California and currently lives and works in New York City. His more than 40 year artistic career has focused on the public and personal construction of the meanings of objects. His first solo exhibition was in 1970 at the Nicholas Wilder Gallery in Los Angeles; over the subsequent decade, he showed work frequently at galleries and museums in Southern California and New York. Notably, he was

included in the 1975 Whitney Museum of American Art Biennial Exhibition in 1975, and moved to New York the same year. McCollum began exhibiting in Europe in the 1980s, showing work in with the Lisson Gallery in London since 1985. In New York, he has been represented by the Friedrich Petzel Gallery since 1996.
http://allanmccollum.net/allanmcnyc

Alissia Melka-Teichroew

Alissia Melka-Teichroew (Netherlands, b. 1976) studied at the Design Academy Eindhoven from 1996 to 2000 and holds a Masters of Industrial Design (2004) from the Rhode Island School of Design. She is the founder and creative director of byAMT, Inc., having worked previously at the design consultancy IDEO and at Puma International. In addition to her own design work, she has curated design exhibitions, including *Bits 'n Pieces* (with Lucas Maassen) at Material Connexion, *Still Life* at Trespa Design Centre, and *Cite Goes Dutch* and *Cite Goes America* at Cite Showroom, all in New York. Melka-Teichroew has also lectured or guest-critiqued at design academies including RISD, the Art Institute of Chicago, Philadelphia University of the Arts, California College of Arts, and Cranbrook Academy of Arts. In 2010, Alissia was a visiting professor at Pratt Institute in New York. *http://byamt.com*

Vivian Meller

Vivian Meller (Germany, b. 1982) apprenticed as a goldsmith in Düsseldorf between 2002 and 2006 before entering the Studies for Applied Arts program at the University of Applied Sciences Düsseldorf, where she received her diploma in 2011. As a student she received several accolabes Swarovski SIERAAD International Jewellery Art Fair. She is part of the design group Formativ (est. 2009), and she currently collaborates with fellow Formativ member Laura Alvarado on the PortraitMe series of 3D-printed jewelry, which was selected for Talente 2012 in Munich and honored at the Ritual 21st Silver Festival in Legnica, Poland. Meller has exhibited in numerous group shows and fairs around the world. *http://vivianmeller.de*

Achim Menges

Achim Menges (Germany, b. 1975) is the founding director of the Institute for Computational Design (2008) at the University of Stuttgart. He graduated in 2002 from Architectural Association in London, where he then acted as Studio Master of the Emergent Technologies and Design Graduate Program until 2009. He has also taught at Rice University in Houston, as Professor for Form Generation and Materialisation at the HfG Offenbach University for Art and Design in Germany, and as Visiting Professor in Architecture at Harvard University's Graduate School of Design. His own design work is highly interdisciplinary, and involves collaboration with structural engineers, computer scientists, material scientists, and biologists. At the Institute for Computational Design, Menges spearheads instruction and research for generative computational design and computer-aided manufacturing processes in architecture. *http://www.achimmenges.net*

Nendo
(Oki Sato)

Nendo (est. 2002) was founded in Tokyo by designer Oki Sato (Japan, b. 1977, Canada) after he graduated with an architecture degree from Waseda University. The firm now has a second office in Milan. Nendo's work ranges from products to furniture design to interiors and installations, and is characterized by the playful and poetic use of materials within minimalistic forms. Nendo's work has been exhibited extensively and is held in the collections of numerous museums, including the Art Institute of Chicago, the

Israel Museum, the Victoria and Albert Museum, the Montreal Museé des Beaux Arts, the Centre Pompidou and Musée des Arts Décoratifs in Paris, in New York, the High Museum of Art in Atlanta, the Museum of Fine Arts Houston, and the Smithsonian Cooper-Hewitt National Design Museum and Museum of Arts and Design, New York.

Nervous System
(Jessica Rosenkrantz and Jesse Louis-Rosenberg)

The design studio Nervous System (est. 2007) was founded by Jessica Rosenkrantz (United States, b. 1983) and Jesse Louis-Rosenberg (United States, b. 1986). Rosenkrantz graduated in 2005 from MIT and holds degrees in both Architecture and Biology. She also studied at the Harvard Graduate School of Design and is currently Nervous System's Creative Director. Louis-Rosenberg studied Mathematics, also at MIT. He has previously worked as a building modeling and design automation consultant for Gehry Technologies and is now the Chief Science Officer at Nervous System. Rosenkrantz and Louis-Rosenberg use computer programs based on natural processes and patterns to realize design objects with the aid of digital fabrication technologies. Their studio is located in Somerville, Massachusetts.
http://n-e-r-v-o-u-s.com

Marc Newson

Marc Newson (United Kingdom, b. 1963, Australia) graduated from Sydney College of the Arts in 1984 with a degree in jewelry and sculpture. In 1986, he received a grant from the Australian Crafts Council and staged his first exhibition, which included the now-iconic Lockheed Lounge. He lived and worked in Tokyo between 1987 and 1991, and Paris from 1991 to 1997, when he moved to London and established Marc Newson Ltd. Recognized as one of the most influential living industrial designers, Newson's clients have included a broad range of prominent furniture companies, including Cappellini, Magis, and Alessi, as well as those in the fields of transportation, jewelry, clothing, and product design. His works are represented in the permanent collections of The Museum of Modern Art in New York, the Victoria and Albert Museum and Design Museum in London, the Centre Georges Pompidou, and the Vitra Design Museum, Germany. Newson has been included in *Time Magazine*'s 100 Most Influential People in the World and has received numerous distinctions, including an appointment as The Royal Designer for Industry in the UK, an honorary doctorate from Sydney University, and Adjunct Professorships at Sydney College of the Arts and Hong Kong Polytechnic University.
http://www.marc-newson.com/intro.htm

Roxy Paine

Roxy Paine (United States, b. 1966) lives and works in New York. He studied at both the College of Santa Fe in New Mexico and Pratt Institute in New York. Paine cofounded the artist collective Brand Name Damages in 1990 and has exhibited work internationally, becoming known especially for his semiautonomous "art-making machines." He has installed permanently-sited works at the Olympic Sculpture Park, Seattle; the National Gallery of Art, Washington, DC; the Nelson Atkins Museum of Art, Kansas City; the Modern Art Museum of Fort Worth, Texas; and the Wanas Foundation in Sweden. He is represented in the permanent collections of numerous other institutions, including the National Gallery of Canada in Ottawa, and the Israel Museum in Jerusalem. Paine has also received several important awards and honors, including a John Simon Guggenheim Memorial Foundation Fellowship, the Trustees Award for an Emerging Artist by the Aldrich Museum of Contemporary Art, and the Brooklyn Museum's Asher B. Durand award for artistic accomplishment. *http://www.roxypaine.com*

Michael Rees

Michael Rees (United States, b. 1958) attended Vassar College and then the Kansas City Art Institute, receiving his BFA in 1982. Between 1983 and 1984, he studied at the Kunstakademie Dusseldorf as part of a Deutscher Akademischer Austauchdienst award, and obtained his MFA from Yale University in 1989. He has exhibited widely, and his work is held in the collections of The Whitney Museum of American Art, New York; the Edelman Foundation, Lauzanne, Switzerland; the Kemper Museum of Contemporary Art, Kansas City, Missouri; and The Science Museum, London. In addition to his artistic work, he has been an active art educator, teaching at Oberlin College, the Kansas City Art Institute, Washington University in St. Louis, the New York Institute of Technology, Rutgers University, and, currently, as Associate Professor of Sculpture and Digital Media at William Patterson University in Wayne, New Jersey. *http://www.michaelrees.com*

Antonio Pio Saracino

Antonio Pio Saracino (United States and Italy, b. 1976, Italy) received a Masters in Architecture from the Sapienza University in Rome in 2003, where he also worked as an assistant professor of architectural design. Since 2004, he has collaborated with New York-based architect Steve Blatz on interiors and conceptual projects. Saracino has won *Interior Design* magazine's Future Furniture design competition four times, and his work has received extensive press in international design publications. In 2007 to 2008, Saracino was selected as the winner of the Agorafolly art competition in Brussels, Belgium, creating an installation in front of the Central Train Station that celebrated the 50th anniversary of the European Union. In 2011, he was honored as one of the Top Ten Italian Architects under 36 by the New Italian Blood award, and participated in the Italian Pavilion in the World at the Venice Biennale.
http://www.antoniopiosaracino.com

Michael Schmidt

Michael Schmidt (United States, b. 1963) is a wardrobing and jewelry designer who has worked with numerous high-profile performing artists. His clients have included Cher, Lady Gaga, Rihanna, the Black Eyed Peas, Janet Jackson, Deborah Harry, Dolly Parton, Steven Tyler, Ozzy Osbourne, and Madonna, for whom he created nearly 300 pieces for her 2012 MDNA World Tour. In 1991, Schmidt was nominated for an Emmy Award for Costume Design for a Variety or Music Program for his work on *Cher... At The Mirage*. His work has been exhibited as part of the *Rock Style* exhibition at The Metropolitan Museum of Art, 1999–2000, and is on permanent display at the Rock and Roll Hall of Fame and Museum in Cleveland, Ohio. His career was also the subject of a 2012 retrospective at the Pasadena Museum of California Art.
http://www.michaelschmidtstudios.com

Ben Shaffer

Ben Shaffer (United States, b. 1977) is a designer at Nike who graduated from the University of Cincinnati in 2001. Following experience gained at design consultancies, Shaffer has been designing Nike products for nearly a decade, ranging from yoga-specific footwear to Nike Free. Nearly four years ago he joined the Innovation Kitchen and his passion for new materials and design techniques have helped engineer product to the exact specifications of elite athletes.

Sakurako Shimizu

Sakurako Shimizu (United States, b. 1972, Japan) is a Japanese artist and designer who lives and works in Brooklyn, New York. She received a BFA in design from Tokyo Zokei University in 1995, and her MFA from the SUNY

New Paltz Metals program in 2002. Her jewelry draws inspiration from digital visualizations of data, whether sound recordings, computer hardware, or programming codes. Sakurako's work has been exhibited and collected extensively, at venues including Gallery Nina Lummer, Milan; Friends of Carlotta, Zurich; the STRP Festival in Eindhoven; The Museum of Arts & Crafts ITAMI, Hyogo, Japan; the Samuel Dorsky Museum (New Paltz), and The Society of Arts and Crafts (Boston). Her work has also been featured in recent publications on contemporary jewelry and digital design, including *Jewelry Design* (Daab Books, 2008), *Digital Aesthetics* (Artist Press, 2008), Data Flow (Die Gestalten Verlag, 2010), and *500 Necklaces: Contemporary Interpretations of a Timeless Form* (Lark Books, 2006). *http://sakurakoshimizu.blogspot.com*

Softkill Design

Softkill Design is a London-based architectural collaborative formed in 2011 by Nicholette Chan (b. 1987, United States), Gilles Retsin (b. 1985, Belgium), Aaron Silver (b. 1984, United States), and Sophia Tang (b. 1984, China/USA). They research methods of generative design, additive manufacturing, and their applicability to architectural spaces. Softkill Design aims to produce intelligent designs which intuitively utilize 3D printing technology. Their research was founded at the Architectural Association School of Architecture's Design Research Lab. In addition to their theoretical work and specialization in 3D printing, Softkill Design provides design consulting for architecture, furniture, product design and fashion. *http://www.softkilldesign.com*

SOMA DESIGN
(Tamae Hirokawa)

Tamae Hirokawa (Japan, b. 1976) studied in the Apparel Design Technique program of Bunka Fashion College in Tokyo, graduating in 1998. She joined Issey Miyake Co., Ltd. soon after receiving her degree, where she worked in knitwear. In 2006, she founded her own studio, SOMA DESIGN, and simultaneously launched the brand SOMARTA at the Spring/Summer Tokyo Collection Week. She was honored with the Newcomer's Prize of the 25th Fashion Grand Prix and the Shiseido Sponsorship Award. SOMA DESIGN has continued to receive accolades in the fashion world, but has also branched into installation artwork, furniture design, sound, and graphics. Hirokawa credits a love of anthropology and biology with a major influence on her designs. *http://www.somarta.jp*

Frank Stella

Frank Stella (United States, b. 1936) studied painting under Patrick Morgan at the Phillips Academy in Massachusetts from 1950 to 1954, and studied art history and history at Princeton until 1958. He moved to New York in 1958 and gained quick recognition for his early paintings, included in the Museum of Modern Art's 1959 exhibition Sixteen Americans. The same year, gallery owner Leo Castelli began representing Stella. Later on, he would experiment with both printmaking and sculpture. Since the 1980s, he has incorporated mathematical concepts and painting techniques in his interdisciplinary, three-dimensional artwork, and more recently has delved into digital fabrication as a means of realizing sculptures. Stella has been the recipient of numerous honors and awards both in the United States and internationally, including the Ordre des Arts et des Lettres from the French Government, 1989, the Gold Medal for Graphic Art Award from American Academy of Arts and Letters, 1998, and the National Medal of Arts from President Barack Obama, 2009.

Rebecca Strzelec

Rebecca Strzelec (United States, b. 1977) is a Professor of Visual Arts at Pennsylvania State University Altoona. She received her BFA (2000) and MFA

(2002) in Metals, Jewelry, and Computer-Aided Design and Manufacturing from the Tyler School of Art, Temple University (2000 and 2002). She creates wearable objects through computer-aided design and rapid prototyping technologies. She was the 2005 recipient of the Nancy Graves Fellowship at The Millay Colony for the Arts, and her work has been published in the recent Lark Books publication *500 Brooches Inspiring Adornments for the Body*, as well as *Metalsmith* magazine, *American Craft* magazine, and the 2007 book *Body of Art*. *http://www.personal.psu.edu/ras39*

Hiroshi Sugimoto

Hiroshi Sugimoto (United States and Tokyo, b. 1948, Tokyo) is best known for his photographic work, but his practice has encompassed architecture and sculpture at times as well. He graduated in 1970 from Rikkyo University in Tokyo after studying politics and sociology, then pursued a BFA at the Art Center College of Design, Los Angeles, graduating in 1974. He moved to New York in the same year. Sugimoto's photographic work is influenced by the Dadaist and Surrealist movements, and informed by a keen interest in late twentieth century modern architecture. He is considered a photographer of very high technical ability, using a large-format camera and extremely long exposures. Sugimoto's work is held in numerous public collections including The Metropolitan Museum of Art, New York; Moderna Museet, Stockholm; Centre Georges Pompidou, Paris; the Museum of Contemporary Art, Tokyo; The Museum of Modern Art, New York; the National Gallery, London; the National Museum of Modern Art, Tokyo; the Smithsonian Institution, Washington, D.C.; MACBA, Barcelona; and Tate Gallery, London. *http://www.sugimotohiroshi.com*

Marloes ten Bhömer

Marloes ten Bhömer (United Kingdom, b. 1979, the Netherlands) received her BA in 3D Design from ArtEZ Institute of the Arts in Arnhem in 2001. She then studied in London between 2001 and 2003 at the Royal College of Art, where she obtained a Masters in Design Products in 2003. Her work is found in the permanent collection of The National Centre for Craft & Design in Sleaford, United Kingdom; the Stedelijk Museum's-Hertogenbosch, Netherlands; and the Dutch Leather and Shoe Museum in Waalwijk. She continues to live and work in London, in addition to acting as a Senior Research Fellow at Kingston University and guest professor in Fashion at the Universität der Künste Berlin. Her work was nominated for the Designs of the Year at the Design Museum London (2009) and was shown in an exhibition on fashion and technology at the Design Museum Holon, Israel and the *Power of Making* exhibition at the Victoria and Albert Museum. She has recently exhibited her Research Fellowship works in an exhibition at the Stanley Picker Gallery. *www.marloestenbhomer.com*

The T/Shirt Issue

The T/Shirt Issue (est. 2008) is a Berlin-based interdisciplinary design collaboration between Mashallah (Hande Akcayli, b. 1974, Turkey and Murat Kocyigit, b. 1974, Germany) and Linda Kostowski (b. 1980, Poland) that combines fashion design and technology to rethink basic apparel. Their work includes wearable pieces as well as conceptual installations, most of them based on a complex polygonal structures designed with a hybrid of digital software and handcraft. Their work has been exhibited including *If/Then Fashion*, Ars Electronica, 2009; the Biennale Internazionale Design 2010 in Saint Etienne; and *After the Bit Rush: Design in a Postdigital Age* at MU Eindhoven, 2011. *http://the-t-shirt-issue.com*

Peter Ting

Peter Ting (United Kingdom, b. 1959, Hong Kong) is a ceramic designer and consultant who has worked for more than two decades in the luxury sector.

He received a BA in 3D Design and an MA in Ceramics, and has designed production lines and special commissions (including state gifts for the Queen and Prince of Wales) for numerous companies and private clients. From 1999 to 2002, he was a professor of 3D Design at the University of Central Lancashire, and a visiting lecturer in Ceramics and Glass at the Royal College of Art, London. He is also a trustee of the British Crafts Council. Collections of his work are in the Victoria and Albert Museum, London and the Museum of Arts and Design, New York USA. *http://www.peterting.com*

Unfold
(Dries Verbruggen and Claire Warnier)

Unfold (est. 2002) is the collaboration of Claire Warnier (Netherlands, b. 1978) and Dries Verbruggen (Belgium, b. 1979). Warnier graduated from the Design Academy in Eindhoven in 2002, then studied at Erasmus University in Rotterdam before obtaining a Masters of Art Sciences from the University of Ghent. In addition to her work with Unfold, she has taught design theory at University College of Art and Design in Brussels and worked as a curator with the Z33 House for Contemporary Art in Hasselt. Verbruggen also graduated in 2002 from the Design Academy Eindhoven, having previously studied architecture at Sint-Lucas in Antwerp. In addition to his design work, he has taught at Fontys University of Applied Sciences Eindhoven, Sint Lukas Brussels University College of Art and Design, and the Design Academy Eindhoven. Together as Unfold, they have received Laureate Henri van de Velde Awards for the Young Talent Selection in 2010 and 2011 from Design Flanders. *http://unfold.be/pages/projects*

Daan van den Berg

Daan van den Berg (Netherlands, b. 1976) received a degree in interior architecture in 2004 from the Academy of Arts Minerva, Groningen, and began to work as an independent designer. He also pursued graduate studies at the Sandberg Instituut, Amsterdam, from 2011-2013. In his work on objects, furniture, and products, Daan van den Berg attempts to play with appearances and the expectations these instigate. He currently works as a freelancer on projects in the fields of interior, architecture, visual arts and product design. *http://www.studiodaan.nl*

Elona Van Gent

Elona Van Gent (United States, b. 1961) studied literature and music and served as Director of the Urban Institute for Contemporary Arts (Grand Rapids, MI) before receiving an MFA in sculpture from the Tyler School of Art at Temple University in 1989. Since then, her practice has gradually expanded to include digitally designed and fabricated sculptures, prints, and animations that depict improbable, monstrous creatures. Her work has been shown at the Exploratorium in San Francisco and numerous university galleries and museums in the U.S., as well as at Peter the Great Museum of Anthropology and Ethnography in Russia, Roda Sten in Sweden, and Sydney's University of Technology. Van Gent has lectured and presented her work at museums, art schools, and conferences across America and Europe, and currently teaches in the School of Art & Design at the University of Michigan. *http://un-tethered.net/eevege*

Dirk Vander Kooij

Designer Dirk Vander Kooij (Netherlands, b. 1983) graduated from the Design Academy in Eindhoven in 2010 and founded his own practice, Studio Dirk Vander Kooij. Much of his work stems from his initial interest, during his studies, in scaling up the capabilities of small-format 3D printers. To do so, Vander Kooij has built and continues to develop his own 3D printing robots to achieve his precise manufacturing capabilities, as well as experimenting with material use and properties—particularly the recycled refrigerator plastic from which many of his furniture piece are made. Vander Kooij has shown work at numerous design fairs and exhibitions, and is represented in the collections of The Museum of Modern Art in New York, the Stedelijk Museum in Amsterdam, and the Vitra Design Museum in Germany. *http://www.dirkvanderkooij.nl*

Jeroen Verhoeven

Jeroen Verhoeven (Netherlands, b. 1976) graduated in 2005 from the Design Academy in Eindhoven and works with his twin brothers Joep and Judith de Graauw in both Amsterdam and Bangalore, India. The trio forms the Dutch design studio Demakersvan ("The Makers Of"), established in 2005, which aims to fuse the work of filmmakers, artists, and scientists into works that act as "storytellers." Works by Verhoeven and Demakersvan have been exhibited globally, in important exhibitions at the Victoria and Albert Museum, London, The Museum of Modern Art and the Museum of Arts and Design in New York, and the Museum of Contemporary Art, Tokyo. He has won several awards in the United Kingdom and the Netherlands, and has taught at the Architectural Association School of Architecture, London and the Art Academy, Maastricht. *http://www.demakersvan.com*

Wertel Oberfell

WertelOberfell was founded in 2007 by Gernot Oberfell (Germany, b. 1975) and Jan Wertel (Germany, b. 1976). Both designers studied Industrial Design at the State Academy of Arts in Stuttgart, under a curriculum based on the principles of the Ulmer Schule and the Bauhaus. They graduated in 2004 and worked for Ross Lovegrove Studio in London before forming their own practice based in London and Munich. WertelOberfell has executed both fully-formed product designs and experimental research pieces for clients including Artemide, Sony, Yamagiwa, MGX by Materialise, DuPont Corian, Issey Miyake, and others. Their work has been exhibited globally and is represented in the permanent collection of The Metropolitan Museum of Art in New York and the Victoria and Albert Museum in London. *http://www.platform-net.com*

GLOSSARY

3D model

A computerised three-dimensional representation of an object. Mathematically accurate, 3D models allow the designer to visualise the finished product as it would appear in real life, so as they can make vital changes to its design before it goes into production.

3D print

A technologically emerging additive printing process in which a material is layered in succession according to an original digital plan, eventually producing a three-dimensional object.

3D scan/3D scanner

A scanner which analyses an object or environment in the real world, using the data in order to create a three-dimensional digital model. This process is useful for documentation of historic artefacts and reverse engineering and has been used extensively in the entertainment industry for the production of animated films and games.

Additive Fabrication (Additive Manufacturing)

A process of manufacture in which an object is created in an accumulative fashion, with material gradually added until the object is completely formed. This is opposed to subtractive process, where the object emerges as material is removed, such as drilling or cutting, for example.

Advanced fiber placement

A technology to manufacture on a large scale complex composite materials by placing very thin bundles of carbon fibers impregnated with epoxy resin at varying rotations to ensure that the final product has good strength in all directions. The produced material is typically of comparable or greater strength than traditional metals and is used where low-weight, high-strength materials are required.

Algorithm

An algorithm, broadly, is a detailed set of instructions that lead to a predictable end from a known beginning. Clear initial definition is essential to an accurate algorithm. A basic example would be the instructions for building a piece of furniture: a considered step-by-step of constituent processes leading to a conclusive whole. Computer programs and elements of mathematics work in the same way, to very differing levels of complexity.

Automatic production

The use of computerised machines in industry to increase productivity.

Bending/scoring/folding

A triumvirate of basic processes used to change the angled shape of a flat sheet. Though bending and folding involve a mere application of force, scoring comprises first cutting partially through the object, and thus compromising structural integrity in that portion and making manipulation easier.

Biomimetic design

The replication of naturally occurring functions and phenomena for the purpose of understanding complicated human problems. Biomimetic design may study the operations of another organism in order to tackle limitations with solutions that have been derived from a human perspective. An object designed in a biomimetic way will utilise efficacious solutions which are present in nature. It may also simply mimic organic patterns.

Bitmap

A format of digital imagery organisation where the file is reduced to an arranged collection of bits. Also known as a bit array or bitmap index.

Body Art

Art which incorporates the human body, as a direct material, a performative element or the subject of exploration.

Boolean

Named after the 18th century mathematician and logician George Boole, 'Boolean' refers to data and algebraic or programming expressions which may only have two outcomes; true or false.

CAD (computer aided design)

CAD (computer aided design) is the use of computer systems to assist in the process of design. CAD software is used by designers, architects, engineers, artists et al. to create plans and drawings with increased productivity and efficiency.

CAM

Otherwise known as 'computer-aided manufacture', CAM removes the need for manual labour, instead using computers to control the industrial devices and tools with which a product is made. The benefits of CAM include speed, accuracy and efficiency during production.

CNC machining milling, lathing, drilling, sawing laser cutting

Computer Numerical Machining (CNC) is the automation of machining by providing the machine used for production with pre-prepared instructions, rather than by manual adjustment. Typically a set of schematics are created on a computer using CAD then loaded onto the CNC machine, which extracts the instructions and proceeds to carry out the predetermined steps. Since one design may require a number of processes, many CNC machines incorporate multiple tools, and can be instructed to use any one of them during the machining process.

Code

Refers to a set of instructions, written in a human-readable language, which once interpreted by a compiler application into machine code understood by the computer will be followed to perform a specific action or sequence of actions.

Computer-numerically-controlled machining

A form of numerical control specifically utilizing computers. During the process, a computer converts the designs produced by CAD software into numbers. These can be considered to be the coordinates of a graph controlling the movements of a cutter. Thus, the computer controls the cutting and shaping of the material.

Constructive solid geometry

A technique used in solid modeling. It is the creation of potentially complex solid shapes through the combination of geometric objects (primitives). The primitives are combined using Boolean operators, which determine how these shapes will interact. The three operators are set union, intersection and difference. The set union is the addition of one object to another; the intersection is the subtraction of one object from another; the difference is the part of the joined shape that is common to the two primitives. Boolean logic allows the created shape to be written in the form of an equation.

Crystallography/crystal system

The study of atoms within a solid structure.

Digital

Information recorded utilising 'digits' of discrete continuous data is referred to as digital. Most frequently it is used to describe computer technology. Computer technology utilises binary digits, taking the discrete values of either 0 or 1, in order to process and relay information.

Digital design

Digitally created visual media, including web design, digital imaging and 3D modeling, and the processes of its creation.

Direct Metal Laser Sintering (DMLS)

An additive metal fabrication technology used to produce metal components. DMLS replicates 3D CAD models through the layering of metal powder. Once a design is completed digitally, DMLS creates the object layer-by-layer. Each level is produced by the dispensing of the powder and its melting via a focused laser. It allows for the real-world creation of complex geometric metal shapes that have been created digitally.

Digital model/digital modeling

A design facilitated through the use of computer technology. Digital modeling allows the user to test the material property of a designed object without physical creation.

Digital scan

A process by which a physical object, most commonly images and text but sometimes three-dimensional objects, are converted into a digital images. This may be done either by using a CCD (Charge Coupled Device) scanning device, a CIS (contact Image Sensing) scanning device or a drum-scanning device, which typically utilises photomultiplier tubes (PMT) to obtain high quality images. By using these devices, a physical image or object can be viewed as a digital file, which may then be viewed, manipulated, reproduced in physical form or electronically distributed.

Digital imaging

Digital imaging is the art of making digital images through the use of a digital camera or imaging machine, or by scanning an image. Each image comprises an amount of pixels—the smallest addressable element in a display device—which are mapped onto a grid and stored in a sequence by a computer, appearing as an image.

Digital manufacture/digital fabrication

The use of three-dimensional modeling software in the manufacturing of an object. Blurring the line previously set between the design and manufacture stages of production, digital manufacture/ digital fabrication uses computer systems to build three-dimensional objects.

Euclidean geometry

Mathematical system derived from the Greek mathematician Euclid's Elements, which describes geometry as a series of theorems and basic truths, and which defined knowledge of geometry until recent centuries.

Evolutionary computation

A branch of computer science that uses biological evolutionary theory to inspire a process of problem solving. In order to resolve a particular problem, possible solutions are selected, either randomly or on the basis of any available knowledge about the problem. These 'parent' solutions then produce 'offspring' by a preselected method of random variation. This process is repeated until the most appropriate final solution is determined.

Extruding

Shaping a material by driving it through a die or shaping tool.

Filament winding

Filament winding involves applying continuous strands of composite fiber on to a rotating mandrel or mold in the form the user desires. The process provides a very uniform structure and exact placement of fibres. The most common composites used here are carbon or glass fibers, coated with synthetic resin as wound. Upon completion, the product is heated to set the resin and the mandrel or mold removed.

Fractal

A fractal pattern is self-repeating, and looks similar or identical at every level of magnification or scale, exhibiting self-similarity, meaning that a whole object has the same shape as one or more of the component parts. They are frequently modeled virtually using one of a number of fractal generating computer programs.

Fused deposition modeling

Fused deposition modeling is a process used by 3D printers to create models by heating thermoplastics to a molten state and extruding them in to the desired forms via computer. This is then cooled and solidified.

Generative art

Art created partly or wholly by use of an autonomous system. This is usually a synthetic, non-human system, making 'decisions' to determine aspects of an artwork that would usually be chosen by the artists themselves, thus creating a work ostensibly random in design.

Generative design

The design of a finished product using an algorithm generated by a computer program. Generative design allows for speed in manufacture due to its ability to explore all possible manufacturing outcomes faster than would be done manually.

Generative systems

A system that produces a pattern output by adhering to a precise set of rules.

Geometric modeling

A branch of applied mathematics and computational geometry, which is concerned with algorithms and methods of describing shapes mathematically. This is most frequently expressed in two-dimensional modeling for use in typography and technical drawing and three-dimensional modelling for Computer Aided Design and Manufacture (CAD/CAM).

Hexagonal tiling

Hexagonal tiling is one of the three regular tilings of the Euclidean plane (the others being triangular and square). Three hexagons meet at each vertex, and the method is the densest way of arranging circles in two dimensions.

Instruction set

The foundational set of commands that a computer's microprocessor will understand. It is fundamental to the architecture of a computer, and is, broadly speaking, the section that deals with programming.

Laminated object manufacturing

A process of producing objects by layering, fixing and cutting sheets of adhesive-coated paper, plastic or metal.

Laser cutter

A means of cutting a material using a high-powered laser to melt, burn or vaporise a given material, leaving an edge with a high quality finish. Laser Cutting is typically used to cut sheet materials (wood, metal and plastic) as well as to engrave patterns on the materials.

Laser sintering

A manufacturing technique using a high-powered laser to fuse materials together to form a three-dimensional shape. Laser sintering is usually used to produce prototype models and components.

Mass-customization

The mass production of a product using computer aided manufacturing (CAM), which also allows for individual customization. Mass-customization combines the low-costs of mass production with the variety associated with individual customization.

Non-Uniform Rational Basis Spline (NURBS) modeling

A form of mathematical modeling in which 2D shapes are transformed into 3D free-form solids by generating curves and surfaces. Their flexibility lends them to use for illustration, animation and manufacturing purposes.

Open-source software

Computer software of which the source code and right to study, change and distribute is freely available.

Open-Source hardware

Open-Source hardware is hardware created using technical drawings, circuit-board design or other instructions, which are released under an open-source license. This ensures that the designs may be modified, circulated and remain freely available and in the public domain. Common Open-Source hardware includes circuit boards, three-dimensional printing devices, and objects suitable to be printed using three-dimensional printers.

Parametric modeling/parametricism

Parametric modeling utilises parameters in order to define and delimit a model. In a parametric model any alteration will affect the model's properties according to the specified parameters. As the modeler manipulates their shape or object, the parameters ensure that all parts respond accordingly.

Perforation

A series of small holes pierced into a material, commonly in a pattern that enables the material to be easily folded or torn.

Pixel

The smallest element in a digitally displayed image. The word is a portmanteau of 'picture' and 'element'. The shape and size of a pixel is dependent on the context in which the image is presented, i.e. high-resolution images will have a higher number of small pixels.

Plasma cutter

Plasma cutting is a process used to efficiently cut heavy-duty materials such as steel and other metals. The plasma cutter functions by ejecting a stream of inert gas (or, occasionally, compressed air) through a small nozzle. A high-voltage, low-current electrical arc is passed through the stream, heating it to a sufficient temperature—in the range of 25,000°C—to turn some of the gas into plasma. A very exact cutting point is created, making this process useful for creating circles or angles.

Play theory

'Play theory' is a term invented by the Dutch historian, cultural theorist and professor Johan Huizinga, devised in his 1933 book *Homo Ludens*. The theory refers to the conceptual space in which social play occurs, one which Huizinga considers essential to cultural development.

Polygonal mesh

A computer-generated three-dimensional object composed of polygonal shapes with vertices, edges and faces. The modeling possibilities of using a polygonal mesh are infinite.

Polygonal modeling

A 3D computer graphics process of creating 3D objects by reproducing their surfaces with polygons.

Polygonal shaping

A process which uses a mesh of polygonal vertices, edges, faces and surfaces in order to create solid objects. Polygons are fitted together in order to construct 3D models. It typically involves the use of simple convex polygons and is prevalent in 3D computer modeling and solid modeling.

Postdigital

A term used in the discourse surrounding contemporary art with particular reference to a movement away from digitally concerned artistic practice.

Process Art (Dupont)

An artistic movement whose primary concern is the process of the creation rather than the final resulting object. Through this, art is viewed as a journey and experience rather than a product.

Rapid prototype

Rapid prototyping is the process of creating 3D models from three-dimensional CAD files. The full design is 'sliced' into two-dimensional sheets, which are then layered and bonded to create the full tangible object. The process is useful for component manufacture, creating sculpture and artworks, and making test prototypes.

Remote manufacture

The manufacturing of an object at a different location to its design. Made possible with the introduction of computerised devices, remote manufacturing is often used to save costs and to utilise the skills and materials particular to a location.

Robocasting

A manufacturing technique used in the freeform fabrication of a ceramic object. Controlled by computerised robotics, robocasting applies ceramic slurries in layers on to a base to form a three-dimensional product.

Self-similarity

A mathematical term used to refer to objects that have the same shape as their parts. For something to be self-similar, the whole must have the same structure as its parts, or at least some of them.

Space truss geometry

An architectural structure composed of a series of geometrically connected frames.

Stereolithography

A method of additive production, where 'printing' creates an object in thin, successive layers. Each layer is drawn onto an ultraviolet-curable material with a UV laser, which solidifies each layer and fixes it to the layer below.

Subdivision surface (Chaiken algorithm)

A way of representing a smooth surface through division of the faces on a polygon into successively smaller polygons. This creates new faces and vertices that better approximate the smooth surface being represented. The Chaikin Algorithm cuts all the corners on the polygon according to a fixed ratio in order to refine the polygons and achieve a smoother curve on the final polygons.

Systems theory

The transdisciplinary study of the abstract organization of different phenomena or systems in general, with the aim of developing principles applicable to all phenomena at nesting levels, in all fields of research. The theory investigates the principles shared by all complex entities.

Topology

Topology is the pure mathematical study of shapes and spaces. It is a basic form of geometry and is used in mathematical disciplines of all kinds.

Voronoi Diagram

A diagram based around a series of points, often referred to as 'seeds'. Indicated around each seed is a delineated area, all points of which are spatially nearer to that seed than any other.

Voxel

A volumetric pixel, or unit, which represents a value on a three-dimensional grid, frequently used in the visualization of scientific data and volumetric displays.

Water jet cutter

A high-pressured jet of water is used to cut materials that might otherwise bow or snap under the pressure of other cutting methods. A high-powered tool, the water used in a water jet cutter is often mixed with an abrasive substance to increase the tool's cutting capability, in particular when used on harder materials such as metal.

ACKNOWLEDGEMENTS

The idea for an exhibition on digital fabrication came from David Revere McFadden, MAD's William and Mildred Lasdon, Chief Curator, and Holly Hotchner, former Executive Director. I am indebted to them both for encouraging creative freedom in shaping the project. I extend my profound gratitude to MAD trustees Marcia Docter, longtime museum benefactor who believed in this exhibition from the start, and Barbara Tober, Chairman Emerita and Chairman, Global Leadership Council, for their enthusiastic support. I am especially thankful to the two project managers, Colleen Germain and Colin Fanning, who only overlapped for a brief period but whose combined efforts made the publication and exhibition possible. Colleen's tireless dedication was only surpassed by her irreproachable work ethic and good humor. Colin's exceptional organizational skills and professional commitment laid a solid foundation to build upon. In addition, Colleen assiduously compiled the artist statements and Colin contributed the artist biographies. Dorothy Globus, Curator of Exhibitions, and Matthew Cox, Exhibition Manager, expertly coordinated the installation in concert with Adam Rolston, Sheena Murphy and Louisa Brown of Incorporated, New York, who provided an inspired exhibition design. Alisha Ferrin, Associate Registrar, diligently and patiently attended to the myriad packing and shipping details, and Elizabeth Edwards Kirrane, Assistant Curator, provided vital structure and organization. I would also like to acknowledge project interns Lee Ramsey, Riva Arnold, and Samantha Rowe who conducted research and assisted in various ways, and Curatorial Fellow, Lyndsay Bratton, who oversaw the planning of the two outdoor installations and composed the bibliography. In Education, Cathleen Lewis, Dia Felix, Jake Yuzna, Molly McFadden, Nakeisha Gumbs, Carli Beseau, and Eric Scott merit special recognition for the related multimedia assets and exceptional programs and events.

Other departments at MAD played a crucial role in the realization of this project. My thanks go to the following: Development and External Affairs (Sophie Henderson, Alan Yamahata, Megan Skidmore, Georgia Wright, Anna Starling, Rafael Flores, Jon Hogan, Claire Laporte, Carnelia Garcia, Sophie May, Stephanie Lang, Rebekka Grossman, Patty Tsai, Rosalinda Wessin, and Stephanie Lovett), Finance (Rob Salemo, Sharon Sabater, Katherine Dever, and Desmond Moneypenny), Registration (Ellen Holdorf and Friese Undine), Facilities and Security (Alex Berisha, Vincent Maldonado, John D'Ambrosio, Raul Rodriguez, Robert Rivera, Senior Bower, Lal Rampratap, and Gool Mohamed), and Retail (Franci Sagar, Jules Jones, Hope Kyser, Judi

Bundick, and Lin Wong). Grateful acknowledgment must be extended to my fellow Curators Lowery Sims and Ursula Neuman for their invaluable advice, support, and collegiality.

I wish to thank the Consulate General of the Netherlands, Creative Industries Fund NL, Dassault Systèmes, Design Flanders, Infor, Japan Airlines, KLM Royal Dutch Airlines, Lucite International, Shapeways, and Toyota for their generous sponsorship of this project. Duann Scott at Shapeways deserves special acknowledgment for championing the exhibition's interactive design and fabrication space.

Many thanks are also due to the essay authors Greg Lynn and Christiane Paul. At Black Dog Publishing, I express my gratitude to Duncan McCorquodale, Kate Trant, and Nick Warner. Sylvia Ugga merits special recognition for her exceptional book design.

Numerous colleagues at other institutions provided information, connections, and other assistance that proved helpful to the planning of the exhibition. Special thanks go to Wendy Kaplan, Bobbye Tigerman, and Amy Wright, Los Angeles County Museum of Art; Benjamin Teague, Maxine and Stuart Frankel Foundation for Art, Bloomfield Hills, Michigan; Catherine Futter, Julie Mattsson, Jan Schall, and Stacey Sherman, The Nelson-Atkins Museum of Art, Kansas City, Missouri; and Stephen Hoskins, University of the West of England, Bristol, United Kingdom.

Both the exhibition and the publication could never have materialized without the talents and generosity of the artists, designers, and architects represented in *Out of Hand*, many of whom lent works to the exhibition and provided images and text that appear in this catalogue. Equally invaluable were the diverse contributions of the following organizations and individuals: Annika Adelman, 21st twenty first, New York; Fernando Alba, Fernando Alda Fotografía, Seville, Spain; Taeko Baba, New York-Tokyo, New York; Corey A. Barr and Lauren Sohn, Phillips, New York; Marc Benda, Nina Embiricos, Kirby Guthrie, and Erica Miranda, Friedman Benda, New York; Sean Boyd, Greg Lynn FORM, Venice, California; Clare Chapman and Peter Lynch, Studio Anish Kapoor, London; Rachel Churner and Renee Bovenzi, Churner and Churner, New York; Katherine Codega, Cambridge, Massachusetts; Emily Colassaco, Colleen Chattergoon, and Courtney Mulligan, New York Department of Transportation; Clarisse Colliard, Société Privée de Gérance, Geneva; Andree Cooke and Elena Checchi, David Gill Galleries, London; Joris Debo and Annelies Meulemans, Materialise, Leuven, Belgium; Doug DeGaetano, and Lilla Fekete, Barry X Ball Studio, New York; Kristin DuFrain, Will Lytch, and Kristin Soderqvist, Graphicstudio, University of South Florida, Tampa; Don and Era Farnsworth, Magnolia Editions, Oakland, California; Poppy Edmonds and Brian Phillips, Black Frame, New York; Ingrid Forster and Amrei Heyne, Roland Halbe Fotografie, Stuttgart, Germany; Ann Freedman, Jessica Freedman, Julia Loughlin, and Sallie Wiggins, FreedmanArt, New York; Cheryl Gold, New York; Tomasz Gudzowaty, Warsaw, Poland; Ante Hellqvist, Sandra Backlund, Stockholm; Wilko Hoffman and Eva Kellerer, J. Mayer H. Architects, Berlin; Aaron Holmes, Nervous System, Somerville, Massachusetts; Alexandra Jenal, Studio Dror, New York; Paul Johnson, Johnson Trading Gallery, Queens, New York; Sarah Jones, Gagosian Gallery, London; Katharina Kayser, Markus Kayser Studio, London; Betty Kim, Mass Studies, Seoul, Korea; Emily-Jane Kirwan, Madeline Lieberberg, Heather Monahan, Nancy Rattenbury, and Taline Toutounjian, Pace Gallery, New York; Matthew Kneller and Howard Lichter, Nike, Inc., Beaverton, Oregon; Murat Kocyigit, The T/Shirt Issue, Berlin; Oliver David Krieg, Institute for Computational Design, Universität Stuttgart, Stuttgart, Germany; Loic Le Gaillard, James Malcolm-Green, and Mathilde Prieur, Carpenters Workshop Gallery, London; Annika Lievesley, Stephen Jones Millinery, London; Patricia Low, Sophie C. Grüne, and Khalil Outassou, Patricia Low Contemporary, Gstraad; Mayumi Marumoto and Akihiro Ito, Nendo, Tokyo; Maria E. Murguia, Artists' Rights Society; Lisa Palm, Naim Josefi, Stockholm; Kat Parker, Petzel Gallery, New York; Cathy Lewis and Alyssa Reichental, 3D Systems Corporation, Rock Hill, South Carolina; Lea Richard-Nagle, Studio Daniel Libeskind, New York; Christian Richters, Christian Richters Photography, Berlin; Stefanie Riegman and Anita Star, Joris Laarman Lab, Amsterdam; Claudine Sablier, Boucheron, Paris; Elaine Shocas and Alexis Keslinke , Albright Stonebridge Group, Washington, D.C.; Jenny Smith, Marc Newson, Ltd., London; Isabel Valembras, Galleria Nilufar, Milan; Willem van der Kooij, Studio Dirk Vander Kooij, Eindhoven; Wilma Wabnitz, Wabnitz Editions, Ltd., Columbus, Ohio; Maarten Willemstein, Willemstein Fotografie, Amsterdam; and Arthur Young-Spivey, New York.

Ronald T. Labaco
Marcia Docter Curator

SUGGESTED READING

BY LYNDSAY BRATTON

Aldersey-Williams, Hugh, Peter Hall, Ted Sargent, and Paola Antonelli: *Design and the Elastic Mind*. London: Thames & Hudson, 2008.

Bohnacker, Hartmut, Benedikt Gross, Julia Laub, et al. Generative Design: *Visualize, Program, and Create with Processing*. New York: Princeton Architectural Press, 2012.

Corser, Robert, ed. Fabricating Architecture: *Selected Readings in Digital Design and Manufacturing*. New York: Princeton Architectural Press, 2010.

Dezeen. Print Shift: *How 3D Printing is Changing Everything*. London: Blurb Books, 2013.

Dunn, Nick: *Digital Fabrication in Architecture*. London: Laurence King Publishers, 2012.

Freyer, Conny, Sebastian Noel, and Eva Ruck: *Digital by Design: Crafting Technology for Products and Environments*. London: Thames & Hudson, 2008.

Hardy, Steve, ed. Environmental Tectonics: *Forming Climatic Change*. London: AA Publication, 2008.

Hoskins, Stephen: *3D Printing for Artists, Designers and Makers*. London: A & C Black, 2013

Iwamoto, Lisa. Digital Fabrications: *Architectural and Material Techniques (Architecture Briefs)*. New York: Princeton Architectural Press, 2009.

Jones, Will. Unbuilt Masterworks of the 21st Century: *Inspirational Architecture: for the Digital Age*. New York: Thames & Hudson, 2009.

Kolarevic, Branko, ed. Architecture in the Digital Age: *Design and Manufacturing*. New Edition. New York: Spon Press, 2005.

Kolarevic, Branko, and Ali M. Malkawi, eds. *Performative Architecture: Beyond Instrumentality*. New York: Spon Press, 2005.

Kraeul, Jacobo, Jay Noden, William George, eds. Contemporary Digital Architecture: *Design & Techniques*. Barcelona: Links, 2010.

Lally, Sean, and Jessica Young, eds. *Softspace: From a Representation of Form to a Simulation of Space*. New York: Routledge, 2007.

Lipson, Hod, and Melba Kurman. *Fabricated: The New World of 3D Printing*. London: John Wiley & Sons, 2013.

Lovell, Sophie. *Limited Edition: Prototypes, One-offs and Design Art Furniture*. Basel: Birkhäuser, 2009.

Maeda, John: *Creative Code: Aesthetics + Computation*. New York: Thames & Hudson, 2004.

McCullough, Malcolm: *Abstracting Craft: The Practiced Digital Hand*. Cambridge, Mass.: The MIT Press, 2008.

Oxman, Rivka, and Robert Oxman, eds. The New Structuralism: *Design, Engineering and Architectural Technologies (Architectural Design)*. London: John Wiley & Sons, 2010.

Paul, Christiane: *Digital Art (World of Art Series). Second Edition*. New York: Thames & Hudson, 2008.

——— *"Renderings of Digital Art."* Leonardo 35, no. 5 (2002): 471-484.

Punt, Michael, and Robert Pepperell: *The Postdigital Membrane: Imagination, Technology, and Desire*. Portland, OR: Intellect, Ltd., 2001.

Quinn, Bradley: *Design Futures*. New York: Merrell, 2011.

Rosa, Joseph: *Figuration in Contemporary Design (A + D Series)*. Chicago: Art Institute Chicago, 2008.

———, ed. Glamour: *Fashion, Industrial Design, and Architecture*. New Haven: Yale University Press, 2004.

———. *Next Generation Architecture: Folds, Blobs, and Boxes*. New York: Rizzoli, 2003.

Sims, Lowery Stokes: *Against the Grain: Wood in Contemporary Art, Craft and Design*. New York: The Monacelli Press, 2012.

Tual, Brice, ed. PROTOtypes: *From Rapid Prototyping to Customised Production*. Paris: Innovathèque, 2009.